Psychotherapy
and
Religious Values

Edited by
EVERETT L. WORTHINGTON, JR.

BAKER BOOK HOUSE
Grand Rapids, Michigan 49516

Published by Baker Book House Company
P. O. Box 6287, Grand Rapids, Michigan 49516-6287

Printed in the United States of America

Library of Congress Cataloging-in-Publication Data

Psychotherapy and religious values / edited by Everett L. Worthington, Jr.
    p.   cm.—(Psychology and Christianity series; ISSN 7)
    Includes bibliographical references and index.
    ISBN 0-8010-9719-3
    1. Pastoral counseling. 2. Psychotherapy—Religious aspects— Christianity
3. Pastoral psychology. I. Worthington, Everett L., 1946–. II. Series.
    BV4012.2.P77 1992
    261.5'15—dc20   92-14187

Psychotherapy
and
Religious Values

Volumes in the
Psychology and Christianity Series

David G. Benner
Series Editor

1. David G. Benner, ed., *Christian Counseling and Psychotherapy.*
2. LeRoy Aden and J. Harold Ellens, eds., *The Church and Pastoral Care.*
3. LeRoy Aden and David G. Benner, eds., *Counseling and the Human Predicament: A Study of Sin, Guilt, and Forgiveness.*
4. LeRoy Aden and J. Harold Ellens, eds., *Turning Points in Pastoral Care: The Legacy of Anton Boisen and Seward Hiltner.*
5. H. Newton Malony, ed., *Psychology of Religion: Personalities, Problems, Possibilities.*
6. LeRoy Aden, David G. Benner, and J. Harold Ellens, eds., *Christian Perspectives on Human Development.*
7. Everett L. Worthington, Jr., ed., *Psychotherapy and Religious Values.*

Contents

Introduction to the Series   7

Preface: Values and Psychotherapy: Not "Whether" But
    "Which" and "How"   9
    David G. Benner

Contributors   13

Introduction: Critical Issues in the Study of Psychotherapy
    and Religious Values   17
    Everett L. Worthington, Jr.

**Part 1 Definitions, the Context of Counseling, and
        Theories of Counseling**

Introduction to Part 1   29
    1. Religious Values in Secular Theories of Psychotherapy   37
        Stanton L. Jones and *David A. Wilcox*

Part 2 Before Counseling Begins

Introduction to Part 2   65
    2. Psychiatric Factors Predicting Use of Clergy   71
        Ann A. Hohmann and *David B. Larson*
    3. Values, Pretherapy Information, and Informed Consent
        in Christian Counseling   85
        Kathleen N. Lewis and *Douglas L. Epperson*
    4. The Relevance of "Religious Diagnosis" for Counseling   105
        H. Newton Malony

Part 3 During Counseling and Psychotherapy

Introduction to Part 3   123
  5. Psychotherapy and Religious Values: An Update   127
      Everett L. Worthington, Jr.
  6. Boundary Areas of Religious Clients' Values:
      Target for Therapy   145
      W. Mack Goldsmith and *Betty K. Hansen*
Appendix: Surveys of Therapists' Religious Values   163

Part 4 Use of and Training in Christian Therapy Techniques

Introduction to Part 4   167
  7. Self-Reported Professional Practices of Christian
      Psychotherapists   171
      Robert A. Ball and *Rodney K. Goodyear*
  8. Practitioners, Religion, and the Use of Forgiveness
      in the Clinical Setting   183
      Frederick A. DiBlasio and *Brent B. Benda*
  9. Training in the Use of Christian Disciplines
      as Counseling Techniques within Christian
      Graduate Training Programs   191
      Gary W. Moon, Judy W. Bailey, John C. Kwasny,
      and *Dale E. Willis*

Part 5 An Eye to the Future

Introduction to Part 5   207
  10. Christian Ethics and Psychological Explanations of
       "Religious Values" in Therapy: Critical Connections   209
       Alan C. Tjeltveit
  11. Religious Values and Interventions in Lay Christian
       Counseling   225
       Siang-Yang Tan
  12. Proposed Agenda for a Spiritual Strategy in Personality
       and Psychotherapy   243
       Allen E. Bergin and *I. Reed Payne*
  13. Psychology and the Christian Faith:
       20th and 21st Century   261
       Everett L. Worthington, Jr.
Index   283

Introduction to the Series

This is the seventh and final volume in the *Psychology and Christianity Series,* a collection of books published cooperatively by Baker Book House and the Christian Association for Psychological Studies (CAPS). Founded in 1952 in Grand Rapids, Michigan, by a group of psychologists, psychiatrists, and pastoral counselors, CAPS is an international society of Christian helping professionals committed to the exploration of the relationship between psychology and Christian faith.

Books in this series draw on the best of previous publications in *The Journal of Psychology and Christianity,* the official publication of CAPS, and supplement these with original articles written for each volume. The purpose of the series is to present psychological and theological reflection on the most important issues encountered in human relationships, particularly relationships of counseling, education, parenting and ministry.

Further information about the Christian Association for Psychological Studies may be obtained by contacting the head office:

Christian Association for Psychological Studies
P. O. Box 890279
Temecula, CA 92589
(714) 695-2277

David G. Benner
Series Editor

Preface

Values and Psychotherapy:
Not "Whether" But "Which" and "How"

DAVID G. BENNER

If the advent of modern psychotherapy can be dated to the development of psychoanalysis in the closing years of the 19th century, psychotherapy's 100th birthday will be celebrated sometime in the latter part of this decade. Birthdays are often occasions for both reflection on the past and a look toward the future, and this seems particularly appropriate as we approach this historic milestone of psychotherapy.

In terms of cultural development, 100 years is, of course, a relatively short time, and viewed from this perspective, psychotherapy is rather young. In fact, in many ways it might be viewed as somewhere in the middle of its adolescent years, displaying ample evidence of the identity crisis that Erikson suggested often accompanies an adolescent pilgrimage. Although a diagnosis of identity crisis might be debated by those who are most impressed by the advances of the past 100 years, the great variety of theories of the nature of the psychotherapeutic process make it clear that we are far from reaching a consensus on the nature, theory, and technique of psychotherapy. A recent listing identified 255 different approaches to psychotherapy (Herink 1980). However, at a much more fundamental level there is a profound absence of agreement about whether psychotherapy is best viewed as a treatment of mental disorders, training in social skills, a growth experience for those seeking self-actualization, continuing education for those seeking self-knowledge, a technique for restructuring personality, guidance for living, or a secular confessional. Or possibly it is some combination of all of these.

These are the sorts of unanswered questions about the essential nature of psychotherapy that lead a number of observers to describe its present state as a crisis of one sort or another. Historian of psychotherapy Jan Ehrenwald is one who uses the language of an identity crisis. Noting that psychotherapy arose as a stop-gap effort to fill the spiritual void left by the demise of religion, he describes its present problems as rooted in the fact that the human needs that confront therapists transcend the frame of reference to which therapy has been confined (Ehrenwald 1966). People consulting psychotherapists seldom simply present symptoms of mental disorders. Much more typically they seek help for difficulties in living.

This represents a serious challenge to the view of psychotherapy that had its beginnings with Freud, namely, the view that therapy is best understood as the skillful application of value-free technical interventions in the treatment of mental disorders. If this were true, questions about the place of values (particularly religious values) in psychotherapy would be quite meaningless. But as the myth of psychotherapy as a value-free technical therapeutic becomes recognized for what it is, questions about the place of values in therapy are not only more common but also more commonly recognized as foundational to efforts to further develop psychotherapeutic theory and practice.

No longer is the question whether or not therapist values influence the therapeutic process. Nor is it whether or not the therapeutic dialogue touches domains of life that are addressed by values. Almost all therapists would today accept these matters as self-evident. Rather, the more pertinent questions now relate to the ways in which values should be addressed in this dialogue. Should therapists disclose significant personal values that may affect therapeutic process and outcome? If so, which values should be judged to be of such importance? And, how and when should they be disclosed? What does respect for client values mean? How should therapists treat client values that may be judged to be a part of their problem? How explicit a part of therapy should value clarification and education become? These are a few of the many value-oriented questions thoughtful psychotherapists are addressing today.

The present volume makes a significant contribution to this reappraisal of the place of values, particularly religious values, in psychotherapy. It includes chapters written by many of the most eminent contributors to the current dialogue on these matters, who bring insightful and often fresh perspectives on both theoretical and clinical aspects of the topic. Several of the chapters (3, 5–10, and 12) were first presented as a special issue of the *Journal of Psychology and Christianity* (1991, issue 2, and continuing into issue 3) devoted to the topic of this book. The remainder (more than half of the total material) has not been previously published and was specially prepared for the present volume.

This book offers important help to all those who are concerned about the direction psychotherapy will take in this next century. If, as I have argued, the crisis currently faced by psychotherapy relates in large part to its historic denial of the personal and value-laden nature of the therapeutic relationship, then efforts to reevaluate the place of values in therapy should be at the very heart of strategies designed to address this crisis. And they are in the present volume.

But more importantly, this book offers help not just to the profession of psychotherapy but to therapists themselves. Its intended audience is Christian therapists, but secondarily all therapists who are interested in the place of religious values in therapy. If this is you, this volume will be immediately recognized as a treasure of great value.

References

Herink, R. 1980. *The psychotherapy handbook.* New York: New American Library.

Ehrenwald, J. 1966. *Psychotherapy: Myth and method.* New York: Grune and Stratton.

Contributors

Judy W. Bailey (M.A., Regent University) is the internship coordinator for the School of Counseling and Family Services at Regent University. Her scholarly interests include student development in high school and higher education.

Robert A. Ball (Ph.D., University of Southern California) is a psychologist with the Idaho Department of Health and Welfare who works with severely emotionally disturbed children and with their families.

Brent B. Benda (Ph.D., University of Wisconsin-Madison) teaches research and delinquency and crime at the University of Arkansas at Little Rock. He has published articles on predicting criminal recidivism, homelessness, and adolescent sexual behavior.

David G. Benner (Ph.D., York University) is professor of psychology at Redeemer College and adjunct professor of psychology and Christianity at the University of Toronto (St. Michael's College). His scholarly interests include the place of spirituality in personality and psychotherapy, pastoral psychology and counseling, and the role of dissociation in trauma disorders.

Allen E. Bergin (Ph.D., Stanford University) is professor and director of clinical psychology at Brigham Young University, Provo, Utah. He is past president of the Society for Psychotherapy Research and recent recipient of the William James Award for Psychology of Religion research by Division 36 of the American Psychological Association.

Frederick A. DiBlasio (Ph.D., Virginia Commonwealth University) is associate professor at the School of Social Work, University of Maryland at Baltimore. His current research interests include adolescent sexuality and the clinical use of forgiveness.

13

Douglas L. Epperson (Ph.D., Ohio State University) is associate professor of psychology and co-director of the APA-accredited program in counseling psychology at Iowa State University. His scholarly interests include values and ethical issues in counseling as well as a general interest in counseling process and outcome research.

W. Mack Goldsmith (Ph.D., Cornell) is professor of psychology at California State University, Stanislaus, with a research specialty in the psychology of religion. He is also a licensed psychologist in a part-time private practice and is a past president of CAPS's Western Region.

Rodney K. Goodyear (Ph.D., University of Illinois) is a professor and the chair, Division of Counseling and Educational Psychology, University of Southern California. His areas of scholarship include counselor training and supervision and professional and ethical issues in counseling.

Betty K. Hansen (M.S., University of California-Davis; M.S., California State University-Stanislaus) is a licensed marriage and family counselor in private practice and does frequent women's conferences and workshops.

Ann A. Hohmann (Ph.D., Rutgers University; M.P.H., Harvard University) is currently chief of special populations and methods development research at the National Institute of Mental Health. Her areas of scholarship include clinical services research, especially the physician-patient interaction.

Stanton L. Jones (Ph.D., Arizona State University) is associate professor of psychology and chair of the department of psychology at Wheaton College. His scholarly interests include theories of psychotherapy, cognitive-behavioral therapies, integration of psychology and Christianity, and human sexuality.

John C. Kwasny (M.A., Regent University) is the program director and head counselor at Mid-Atlantic Teen Challenge. His scholarly interests include Christian counseling theory and techniques and adolescent counseling.

David B. Larson (M.D., Temple University; M.S.P.H., University of North Carolina-Chapel Hill) is a research scientist and adjunct assistant professor at the department of psychiatry at Duke University Medical Center. His scholarly interests include the impact of religious commitment and traditional values on health, mental health, and social status; systematic reviews of research literature; and provision, delivery, and quality of mental health services.

Kathleen N. Lewis (Ph.D., Ohio State University) is an adjunct faculty member at Robert Morris College in Pittsburgh, Pennsylvania. Her scholarly interests include the impact of values on psychotherapy process and outcome; values, education, and home schooling; and the integration of Christianity and psychology.

H. Newton Malony (Ph.D., George Peabody College) is professor of psychology in the Graduate School of Psychology at Fuller Theological Seminary. His scholarly interests are centered around the psychology of religion.

Gary W. Moon (Ph.D., M. Div., Fuller Theological Seminary) is director of the School of Counseling and Family Services at Regent University. His scholarly interests include spiritual direction in psychotherapy and individual differences and Christian formation.

I. Reed Payne (Ph.D., Pennsylvania State University) is professor of clinical psychology at Brigham Young University and a practicing clinician. His interests include religious values and psychotherapy, psychology of music, and corrections.

Siang-Yang Tan (Ph.D., McGill University) is director of the program in clinical psychology and associate professor of psychology in the Graduate School of Psychology at Fuller Theological Seminary. His scholarly interests include lay counseling and lay counselor training, intrapersonal integration and spirituality, cognitive-behavioral therapy, epilepsy, pain, and cross-cultural counseling, especially with Asian-Americans.

Alan C. Tjeltveit (Ph.D., Fuller Theological Seminary) is assistant professor of psychology at Muhlenberg College. His scholarly interests include values, ethics, and psychotherapy, philosophical and theoretical psychology, and the integration of psychology and Christian faith.

David A. Wilcox (B.A., Belhaven College) is a graduate student pursuing the M.A. in clinical psychology at Wheaton College Graduate School. His interests are in the areas of Christian existential psychology and psychotherapy, psychological assessment, and religious values in psychological theories.

Dale E. Willis (M.A., Regent University) is an outpatient therapist at East Central Missouri Mental Health Center. His scholarly interests include Christian counseling and the application of Christian disciplines in mental health settings.

Everett L. Worthington, Jr. (Ph.D., University of Missouri-Columbia) is professor of psychology at Virginia Commonwealth University. His scholarly interests include religious values in both psychotherapy and the family and marriage and family dynamics and therapy.

Introduction

Critical Issues in the Study of Psychotherapy and Religious Values

EVERETT L. WORTHINGTON, JR.

Psychotherapy and Religious Values will excite both scholar and practicing psychotherapist, giving them ideas about how to deal with religious issues in psychotherapy. It is aimed at the *thinking* psychotherapist. While not every article will be relevant to every therapist or scholar, each reader should find chapters that make the book well worth reading.

At the end of the 20th century, we are at a critical juncture in religious counseling and psychotherapy. This book is a crucial step toward meeting the needs faced in the field.

Speculations about the Future

Insurance costs are running rampant. People are becoming increasingly disgruntled about insurance costs, medical costs, and the annoyances associated with paying for treatment of physical and psychological problems. Physicians and psychotherapists often treat patients like numbers rather than people. The general population is increasingly dissatisfied with the health care industry.

On the other hand, insurance companies try to limit insurance costs so premiums can become manageable. To limit costs, they often limit the number of sessions people are allowed per year for mental health problems (and some companies even limit individuals' lifetime insurance expenditures). Independent review boards of psychiatrists and psychologists, hired by insurance companies, review mental health records and make decisions that limit mental health care of patients. Managed health care limits patients' access to mental health workers who are not on approved lists.

Mental health service providers and insurance companies fence—thrusting, parrying, and riposting. Patients and nonpatients who see their insurance premiums skyrocketing are caught in the middle. They are angry, and their anger emerges within a litigious climate that induces distraught, angry consumers to initiate lawsuits.

A clamor has arisen demanding government intervention. In 1991, the National Association of Social Workers (NASW) proposed a plan for nationalized mental health insurance that would be administered by the government. Although I doubt that the NASW's proposal will be adopted, other voices sing a similar tune. The pressure for national control over physical and mental health services mounts yearly. As we have seen with public education, whenever governmental involvement occurs, religious programs are relegated to the private sector or eliminated altogether.

If nationalized health care is adopted, will Christian psychotherapy be allowed? I cling to the hope that scientists can show that Christian psychotherapy is effective with Christian clients. While I do not believe that any current studies show that Christian psychotherapy is *superior* to secular psychotherapy on purely mental health outcomes, I believe we are beginning to show that mental health outcomes of secular and Christian psychotherapies are essentially equal. We must also show that other outcomes—enhanced spiritual life and preference for religious counseling—are better when strongly Christian people are matched with Christian therapists practicing Christian therapies.

Even without the specter of nationalized mental health services, insurance companies are demanding accountability of psychotherapies. Which are truly effective? Again, research is the language of persuasion for insurance companies.

A Metaphor

In chapter 6, Goldsmith and Hansen propose an elegant metaphor to describe how religious values operate in the life of a troubled person. They describe religious values to which the person is firmly committed as being like a castle on a solid island. Values to which a person is firmly opposed are like a forest surrounding the island. A marshland, consisting of values that are especially vulnerable to change during psychotherapy, lies between the two areas.

The picture they draw is also pertinent to viewing Christian counseling, or even religious counseling in general, and psychotherapy. There are those in the forest who attack religious psychotherapy—either as presumably ineffective or as morally or philosophically repugnant. There are those of us who would defend religious psychotherapy and even promote it for use with highly religious people. Often we feel as if we are in a fortress near the hostile forest. Under siege, we defend our explicitly religious approach to psychotherapy and attempt to survive the varieties of attack.

Research and theory in the practice of religious psychotherapy are among the weapons and ammunition with which future battles will be fought. Our faith and supernatural influences are other weapons, but one important job of the Christian mental health professional is to prepare for potential battle using the weapons available, namely, research evidence.

Adequacy of Current Evidence

If asked to adduce the evidence for the effectiveness of a distinctly Christian approach to psychotherapy, the result would be a meager smattering of studies (Johnson and Ridley 1989; Peucher and Edwards 1984; Propst 1980a, 1980b; Propst, Ostrum, Watkins, and Morris 1984; Wilson 1974; Worthington, Dupont, Berry, and Duncan 1988). Of course, there would be vociferous protest from the Christian community if Christian psychotherapy were suddenly not funded by insurance or by the federal government. Yet, outrage in the Christian community has not previously been notably effective at bending the will of government or insurance companies.

What We Need

If we are to have the ammunition to combat the attacks that we may soon face, we must be able to adduce scientifically credible research to support our position. Yet, historically, Christians have conducted little empirical research on Christian psychotherapy.

Most of the articles in the present volume deal with the empirical investigation of religious values in psychotherapy. As such, they undergird the empirical justification for Christian psychotherapy that we as a profession may some day be required to make.

An Introduction to the Book

Most chapters consider specifically Christian counseling or psychotherapy, but a few are more general, dealing with religious values and psychotherapy. Six chapters report original studies; three use research in making conceptual points; one asks serious questions about the proper ethical and scientific uses of empirical approaches to knowing in Christian psychotherapy; one investigates values inherent in the theories of psychotherapy; others examine values, research, and practice in the future.

This book is one of new ideas, theories, and methods. Its chapters address the full range of psychotherapy—from formation of first impressions, to outcomes, to Christian techniques. It theorizes about and investigates the role of religious values in both the client's personality and treatment.

A Literary Meal

When you get ready to go to a fine restaurant, your mouth may water when you merely think about the tastes, smells, sights, and sounds you are about to experience. If you have never been to the restaurant, you may have many questions about what it will be like. What will the menu be? How are the prices? Will the staff provide good service? Will someone dance on my table? (No. Maybe we go to different types of restaurants.) But mostly you may think, How will the food be? Will we get enough to eat? Will the meal be satisfying?

You are holding the literary equivalent of a variety of excellent meals for your mind. These meals deal with religious (in many cases, specifically Christian) values in both Christian and secular counseling.

Many people think that religious values and psychotherapy (or counseling) do not mix. They may not like beef and sour cream mixed together either. But other people like to blend beef and sour cream into stroganoff or in spicy Mexican food. Like these dishes, religious values and counseling may mix—when done artfully and tastefully in the right proportions, at the right time, and with the proper care. This book deals with some of the ways to make a tasteful mix of religious values and psychotherapy.

Questions about the Menu

The first decision we make about eating out is, What type of food are we going to eat—Mexican, Chinese, Italian, steak and potatoes, or something different? The type of "food" that we discuss in much of this book is Christian counseling. What is Christian counseling? There is no simple answer.

Worthington, Dupont, Berry, and Duncan (1988) surveyed 7 therapists and 19 of their clients over 91 sessions of outpatient psychotherapy. All of the therapists were identified as explicitly Christian psychotherapists. The major finding from the study of these therapists, though, was that they all conducted therapy differently. Some used many religious techniques and dealt with religious topics frequently. Others never dealt with religious topics directly. Some dealt with religious topics with some clients but not with other clients. In practice, a definition of Christian psychotherapy was elusive.

Often, Christian counseling has been strictly prescribed. Professional therapists, pastoral counselors, and lay counselors have adhered rigidly to a formula, usually advocated by an articulate theoretician or prescribed by a church authority. At other times, Christian counseling has been mysterious. The practitioner has relied on the leading of the Holy Spirit, intuitive feelings of how Christianity and psychotherapy should be integrated, or unsystematic and unintentional eclecticism. While the first (prescriptive) approach makes it easier to define what Christian counseling is, the approach is narrowly conceived and often forces clients into uncomfortable Procrustean beds. While the second (mysterious) approach may even sound more "spiritual," its flexibility has often meant theoretical chaos.

Questions about the menu are not limited to definitional questions. We also want to know how the food will taste. Will it be of high quality? Will it be effective? Will there be a good blend of spices and basic foods, aromas and environment?

Similarly, we want to know whether Christian counseling—however we define it—will work. Historically, there have been few attempts to answer that question beyond reliance on testimonials of therapists or clients (see Worthington 1986, 1989, for reviews).

We want to know what place religious values has in psychotherapy, counseling, pastoral counseling, and lay counseling. We want to find out how Christian counselors use religious values with religious and non-religious clients and how non-Christian counselors might deal with religious issues with Christian and non-Christian clients. We want to determine the effects of discussing and of not discussing religious values with clients under a variety of conditions. These are some of the practical questions that beset those who are attuned to religious issues and who espouse religious values.

Answering the Questions

How does one answer such a sweeping array of questions? Answers to such questions depend on our values. Hunter Lewis (1990) identified six ways that people make personal choices.

First, they may rely on authority. The authority may be another person with either attributed or earned expert status. The expert may be a charismatic teacher, authoritative supervisor, or learned author or speaker. The authority may be God, through direct revelation; or, the authority may be an institution (such as the church or one's denomination), a book (such as the Bible or another religion's scriptural writings), or a graduate program in psychology or theology.

Second, they may use deductive logic. Beliefs are subjected to a variety of tests of their internal and external consistency. The rules of logic, of course, may differ from person to person. Some may use dualistic Aristotelian logic; others may use Hegelian dialectical logic.

Third, they may rely on sense experience. People may trust their own experiences as the ultimate authority. What they see, hear, feel, touch, and smell may become unquestionable, or at least become the final arbiter of truth. Such people would likely rely on their own experiences with clients as the final word about how religious values are best dealt with in counseling or psychotherapy.

Fourth, people may rely on emotion to make difficult decisions. Decisions about how and when to intervene in counseling and psychotherapy and how to integrate our faith with our practice may depend on what feels right. Feelings of emotional harmony may be valued above all else. Such people may also give primacy to clients' feelings in their counseling.

Fifth, people may rely on intuition to make decisions. Lewis describes intuitive decision making as logical, but as able to integrate more sources of information simultaneously than our conscious, logical reasoning. Logic is linear, while intuition involves simultaneous information processing. Lewis attributes more power to intuitive reasoning than to logical reasoning but more control and discipline to logical reasoning than to intuitive reasoning.

Sixth, people may rely on "science" (the quotation marks are Lewis's) to make decisions. "Science" is actually a technique that synthesizes a variety of ways of knowing. It uses the authority of well-known and verified theories. (Authority, within the scientific method, is treated as fallible, but nonetheless, well-supported theories are not easily overturned by a single study or even by a series of studies; see Kuhn 1970). "Science" uses logic to trace paths between experience and conclusions. "Science" uses sense experience in collecting observations. "Science" uses emotion to guide scholars and researchers into areas that they care about with passion. "Science" uses intuition to develop creative hypotheses that beg attention. Thus, "science" is a socially-arrived-at method for determining what is valuable and what may be true.

The Type of Food at This Restaurant

To extend our metaphor, once we have decided the type of food we desire, we must select a specific restaurant. The present volume attempts an answer to questions about Christian counseling and religious values in counseling and psychotherapy by relying mostly on logic and "science." Many people view scientific studies as dry and lifeless. Some look cynically at science and at attempts to quantify human experiences. For example, Benjamin Disraeli said, "There are three kinds of lies: lies, damned lies, and statistics"—in that order (attributed to Disraeli by Mark Twain in his autobiography). Noted family therapist Paul Watzlawick said, "Statistics are like bikinis; what they reveal is suggestive, what they conceal, vital" (cited in Gurman and Kniskern 1978). I prefer the more sympathetic approach by an unknown author who said, "Statistics are human experience with the tears wiped dry." Scientific approaches to answering questions about religious values in counseling and psychotherapy rely on measuring the experiences of real people, many of whom are in psychological distress. Although the articles you will read do not have the emotional appeal of a *Guideposts* article, the people on which the conclusions are based are as real as your clients or parishioners, and they each have their story to tell.

As effective counselors, we need to use all six ways of knowing. If we reject any, we risk short-changing our clients. Thus, to the extent that you incorporate the ideas in this book, this volume will contribute to your understanding of religious counseling and of counseling as a whole.

Types of Scientific Articles

In general, there are three types of scientific articles. Each is represented in this book.

The scientific study. The cornerstone of science is the scientific study. Several original studies are reported in this volume. For example, Kathleen Lewis and Doug Epperson have reported an experiment in which the authors try to equate several treatments of clients on all dimensions except the critical dimension that is being studied. Newton Malony reports a series of studies and experiments concerning assessment of spiritual maturity. His work is important because it represents a program of research. A program of research involves a set of studies about a single topic. Programs of research—like those by Lewis and Epperson and by Malony—are ways that science advances.

Gary Moon and his colleagues and Fredrick DiBlasio and Brent Benda also offer survey studies that are part of their programs of research.

A different method of conducting original research is the interview. Robert Ball and Rodney Goodyear report two interview studies using creative methods of research to study the practices of Christian counselors. Mack Goldsmith and Betty Hansen interweave interview transcripts with theoretical speculations. They develop a memorable metaphor about types of religious values in therapy.

The integrative review of research. Besides original research, a second type of research is the integrative review of research. While such work does not add new data to one's knowledge of religious counseling, it adds perspective by considering a variety of research studies and identifying themes in the research and pointing to new directions for research. The chapter I wrote concerning an update of research on religious values in counseling attempts to provide an integrative review.

Theoretical reflection. A third type of work necessary to a scientific understanding of religious values in counseling or psychotherapy is theoretical reflection. Kurt Lewin said, "There is nothing so practical as a good theory." Good theoretical work guides future research and focuses attention of scholars and psychotherapists on what is important.

In this book, several people approach theory in different ways. Stanton Jones considers the values relevant to religious people inherent in secular theories of counseling and therapy. Allen Bergin and Reed Payne make a reasoned plea for a theory of personality and psychotherapy that incorporates the spiritual, rather than being simply a secular look at religious values. Finally, Alan Tjeltveit challenges the empirical way of knowing, giving a thoughtful reflection on religious values and psychotherapy.

Various methods of science are thus sampled within this book. This variety of approaches gives different perspectives to researcher-scholar and practicing counselor or psychotherapist.

Organization of the Menu

A menu is organized to parallel the meal. Appetizers are selected first, then soups or salads, then entrees, and finally desserts. The chapters of this book are organized in a way that logically parallels the therapeutic process. After this introductory chapter, we will examine the context of counseling and psychotherapy by examining theories of counseling

When a client decides to attend counseling or psychotherapy, the client usually has attitudes and beliefs about the therapist and about what is likely to happen in counseling. Those attitudes and beliefs often affect how counseling is conducted and what outcomes are achieved. Three papers are included in the section on the preliminaries to counseling. In one, Hohmann and Larson investigate factors that predict who uses pastors for psychological counseling. In a second, Lewis and Epperson, using a rigorous experimental design, examine pretherapy attitudes and beliefs about Christian counselors. Even those who are not enamored with experimental psychology will benefit by their thoughtful consideration of the issues and the interpretation of their results. Malony's chapter deals with assessing clients after counseling has begun. Malony examines the appropriateness of assessing and diagnosing Christian maturity in pastoral and professional counseling.

Two chapters give a conceptual overview of ways that religious values might be used during therapy. I describe previous research in religious values in psychotherapy, and Goldsmith and Hansen describe how religious values might be challenged and defended within therapy. They illustrate their ideas with several interesting clinical interviews.

In psychotherapy, theories are actualized by using techniques. Ball and Goodyear surveyed members of CAPS to determine when and how they employed religiously-oriented techniques in their therapy with Christians. DiBlasio and Benda surveyed members of the American Association of Marital and Family Therapists (AAMFT) to determine their attitudes toward and use of forgiveness as a therapeutic strategy. Therapists learn their techniques through their experience, their reading, and their training. Moon and his colleagues surveyed explicitly Christian training programs to determine how much training was given in explicitly Christian counseling techniques, which Moon and others call spiritual disciplines.

In the final essays in this book, Tjeltveit discusses the limitations of empirical investigations of Christian counseling. He argues for a broader methodology—a point that all the authors in this book would likely support.

The chapter by Tan examines religious values in lay counseling. Lay counseling, a valuable part of the psychotherapeutic enterprise, focuses on prevention of severe mental health problems that require the attention of psychotherapists. As such, it deserves our attention, and it will likely receive increasing attention in the future.

Bergin and Payne point our investigations toward the future by issuing a call for developing a personality theory and treatment theory that adequately accounts for the spiritual perspective. In the final essay in this book, I speculate about the future and look at the prospects for Christian psychotherapy in the 21st century.

Your Choice

The purpose of this book is not to teach you how to do Christian counseling. The purpose is to promote hard thinking about religious counseling in people who intend to practice it—lay counselors, pastors who disciple lay counselors, pastors who counsel, professional therapists (pastoral counselors, licensed counselors, psychologists, and psychiatrists), and people who do research and build theories in effective counseling and psychotherapy.

Not every chapter in this book may be for you, just as every dish on a menu may not be to every patron's liking. Some are heavy with the meat of original data. Others are varied, like a spicy, succulent casserole. Others are sweet with reflection. Nonetheless, the papers in this book are like dishes found in a gourmet restaurant. They are to be tasted, savored at your leisure, and recalled as stimulating nourishment.

Bon appetit.

References

Gurman, A. S., and D. P. Kniskern, eds. 1981. *Handbook of family therapy.* New York: Brunner/Mazel.

Johnson, W. B., and C. R. Ridley. 1989. Christian and secular rational-emotive therapy with depressed Christian clients: An exploratory study. Paper presented at the meeting of the American Psychological Association, New Orleans, August.

Lewis, H. 1990. *A question of values: Six ways we make the personal choices that shape our lives.* San Francisco: Harper and Row.

Pecheur, D. R., and K. J. Edwards. 1984. A comparison of secular and religious versions of cognitive therapy with depressed Christian college students. *Journal of Psychology and Theology* 12: 45–54.

Propst, L. R. 1980a. The comparative efficacy of religious and non-religious imagery for the treatment of mild depression in religious individuals. *Cognitive Therapy and Research* 4: 167–78.

———. 1980b. A comparison of the cognitive restructuring psychotherapy paradigm and several spiritual approaches to mental health. *Journal of Psychology and Theology* 8: 107–14.

Propst, L. R., R. Ostrum, P. Watkins, and M. Morris. 1984. Preliminary report of the comparative efficacy of religious and non-religious cognitive-behavioral therapy for the treatment of clinical depression in religious individuals. Paper presented at the meeting of the Society for Psychotherapy Research, Banff, Canada, June.

Wilson, W. P. 1974. Utilization of Christian beliefs in psychotherapy. *Journal of Psychology and Theology* 2: 125–31.

Worthington, E. L., Jr. 1986. Religious counseling: A review of published empirical research. *Journal for Counseling and Development* 64: 421–31.

———. 1989. Religious development across the life span: Implications for counseling and research. *The Counseling Psychologist* 17: 555–612.

Worthington, E. L., Jr., P. A. Dupont, J. T. Berry, and L. A. Duncan. 1988. Therapists' and clients' perceptions of religious psychotherapy in private and agency settings. *Journal of Psychology and Theology* 16: 282–93.

Part **1**

Definitions, the Context of Counseling, and Theories of Counseling

Introduction to Part 1

Different types of counseling intimately affect how religious values are used in counseling. Expectations and norms are completely different for the pastor counseling in his study and the psychotherapist conducting psychotherapy in her secular agency office.

Types of Counseling or Psychotherapy

We can distinguish among three primary types of counseling or psychotherapy: outpatient psychotherapy or counseling, psychiatric inpatient treatment, and community counseling.

Outpatient Counseling or Psychotherapy

Within outpatient counseling or psychotherapy several activities could occur. The activities overlap with one another to some degree and make it difficult to distinguish among them at times. Nonetheless, when we use the different terms, we generally mean different things.

Psychotherapy is generally systematic helping that intends to assist the client deal with problems in living that are extremely bothersome or that interfere with the person's ability to function personally, socially, or occupationally. Psychotherapy is generally concerned with psychopathology, assesses clients or patients using formal diagnosis, and attempts to make long-term personality changes more frequently than do other forms of counseling. Psychotherapy may include individual therapy, group therapy, marital therapy, or family therapy.

Counseling is generally systematic helping that assists the helpee deal with troublesome problems in living that have produced emotional distress, interpersonal tensions, or other disruptions in normal living. While counseling frequently deals with highly disruptive situations and personal problems, counseling does not usually aim as frequently at long-term personality reorganization and at ameliorating psychopathology as does psychotherapy. Counseling often deals with people who are troubled but not incapacitated. Individual, group, marital, and family counseling may be included.

Pastoral counseling is counseling by an ordained pastor (or other member of the clergy). There are two varieties of pastoral counseling—agency pastoral counseling and counseling by individual pastors. Agency pastoral counseling is generally performed within an agency of ordained and credentialed pastoral counselors. Counseling by pastors usually takes place within the congregational boundaries and is one part of pastoral care by clergy for their parishioners. Pastors who counsel may have substantial counseling experience, but many pastors have little formal training in counseling. Generally, pastoral counseling is expected to offer an approach to counseling that considers the spiritual perspective. Pastoral counselors and pastors differ widely in their interpretation of what that means, sometimes violating expectations of their helpees, who may expect more or less of an orthodox religious approach from the pastor than the pastor provides. Most pastoral counseling, especially that done by a congregational pastor, is time–limited (one to five sessions) and deals with problem solving within a religious framework.

Spiritual direction has traditionally been another helping interaction as part of the pastoral care of congregational clergy. In general, spiritual direction is less problem–centered than pastoral counseling. Spiritual direction is directed reflection about one's life, especially the spiritual and religious aspects of one's life. While the person receiving spiritual direction may consider various personal problems, the main thrust of spiritual direction is not to solve problems but is to improve the helpee's spiritual life.

Psychiatric Inpatient Treatment

Recently, several comprehensive residential Christian psychiatric treatment programs have developed. The two most well known are the Minirth-Meier clinics and the Rapha hospital programs. These, and other less nationally distributed clinics, provide for the total psychiatric care of people who are unable to function as outpatients or people who desire total immersion in a psychiatric community to speed their recovery from serious psychological difficulties.

The fundamental characteristic of such programs is that 24 hours of the day must be accounted for. Treatment usually consists of at least some daily contact with an individual psychotherapist or counselor, regular visits and oversight from an attending psychiatrist, and much group psychotherapy. Other managed activities are also planned, which may include Bible-study groups, sports, other recreational activities, and even school (and enforced study periods) for disturbed children and adolescents. The helpee functions within a community of other patients. When the emphasis is Christian, then activities, counseling or psychotherapy, and groups are explicitly Christian and teach Christian concepts within the total psychiatric care of the person.

Community Counseling

Defining community counseling is not something that community psychologists easily do. It involves an array of (usually, but not always) preventative, psychoeducational, and counseling interventions that seek to prevent mental health problems, promote positive mental health, and treat mental health problems within the resources of the community. With that definition, pastoral activities such as sermons, premarital counseling, educational groups, and even discipleship or Bible-study groups might be legitimately considered community counseling.

A community counseling function of growing importance is counseling of the laity within a congregation by other lay people. Generally this involves either paraprofessional, trained lay counselors or friendship counselors. As mega-churches, churches with membership from 1000 to 7000 or more, have become more popular, pastoral staff members have been swamped with the demand for counseling among their parishioners. In response to that demand, formal programs have been established within large churches to train lay people to offer effective Christian-based counsel. Recently, a comprehensive book (Tan 1991) and a national convention at Elmbrook Church in Waukesha, Wisconsin, have summarized some of the work.

Friendship counseling generally involves untrained people who counsel friends and relatives. People who develop a reputation as good helpers often seek what training they can find through self-help books.

An entire book could be written addressing the state of religious counseling within each of these types of religious counseling. In the present volume, you receive a sample of several areas: psychotherapy (Jones; Worthington; Goldsmith and Hansen), psychiatric treatment (Hohmann and Larson), pastoral counseling (Malony), and lay counseling (Tan).

In each instance, theories of counseling are either explicit or implicit. Regardless, theories guide research and psychotherapy. Theories shine light on aspects of counseling that should be attended to. Consequently, the role of theorizing in understanding counseling is crucial.

Theories of Counseling

Theories about religious values come in a variety of packages. Among those are academic/research theories, analyses of secular theories from a religious perspective, religious versions of secular theories, and religious theories using explicitly religious concepts, terms, and interventions.

Academic/Research Theories

Some academic/research theories, such as Beutler and Bergan's (1991) theory about value change within counseling and psychotherapy, are broad frameworks that may apply to many types of values. Beutler and Bergan propose that value *similarity* in terms of self-definition may affect client identification with the counselor but value *difference* (especially with respect to views of God and the nature of people) more strongly affect positive counseling outcome.

Other theories, such as Worthington's (1988) theory of important religious values in therapy and Bergin's (1980) identification of fundamental assumptions in a theistic worldview, provide more specific hypotheses for religious counselors.

At a different level of theory, Robert Lovinger (1984, 1990) has examined ways that therapists of different (or no) religious persuasion explore religious issues with clients who are of different faiths. His main contribution has been sensitizing therapists to the variety of religions and to varieties of belief within similar religions. He cautions therapists that religious issues contain a wealth of information about the client and that the informed religious therapist will make fewer blunders with the religious client than the religious therapist who avoids religion or is uninformed or misinformed about clients' fundamental religious beliefs.

Analyses of Secular Theories from a Religious Perspective

Secular theories of counseling and psychotherapy are practiced and taught throughout the country. Many counselors and psychotherapists who are deeply religious are trained in secular theories. It is helpful, then, when scholars analyze popular secular theories of counseling for their religious implications. It is important to examine all levels of impact of the theory—at an assumptive level, the level of explicit theoretical propositions, and the level of techniques—on the religious and nonreligious client and therapist.

An excellent example of such a scholarly examination is the recent volume by Stanton Jones and Richard Butman (1991), *Modern Psychotherapies: A Contemporary Christian Appraisal*. In the following chapter, Jones and Wilcox summarize additional reflections about secular theories from a Christian point of view.

Religious Versions of Secular Theories

An analysis of secular therapies from the point of view of a particular religion naturally leads religious therapists to theories of counseling and psychotherapy that they are comfortable with. Many have adapted such secular theories to a religious clientele.

Cognitive and cognitive-behavioral theories have been the most popular theories with Christians, especially more theologically conservative Christians. Propst's (1988), Crabb's (1977), McGee's (1990), Wright's (1981), and Worthington's (1989) adaptations for individual and marital therapy have been the most widely used.

Other secular theories, such as transactional analysis (by Newton Malony) and Rational Emotive Therapy (by William Backus), have been adapted by Christians.

Several theorists have proposed Christian adaptations of eclectic models of counseling. The most recent is Smith's (1990) integrative therapy, but others include Meier, Minirth, and Wichern's (1982) and Clyde Narramore's (1960) approaches.

Specifically Religious Theories

A variety of approaches have been specifically Christian. Notable among these has been Paul Tournier's (1965) work, integrity therapy (Mowrer 1961; see also Drakeford 1967), Solomon's (1977) spirituotherapy, and Adams's (1973) nouthetic counseling.

Gary Collins has been a pioneer in disseminating theories of Christianized secular therapies and specifically Christian psychotherapies. *Helping People Grow* (1980) was an initial effort, and his recent book, *Case Studies in Christian Counseling* (1991), adds to the collection of Christian therapies. David Benner has also actively compiled collections of Christian theories, with *Christian Counseling and Psychotherapy* (1987) and *Psychotherapy in Christian Perspective* (1987).

General Comments

Theoreticians use a variety of sources to derive their theories. Most notably, Christian theories are based on the theorist's understanding of the Bible, the theorist's experiences conducting (and possibly undergoing) therapy, and (less popularly) research findings. The theories of the 21st century that gain the respect of practitioners, clients, and insurance companies will necessarily involve elements from various sources of experience, not from a single primary source as is so often the case today. This is the challenge before our profession: to fashion a truly integrated set of Christian counseling theories, supported by Scripture, experience, and research.

References

Adams, J. E. 1973. *The Christian counselor's manual.* Nutley, N.J.: Presbyterian and Reformed.

Benner, D. G., ed. 1987. *Christian counseling and psychotherapy.* Grand Rapids: Baker.

_____. 1987. *Psychotherapy in Christian perspective.* Grand Rapids: Baker.

Bergin, A. E. 1980. Psychotherapy and religious values. *Journal of Consulting and Clinical Psychology* 48: 95–105.

Beutler, L. E., and J. Bergan. 1991. Value change in counseling and psychotherapy: A search for scientific credibility. *Journal of Counseling Psychology* 38: 16–24.

Collins, G. R. 1980. *Helping people grow: Practical approaches to Christian counseling.* Santa Ana, Calif.: Vision House.

_____. 1991. *Case studies in Christian counseling.* Dallas: Word.

Crabb, L. J., Jr. 1977. *Effective biblical counseling.* Grand Rapids: Zondervan.

Drakeford, J. W. 1967. *Integrity therapy.* Nashville: Broadman.

Jones, S. L., and R. E. Butman. 1991. *Modern psychotherapies: A comprehensive Christian appraisal.* Downers Grove, Ill.: InterVarsity.

Lovinger, R. J. 1984. *Working with religious issues in therapy.* New York: Jason Aronson.

_____. 1990. *Religion and counseling: The psychological impact of religious belief.* New York: Continuum.

McGee, R. S. 1990. *The search for significance.* 2d ed. Houston: Rapha Publishing.

Meier, P. D., F. B. Minirth, and F. Wichern. 1982. *Introduction to psychology and counseling: Christian perspectives and applications.* Grand Rapids: Baker.

Mowrer, O. H. 1961. *The crisis in psychiatry and religion.* Princeton, N.J.: Van Nostrand.

Narramore, C. M. 1960. *The psychology of counseling.* Grand Rapids: Zondervan.

Propst, L. R. 1988. *Psychotherapy in a religious framework: Spirituality in the emotional healing process.* New York: Human Sciences.

Smith, D. 1990. *Integrative therapy: A comprehensive approach to the methods and principles of counseling and psychotherapy.* Grand Rapids: Baker.

Solomon, C. R. 1977. *Counseling with the mind of Christ.* Old Tappan, N.J.: Revell.

Tournier, P. 1965. *The healing of persons.* New York: Harper and Row.

Worthington, E. L., Jr. 1988. Understanding the values of religious clients: A model and its application to counseling. *Journal of Counseling Psychology* 35: 166–74.

_____. 1989. *Marriage counseling: A Christian approach for counseling couples.* Downers Grove, Ill: InterVarsity.

Wright, H. N. 1981. *Marital counseling: A biblical, behavioral, cognitive approach.* San Francisco: Harper and Row.

1

Religious Values in Secular Theories of Psychotherapy

STANTON L. JONES
AND DAVID A. WILCOX

Behind the worlds we construct, coloring both our logic
and our rhetoric, are the ideologies that give our world
views their dominant cast. Such ideologies are complex
and not easily analyzed.—William Bevan, 1991

We are accustomed to thinking of individual people as
having values. Both psychotherapists and clients are people, and both
therefore may have values, including religious values. Psychologists
have begun to study values as they are operative in the therapist-client
interchange. Particularly noteworthy are the empirical explorations of
the influence of the convergence of therapist and client values on initial
selection of and expected comfort with a therapist (Lewis and Epperson) and of the role of values in shaping the therapist's usage of reli-
giously-grounded intervention techniques (Ball and Goodyear; DiBlasio
and Benda). These efforts to understand how values influence therapist,
client, and the process of their interaction should be applauded and
continued.

But values are not just held by individuals. Groups of persons such as
cultures, families, races, communities, religions, political groups, and
organizations embody differing values (e.g., see the discussion of organizational values in Katz and Kahn, 1966). Further, values are also sys-

temic and institutional, existing in structures created by persons, as well as in individuals and groups of persons. A football playoff system involving differential payoffs for losers and winners, for example, is an institution created by persons that reflects values in its very structure that are independent of the values of the persons in that system. This is also true for psychological theories. Each theory will embody its own particular values about human personality, especially in regard to its view of psychological health and abnormality. It is this element—the values inherent to psychotherapy theories—that we discuss in this chapter.

We hope to explore in our first section why values in general, and religious values in particular, are embedded in the psychotherapy theories that we currently utilize in professional circles, and also why such a "value encrustation" is in fact inevitable or intrinsic to the process of forming psychotherapy and counseling theories. We will then construct three case studies of a critical analysis from a Christian perspective of the values embedded in three very different psychotherapy theories: cognitive-behavior therapy, psychoanalysis, and existential therapy. In the conclusion, we will explore briefly how the values embedded in psychotherapy theories interact with the values of psychotherapy students and teachers, as well as with the entrenched values of the professional mental health establishment.

We have deliberately side-stepped here the thorny issue of defining either values in general or religious values in particular. In common usage, the term *values* has both expansive and restrictive meanings. For one example of an *expansive* meaning, we might point to the concept of a "facts-values dichotomy," which would suggest that everything that is not a fact, a narrow category indeed, would be a value. By this definition, values would include perceptions, assumptions, impressions, emotions, presuppositions, theories, stories, and basically everything except the strictly logical and scientific assertions of life. Belief in God, or the belief that human beings are created in God's image, would be values by this definition. A more restrictive definition of value was used by Tjeltveit (chap. 10 in this volume) when he defined a value as "what is felt or believed to be valuable." By this definition, a value would have to be consciously experienced in some form or another, and it would have to reflect a preferential ordering of some dimension of human life. Strictly interpreted, this would ascribe a narrow range to what we would call values. Belief in God would not be a value by this definition, though believing that "serving God is the highest good" would be a value.

In this chapter, we will use the term *values* imprecisely and nontechnically. In the first section, we will tend to use the term in its broader context to understand the way in which a broad range of "nonfactual" issues become operative in psychological theory. In the later case studies, we will try to emphasize the more restrictive usage that implies preferential judgments that some states of human affairs are better than others.

The Necessity of Values in Psychological Theory

The Emergence of Studies of Therapist and Client Values

The formalization of psychotherapy theory seems to have begun under assumptions that made examination of values of any sort unlikely. From the early until the mid-20th centuries, the two dominant psychological paradigms in America were behaviorism and psychoanalysis. In different forms, both approaches embraced a naturalistic worldview that denied transcendent or supernatural reality, with the result that the domain of "values" was reduced to a purely psychological status within the minds of individuals. Curiously, each system in its own way went even further in depreciating the causal efficacy of such values; in psychoanalysis because the real causes of behavior were believed to be remote psychosexual events, and in behaviorism because values were regarded as causally inefficacious mentalisms. Each of these paradigms embraced an epistemology (in very different forms) that elevated the empirical method above all other ways of human knowing, with the result that human knowing was seen as a neutral methodological process upon which "personal" factors (such as values) should have little or no effect. The theories, in other words, were themselves value-neutral because they were the result of empirical study. Finally, and most significantly, each of these paradigms embraced the concept of the neutrality of the psychotherapist. Ideal psychoanalysts, it was assumed, had derived sufficient self-understanding from their own analysis that they were able to analyze both their client's and their own transferential reactions with utter objectivity. Ideal behaviorists, on the other hand, were presumably objective implementors of a purely neutral, scientific method of behavior change which was not significantly affected by the mentalisms of either clients or therapists.

It seems anything but coincidental that the discussion about values in therapy began in earnest when the domination of behaviorism and psychoanalysis on the field began to wane. The rather rapid demise of logical positivism in the 1930s and 1940s emboldened many to regard nonempirically derived assertions and beliefs as significant. The rise of "Third-Force" humanistic psychologies, beginning with Adler and the existentialists in Europe and with Rogers in America, forced the field to reexamine the role of the person of the therapist upon the process of psychotherapy, as it was believed that it was the person of the therapist, rather than any particular technique that he or she implemented, who was the true instigator of change in the client. Finally, the various "Third-Force" psychologies shared a view of the human person, therapist, or client, as teleological, as a responsible agent who chooses based upon personally held goals that are expressions of one's values and phenomenological understanding of one's world.

Psychodynamic psychology (the descendent of classical psychoanalysis), cognitive-behavioral psychology (or "behavior therapy," the descendent of classical behaviorism), humanistic psychology, and family therapy are the four major paradigms in the mental health field today. Under the influence of the humanistic psychologies and recent changes in philosophy of science, the psychodynamic and cognitive-behavioral psychologies have become increasingly open to the examination of nonscientific factors that shape therapy outcomes. The humanistic psychologies, on the other hand, still often strive to document their efficacy scientifically and attempt to articulate their understandings of human personality in forms at least partially accessible to empirical study and falsification/verification. These changes have necessitated (or at least legitimated) a careful examination of how the values of the client and the therapist influence the therapy process across the field of mental health.

The Emergence of Studies of Values in Theories

This discussion helps to clarify why psychologists are now excited about exploring the role of therapist and client values in psychotherapy. But why has there been practically no discussion of values in the theories of psychotherapy themselves? We believe that the most important reason is that the empiricist understanding of knowing that has been dominant in psychology has not facilitated awareness of the influence of values and other "nonscientific" factors upon the very "scientific" process of understanding personality and psychotherapy itself. Such an empiricist presumption leads one to use science to look at values and related phenomena in clients and therapists, but not necessarily to use conceptual methods to look at values in our scientific theories themselves.

But advances in philosophy of science have, over the last four decades, led many to recognize the human nature of even the most rigorously empirical programs of human inquiry. There is now a long tradition of work in "post-positivist" philosophy of science, which has its roots in the 19th-century work of Kant and others, which was heavily influenced by Wittgenstein, and which has become most recognizable to psychologists in the work of Thomas Kuhn (1962/1970) in his *Structure of Scientific Revolutions*. The contemporary post-positivist tradition in philosophy of science is enormously larger than the work of Kuhn, and has itself become very complex and difficult to penetrate. It is this tradition that illuminates the necessary and intrinsic role of values and other nonempirical human factors in the conduct of all science, and hence in psychological theory in particular. We will attempt to summarize the core elements of this tradition here. We have previously and casually discussed the role of such factors in the process of doing science (Jones 1988, also 1986; Jones and Butman 1991), but would direct the reader primarily to the excellent summary of O'Donohue (1989) for a more detailed explication of these issues (see also Barbour 1974; Bevan 1991; Brown 1977; Evans 1982; Gholson and Barker 1985; Howard 1985; Koch 1981; Mahoney 1976; Manicas and Secord, 1983; Toulmin and Leary 1985; Wolterstorff 1984).

O'Donohue (1989) calls for an "(even) Bolder Model" of clinical training that recognizes the clinical psychologist to be more than a scientist, more than a practitioner, and more than a scientist-practitioner; but to be a "metaphysician-scientist-practitioner." He also suggests that all scientists are metaphysician-scientists. While traditional empiricist understandings of science would put values and other metaphysical statements outside of the domain of science, O'Donohue argues "there can be no rigid demarcation of science and metaphysics" precisely because "metaphysical sentences are internal to all the sciences" (1465). Metaphysical sentences, according to O'Donohue, have two characteristics: they cannot be directly challenged by any one piece of empirical evidence, though experience is of value in suggesting if our metaphysical beliefs are true; and they are central and integral to the person's cognitive belief structure— "they are deeply entrenched in our web of belief" (1461).

O'Donohue only hints at whether he would regard traditionally religious beliefs to be "metaphysical statements," but it seems clear to us that they are. First, religious beliefs, while not immediately falsifiable, are "experientially-relevant." Beliefs about God, it would seem, are rarely made in a conceptual vacuum untouched by experience. Rather, all sorts of experiential realities, such as the need for transcendent meaning, influence our believing or failure to believe. Experience indirectly shapes our judgments about the truthfulness of religious belief. Second, religious beliefs seem self-evidently a crucial part of the most central portions of our belief networks. O'Donohue, for example, notes that a psychologist's assertion that a certain state of affairs is problematic (i.e., psychologically abnormal) is influenced by "metaphysical views concerning such issues as what constitutes the good life, human nature, and morality" (1467). These are certainly beliefs influenced by our religious commitments.

According to the post-positivists, all science exhibits an infrastructure of what O'Donohue calls metaphysical sentences. Such metaphysical sentences serve two clear roles. First, scientists understand any isolated fact only in the context of a comprehensive web of beliefs, many of which can never be directly tested empirically. All facts are thus "theory-laden," perceived through our broader understanding of reality. Secondly, theories gain support both by the factual evidence they garner and by how well the theory comports with the broader web of belief to which the scientist is committed. Post-positivists have convincingly argued that neither the data nor the "rules of inquiry" ever fully determine one's choice of theory; theories are thus "under-determined by the data." Further, our metaphysical assumptions influence our general view of our subject matter, our choices of problem statements, the types of hypotheses we generate, and our degree of tenacious commitment to our theories. Thus, O'Donohue concludes that "psychologists' research and therapy efforts do not involve merely a circumscribed set of isolated beliefs concerning 'clinical psychology.' No firm barrier separates our beliefs qua clinical psychologists from all our other beliefs. The results of our efforts to understand and help other human beings are a function of our entire web of belief" (1468). This brief summary of the results of post-positivistic philosophy of science can help us to see how values are a part of our psychological theories. By our expansive definition of values earlier, clearly the assumptions or presuppositions that form the backdrop of the various psychological theories qualify as values, whether these are the naturalism of Freud, the pragmatism of behaviorism, or the individualism of Gestalt psychology (see Jones and Butman 1991).

But psychotherapy systems go beyond normal science in embodying values. We concur with Browning (1987), who argues that theories of psychotherapy *necessarily* go beyond the typical limits of scientific theories to answer questions of ultimate meaning and of human obligation. Any system, he argues, that is used as a guide to shape, heal, or reform human life cannot avoid metaphysics or ethics. In this way, psychological theories go beyond the basic scientific need for a metaphysical infrastructure. "Our new scientific myths are modern forms of religious thinking in so far as they attempt to answer our insecurities, give us generalized images of the world, and form the attitudes we should take toward the value of life, the nature of death, and the grounds of morality" (120). Thus, even by the narrower understanding of values as preferential judgments, psychotherapeutic theories embody values, in that each includes explicit or implicit judgments about the nature of the human life that is "good" (healthy, whole, realistic, rational) and that is "bad" (abnormal, pathological, immature, stunted, self-deceived).

One specific example of this point is the article by Woolfolk and Richardson (1984), who present a sophisticated and sympathetic critique of behavior therapy, not as a psychotechnology, but as a socioculturally-based system of belief. Their conclusion, at the broadest level, is that behavior therapy is a worldview of sorts, one that is "closely linked with the values and patterns of thought characteristic of modernity" (777) and is "implicitly predicated on modern epistemological and ethical assumptions" (778). They suggest that behavior therapy contains "a prescriptive, ideological component: a favored mode of thinking and implicit criteria for making judgments that guide behavior therapists in their activities and also represent a vision of reality underlying those activities that justify and support them" (777). Our point here is that all psychotherapy systems are founded upon subtle and often implicit assumptions that overlap into the domain we call values. As such, we must understand and evaluate those values for their compatibility with Christian belief.

Methods of Ascertaining Values

How, then, do we determine what the values inherent to a psychotherapy system are? What steps can be taken to critically understand the values of a particular psychotherapy? In Jones and Butman (1991), we used the method of sequential examination of an approach's philosophical presuppositions and its assumptions about the nature of personality, mental health, abnormality, and the process of change. Two alternative methodologies for critically evaluating psychotherapy approaches with regard to their comportment with Christian belief merit careful examination: the "virtues" approach of Robert C. Roberts and the "deep metaphors" approach of Don S. Browning. All three of these approaches are not merely strategies for detecting "values" in some narrow sense, but are broader evaluative schemes. In the process of using each approach, however, one quickly comes to grips with the values embedded in the psychological theories, in both the restrictive and expansive senses discussed earlier. Elements of each method will be used in the case studies below.

Roberts (1991, 320) has summarized his approach by saying that "therapies can be construed as virtues-systems [which] project, as ideals of human well-being and ideal outcomes of therapy, sets of traits which parallel the traits conceived, recommended, fostered and exemplified" in traditional morality or ethical systems such as Christianity. Roberts commends the careful study of the "grammar" of the virtues extolled by each therapy approach. By grammar, Roberts is referring to the intricate interconnections, in a web of belief, that necessarily exist between the way a particular therapeutic virtue is conceived and the background assumptions of the theory about the nature of human existence and personality.

Roberts (1987) outlines several steps for Christian psychotherapists to follow in order to identify essential "virtues" of a particular psychotherapy system. The core procedures are to identify the therapeutic virtues of the psychotherapy that are projected by it as positive outcomes of therapy or simply as the ideal personality and to identify the Christian counterpart virtues. One then strives to develop a critical understanding of the relationships that exist between the virtues and the related conception of human nature implied by the system, the concepts by which failures to be whole are explained, and the means by which the virtuous goals are achieved. Finally, careful analysis of the respective grammar networks of the psychotherapeutic virtues and the Christian virtues will reveal compatibilities and incompatibilities between the two, including ways the psychotherapy in question would tend to promote traits that are at odds with Christian spirituality.

Browning (1987) conducts a "critical conversation" between theology and psychology in such a manner as to illuminate the "deep metaphors and implicit principles of obligation [i.e., ethics] in the modern psychologies" (17). Because the psychotherapy systems have been presented as scientific theories (which they are in part), the moral/ethical/religious horizon of the theories has typically been implicit rather than explicit, embedded as what Browning calls "deep metaphors" or "metaphors of ultimacy" in each system. Metaphors, such as Freud's instinctualism or Skinner's use of evolutionary natural selection, serve the function of proclaiming the system's metaphysical commitments, but in a way that does not cause the system overtly to appear to be religious in nature. Exegesis of the deep metaphors becomes critical in this view.

In addition to being metaphorically packaged views of ultimacy, therapy systems are also (incomplete) ethical systems. One primary way in which this occurs is in the ordering of human "nonmoral goods" (Browning 1987, xi). A moral good is what we commonly understand as a virtuous, right, or commendable human action or trait, as when we extol honesty, chastity, or charity. A nonmoral good might be described by such statements as "that was one good pizza" or "that is a terrific painting!" A "good" runner is not necessarily a morally virtuous person. As Browning points out, psychotherapy theories systematize human nonmoral goods in such forms as prescribing desirable emotional responses (such as empathy, genuineness, and positive regard), desirable character traits (such as autonomy, self-understanding, rationality, or efficacy), and desirable behaviors (certain family or marital interactions, taking personal responsibility, or expressing one's feelings). When the theories prioritize human nonmoral goods and then implicitly embrace an ethical stance that it is good (in a moral sense) to promote more human nonmoral goods (utilitarian ethics), then our therapy approaches become moral systems, value systems; they implicitly prescribe that the individual, to be a virtuous person, should optimize the degree to which they manifest these nonmoral goods (72ff. and other places). In short, the specification and prioritization of human "nonmoral" goods quickly evolves into an informal and often unexamined moral system. Browning urges the examination of the principles of obligation of the psychologies in addition to that of their deep metaphors.

Case Studies in Values in Counseling Theories

Below we discuss some of the values embedded in three modern psychotherapy theories. As we clarify the values embedded in the theories, our method will not just be to describe the values, but rather to evaluate those values critically, in the manner urged by Evans (1989).

For very brief illustrative purposes, we will utilize a recurrent imaginary case vignette in each of the cases. The case will be of a married female client, Mrs. H, who is depressed and agitated, with her distress being most directly attributable to her long-standing dissatisfactions with her marriage.

Cognitive-Behavioral Psychotherapy

We have discussed elsewhere (Jones and Butman 1991) the manner in which cognitive-behavioral psychology is premised upon the following assumptions: empiricism as a way of knowing; naturalism or materialism as the overarching metaphysical assumption; reductionism as a cognitive value that guides judgments of explanations of complex human behavior to favor explanations by elemental or basic principles of learning; determinism, which rules out true human agency and moral responsibility in favor of an a priori commitment to the belief that all behavior is caused (in the strongest of senses); environmentalism as a preference for the location of the ultimate causes of human behavior in the external environment (though this is less true of cognitive-behavioral psychology than classic behaviorism); and atomism, the belief that the person can be "decomposed" into her constituent behaviors and controlling causes without the essence of the "person" being lost in the process, because the person is regarded as nothing more than her constituent behaviors and controlling causes.

Any of these assumptions would bear extended discussion and analysis, and each has points of compatibility and incompatibility with Christian belief. But we have chosen to focus upon three values of cognitive-behavior therapy that are more clearly values in the restrictive sense of preferred actions or aspects of the human condition. These are the prizing of response efficacy, of reciprocity in human relationships, and of rationality and action over emotionality and experiencing.

Our hypothetical Mrs. H would probably be treated by behavioral marital therapy (Jacobson, Dobson, Fruzzetti, Schmaling, and Saluska 1991). In the behavioral paradigm, depression is often conceptualized as the result of the person not receiving the personal satisfactions, the reinforcers, that they desire or need to maintain normal mood. The primary work of marital therapy is to increase the effectiveness, the efficacy, of the behavior of the client to help her get what she needs through such means as increasing her assertive behavior.

This concept of response efficacy is basic to the behavioral understanding of human action. Most of our actions are examples of operant behavior, responses that operate upon the environment and produce some outcome for the acting organism. Classic behaviorists do not view humans or any behaving organism as teleological, as acting for the purpose of obtaining some end in the future, though cognitive-behaviorists do tend to use teleological language (see Jones and Butman 1991, chaps. 6, 8). Nevertheless, for both groups, responses are judged to be sustained by the outcomes, the consequences, that they produce. Behaviorists do not typically regard this as a prescription for reality but a description of it, and hence this is not regarded as an ethical statement of what ought to be but a scientific description of what is.

As Browning suggested, however, when a psychological theory suggests the ultimate relevant context for understanding human action, it is very easy for a nonmoral good to become a moral good. We see this transformation in many of Skinner's writings when, because there is no ultimate context for evaluating behavior other than the consequences it elicits from its environment (due to the naturalism assumption), the consequences become the only reason for the behavior to exist. This leads to the collapse of all transcendent moral standards into the consequences produced by behavior, as when Skinner declares that any moral norm, any judgment of what is good, "is simply a statement of the contingencies" (Skinner 1972, 110). Everything that we judge as good is simply that which is reinforced, and, equally, behaviors that get reinforcement become those that are good. Thus behavior therapy attempts to guide clients to become able to respond more effectively to obtain the satisfactions they desire.

We do not have the space here to present a more sophisticated analysis of this behavioral valuing of response efficacy. An elaboration would involve turning to such resources as the literature on measurement of social skill "competence" (e.g., McFall 1982) or the increasingly central role that the cognitive constructs of expectancies of response efficacy and response outcomes play in determining performance (Bandura 1986).

A second value of the behavioral paradigm, the value of reciprocity, can be seen in the behavioral marital therapy literature. It was recognized fairly early in the behavioral literature that the concept of operant response efficacy was problematic for the analysis of behavior in groups of people (see Skinner's utopian novel *Walden Two*). Persons who pursue the acquisition of desired consequences for themselves with no regard for others will soon be working at cross-purposes with other persons. Those persons would undoubtedly soon find their interpersonal behavior to be less effective as others began to regard them as selfish, boorish, and manipulative, and to respond accordingly. This led behavioral theoreticians to predict that the natural tendency in relationships would be that patterns would become established that would allow both persons in a dyad to receive the maximal rewards and minimal punishment through exerting the minimal amount of effort. The assumption is that we give in order to get; Stuart (1980, 370) has popularized this descriptive concept as the "best bargain principle: The behaviors that all parities in relationships display at any given moment represent the best means that each person believes he or she has available for obtaining desired satisfactions." Husbands, for example, who want to continue to receive reinforcers such as delicious meals, clean laundry, and sexual relations need to reinforce their wives for those events by giving the wives the reinforces they value, such as attention, affection, sexual pleasuring, and flowers.

Again, behavioral theoreticians view this as a description of reality and not as a moral rule. Jacobson and Margolin (1979) call this the principle of reciprocity, the concept that every relationship tends to stabilize at the point at which persons are approximately balanced in how many positive and negative behaviors they are exchanging. Behavioral researchers have actually produced empirical evidence suggesting that there is some descriptive validity to this concept; spouses do tend to give to their spouse to about the extent that they perceive that they are given to, whether the mix of positives to negatives tends to be 80% to 20% or 20% to 80%. Marital satisfaction, it is argued, increases as the rates of positive exchanges increase and negative exchanges decrease.

In line with Browning's analysis, we again see that because there is no other ultimate context for understanding human action than that of consequences, the only moral good that can guide us in our relationships is the maximization of nonmoral goods, and the only rule we have for relationships is the reciprocity principle. If we are in relatively nonrewarding marriages, this rule would tell us first to try to increase our positive exchanges, and if change (i.e., increased returns) is not forthcoming, to curtail our efforts to more closely match what we feel we are receiving in the marriage.

In our hypothetical case, Mrs. H would be guided in her efforts to increase the effectiveness of her behavior guided by this concept of reciprocity. She would probably be told about this concept in layman's terms. She would be urged to be mindful that for her to get more of what she wants from the marriage, her husband will have to continue to receive as much or more of what he wants. Alternatively, she might be urged to "not pour good money after bad" and to put her efforts into acquiring satisfactions outside of the marriage. Reciprocity might actually be turned into an action principle that directly guides therapy if the therapist chooses to use either explicit or implicit forms of the intervention of contracting, wherein explicit contingencies in the from of "if I do X, then you will do Y" are negotiated. Whether contracting is explicitly used or not, we can see that a descriptive concept (reciprocity) becomes a guide for action, a value that prescribes the best state of human affairs in this marriage, when there is no other ultimate context to guide choice. Even the behavioral marital therapist who urges the couple to express their own values will still understand the marriage conceptually as a behavioral bartering system for exchanging reinforcements, and this understanding will inevitably be communicated to clients, whether explicitly or implicitly.

What kind of behavior is Mrs. H encouraged to manifest in order to develop more efficacious behaviors and a more satisfying ratio of positives to negatives in the reciprocity pattern of her marriage? The behavioral literature clearly favors our third value, actions and rationality over emotionality and experiencing. Valued patterns do not include the pursuit of insight, an inward journey, or a more nuanced experiencing and celebration of one's emotions. Rationality is urged as a route to mastery over one's unruly emotions. Overt behavior, action, is prized. Woolfolk and Richardson (1984, 780) are correct in their pointed summary about the behavioral stance toward emotions: "Helping clients 'get in touch with,' develop, or explore feelings is not a high priority in behavior therapy. Even in those instances in which emotion is purposefully aroused, such as in flooding or implosive therapy, the aim is the extinction rather than the exploration or cultivation of emotional responsiveness or sensitivity. . . . [F]eelings are phenomena to be 'averted, regulated or otherwise controlled.'" This goal of managing emotion is also seen in the work of Baucom and Epstein (1990, 248), who summarized all cognitive-behavioral interventions targeted at affect by saying, "the therapist attempts to change the spouses' affects by asking them to behave differently toward each other and think differently about their relationship." Feelings are to be the managed product of actions and thoughts.

In this vein, our client, Mrs. H, might be exposed to cognitive therapy techniques to help her see her marital reality in a more "adaptive" light. She might be helped to lower her expectations of her husband, stop her catastrophizing, eliminate negative habitual thoughts, and so forth (Beck 1988). She might be introduced to problem-solving methods that would hopefully eliminate the necessity of negative emotions by eliminating the types of events that seem to trigger them (Jacobson and Margolin 1979). She might be taught to more effectively label and communicate her feelings if that is something she and her husband value (Baucom and Epstein 1990). All of these are methods of managing emotion, of "eliminating the static of dysfunctional feelings." A careful examination of the corpus of behavior therapy will reveal little constructive place for the emotive, experiencing side of human life.

How do these values of response efficacy, reciprocity, and a prizing of rationality and action appear when examined in Christian perspective? Briefly, we would first note that response *in*efficacy is certainly not a value in Christianity; we are not morally advantaged when we are incompetent. The key to Christian evaluation would seem to focus on the absence of a behavioral understanding of the ends to which effective behaviors are applied. The grammar of the behavioral concept of efficacy suggests that behaviors can be evaluated only by the consequences they procure, but a Christian virtue of efficacy would judge behavior by the ends that are being served and the motives from which action flows. A virtuous response of humility for the proper reasons (e.g., not due to weakness or self-denigration) that results in the consequence of suffering is to be preferred over an "effective" act of self-exaltation that is motivated out of pride and achieves the end of vaulting one over other people.

Reciprocity as a descriptive concept has some compatibility with Christian understanding. God seems to have made marriage to be a context wherein spouses are to give substantially to one another and thus empower each other to greater service to God and humans. Marriages that are models of mutual submission and sacrificial love (Eph. 5) would probably be good examples of reciprocity, with both spouses giving much and working hard to please each other. Also, it would not be counter to Christian understanding to suggest that under their own power, spouses find it difficult to give more to their partners in the long run than they feel they are receiving from them. Negatively, reciprocity is a concept that embodies no vision of persons being able, with the Spirit's help, to image God's enormous capacity for sacrificial love, to rise above a marital or relational accounting exchange system that gives only to get.

Finally, Christians value rationality and action. Scripture is full of exhortations such as to change our thinking according to more biblical standards. But the scriptural view of persons is a wholistic one that values all aspects of the human person, including the emotional. The human heart, in Scripture, is not a synonym for the mind, but rather refers to the wholistic core of the person. In short, our thoughts and our actions are of central importance, but our capacities to be rational and to act are not vaunted above the other dimensions of human life.

Psychoanalytic Psychology

Classical psychoanalysis shares many metaphysical assumptions in common with behaviorism. It embraces empiricism, though of a more biological, ethological, and/or anthropological style compared to that of behaviorism, which is modeled upon the physical sciences; naturalism or materialism; reductionism, though human action is reduced to psychic processes understood by hydraulic metaphors rather than to basic processes of learning; and determinism. Unlike behaviorism, it locates the ultimate causes of behavior in the psychological unconscious rather than in the environment. It is the structure of the hypothesized psychological structures and processes that gives psychoanalysis its distinct character compared to behaviorism.

Psychoanalysis conceptualizes all human problems as the result of internal conflicts between our incompatible biological drives or instincts, and between our drives and our social responsibilities; this is the irreducible dynamic of the human condition. Strong internal drives cause us to constantly strive towards satisfying our personal needs. These contentious fundamental drives inevitably conflict because they do not naturally complement one another. At the same time, however, we must live within the boundaries of our respective society's norms for behavior. Finally, psychosexual fixations distort one's experiencing of one's drives and of the demands of society. Out of this metapsychology emerge three important values for psychoanalysis: the vital importance of gratification of the libidinal drives, the ultimate autonomy of the individual, and the value of work in human life.

A fundamental principle of psychoanalytic theory is that human psychology is governed by a tendency to seek pleasure and to avoid pain: the pleasure principle (Arlow 1989, 20). The basic drives of sexuality and aggression that motivate human beings are irrational and strong, and assume a vital psychological role early in life—they are the source of all psychological energy in life and are located in the id, the foundational psychic structure. As the personality develops, a second structure, the ego, emerges. Based on the reality principle, the ego's primary task is to satisfy the id impulses, but in socially acceptable ways. The third psychic structure, the superego, is the internalization of the demands of external reality. Both the ego and superego, in classic Freudian thought, are dependent upon the id as a source of basic psychic energy. As in behavior therapy, such gratification is not declared a value by Freud but rather a descriptive need; but in the absence of any other ultimate context for ordering human choice, the pursuit of this "need," this nonmoral good, becomes a moral end, a value. In spite of Freud's gradual elevation of the importance of the ego in his later writings, instinct gratification remained his fundamental explanatory mechanism. Browning (1987) quotes Freud's late claim that "the nucleus of the [unconscious] consists of instinctual representatives which seek discharge of their cathexis" (40). Browning goes on to say that human psychology, in Freud's theory, works "on the basis of tension reduction patterns of the pleasure-pain mechanism" (40). Ego gratification is fundamentally based upon instinctual gratification mechanisms. Thus, gratification of id drives is an irrevocable value in this theory.

Persons such as Mrs. H invest great amounts of energy into their marriages, with few basic needs being gratified. Expressing and receiving pleasure (gratifying drives) from spouses must occur in ways that are acceptable in the culture of the marriage and the broader society. Satisfactory marriages, in the psychoanalytic view, will manifest reciprocity. Reciprocity in psychoanalytic thinking is not the same as it is in behavior therapy; here, reciprocity deals with the amount of psychic energy within the individual and the process of releasing that energy in order to "balance the books." This is accomplished through the twin drives of libido and aggression. Partners give to their spouses only enough libidinal energy to maximize what will be received in return. Failure to gratify needs results in depression, anxiety, and dissatisfaction with the marriage.

This hypothetical example highlights the interaction between the first and second values. Individual autonomy is view as a metaphysical given; the person ultimately must achieve a workable resolution of the difficulties in gratifying her fundamental drives herself. Yet each of us is dependent upon others (or at least must interact with others) in gratifying those drives. The sexual and aggressive instincts each find their most natural gratifications in interaction with others. But how are interpersonal transactions to be ordered? Any reply will be an ethic. Browning (1987, 48) writes:

> Philip Rieff has presented an influential interpretation of Freud which depicts his implicit ethic as a kind of philosophical ethical egoism. The ethical egoist, according to the moral philosopher William Frankena, answers the question of what he is obligated to do with the principle that he is to produce as much good over evil as possible *for himself.* Furthermore, in view of the centrality of the pleasure-pain principle in the Freudian economics, it might be argued that Freud's basic ethical commitments were in the direction of an ethical egoism of a hedonistic kind and that he felt that this was the only ethic genuinely possible by virtue of the way we human creatures are actually made. . . . There is clearly a rather well thematized ethical egoism that runs throughout his writings.

In other words, Freud embraced an implicit ethic that flows from the values in his theory. It is an egoistic and hedonistic ethic of doing good for oneself in the context of a realistic appraisal of one's relationships, an ethic of maximizing pleasure and minimizing pain.

A psychoanalyst would not give injunctions for this client to "do a better job of looking out for number one." But the fundamental conception undergirding therapy is that client defenses and perceptions of the constraints of reality must mature in order to facilitate reasonable and socially acceptable drive gratification. Mrs. H may be too "other" directed, not paying enough attention to herself and to understanding who she is as a person in order to develop self-control over the vicissitudes of life. Within the constraints of reality, instinctual gratification, discharge of cathexis, must occur in order for Mrs. H to overcome her present depression and anxiety. This will result not from changes in her environment, but from examining her past, dealing with her intrapsychic conflicts, and translating her newfound understanding into actions that have meaning and value to her.

The final value in psychoanalysis is that of work. Work is a primary domain in which drive gratification occurs (Fine 1990). Gay (1989, 732) provides an excellent summary of this point:

> No other technique for the conduct of life attaches the individual so firmly to reality as laying emphasis on work; for his [or her] work at least gives him [or her] a secure place in a portion of reality, in the human community. The possibility it offers of displacing a large amount of libidinal components, whether narcissistic, aggressive, or even erotic, on to professional work and on to the human relations connected with it lends it a value by no means second to what it enjoys as something indispensable to the preservation and justification of existence in society. Professional activity is a source of special satisfaction if it is a freely chosen one—if, that is to say, by means of sublimation, it makes possible the use of existing inclinations, of persisting or constitutionally reinforced instinctual impulses. And yet, as a path to happiness, work is not highly prized by men. They do not strive after it as they do after other possibilities of satisfaction. The great majority of people only work under the stress of necessity, and this natural human aversion to work raises most difficult social problems.

The analyst would go about developing these values in Mrs. H by helping her to realize that to one extent or another everyone is pathological due to the inevitable conflicts that arise in life. In other words, problems in living are universal. This would pertain not only to Mrs. H, but also to her husband, children, and friends. Her symptoms are signals that may allow her to cope better with the demands of daily living, even though some of these symptoms may be self-defeating or self-destructive. One primary way in which to "do better" is to better meet drive needs through more efficacious sublimation through meaningful work. Mrs. H's analyst would also attempt to get her to recognize that she only needs to develop enough understanding and insight to bring some closure to her present situation. Again, psychoanalytically speaking, there will be no perfect closure to any problem, but just enough to restore normal levels of functioning.

Some of the "values" of psychoanalysis are compatible with Christianity. For instance, an inner struggle over the nature and acceptability of our motives is something that is basic to every human being. Freud's notion that inner conflict is endemic to the human condition comports well with Christian belief. Christians would not necessarily agree that our most basic nature is a struggle between the erotic and aggressive drives, but could see this as part of the greater struggle we live with: the struggle between good and evil (see Rom. 7:15–23).

Second, although Christians are admonished to honor God with our bodies, love our neighbors as ourselves, and bear one another's burdens, we are to do so out of a heart filled with gratitude for what God has freely done for us out of his infinite love and mercy, not only to fulfill our individualistic needs. Christians are to live in interdependence upon one another as well as dependently upon God, and are enjoined to form deep attachments with others, even to be "one" with others. The individualism of psychoanalysis would have us to understand our interpersonal task as aimed primarily at gratifying our personal instinctual needs. Relationships thus become means rather than ends. "Psychoanalysis is actually so oriented to understanding the person as a self-contained psychological system that even for the healthy person, 'relationships with other human beings are of value only in so far as they facilitate instinctual gratification'" (Jones and Butman 1991, 82). The best description of psychoanalysis's implicit ethic might be that of a "cautious but fair reciprocity" (Browning 1987, 49). Based upon this reciprocity, we may work with others and love others, but the fundamental motivation for such action is always the person's own needs.

Finally, Christians will no doubt applaud Freud's thoughts concerning the importance of work in one's life. One of Christendom's most important individual and corporate responsibilities is to fulfill the cultural mandate (cf. Gen. 1:28–30), and thus meaningful work is a value. For Freud work has value because it is a means of sublimation. Yet Christians must remember that one's work is done primarily in gratitude and obedience to God's call on one's life, and secondarily as a means for self-gratification, financial independence, or self-identification. What Christians receive from God by virtue of their work is just as much a gift from God as is one's salvation. We are called to be good stewards of that which God has entrusted to us, and we are blessed or judged in accordance with how we obey or disobey his commands to us concerning what he has entrusted to us.

Existential Psychotherapy

Existential therapy is unique, in that it does not pretend to be a "scientific" account of human beings, nor does it claim to be value-free. It is quite open about its values and the types of personal characteristics it wishes to propagate. As with cognitive-behavioral therapy and psychoanalysis, existential therapy begins with a number of key assumptions. First, persons come to know things phenomenologically. Second, human behavior is free, so proponents are libertarians, not determinists. Third, persons are indivisible and nonreducible; they cannot be fully understood just by studying the myriad of parts that make up the whole. Fourth, meaning in life is relative, not fixed or predetermined. And fifth, existential therapy advocates individual idealism where there is no ultimate objective reality (or at least we cannot know that reality); therefore, we create our own reality through our choices.

While both behavior therapy and psychoanalysis are quite deterministic (albeit for different reasons) in their respective understandings of human behavior, existential therapy explicitly embraces the valuing of freedom of choice, individual autonomy, and emotional experiencing, as these are among the most important foundations to an individual's search for authentic personhood. Existential therapy sees normal anxiety (as opposed to neurotic anxiety) as the means through which authentic living is possible (May and Yalom 1989, 364–65). True human freedom comes about not by being "free from" choosing responsibly, but by being "free for" choosing responsibly (Hurding 1985, 133). In virtually all existential therapies freedom is not only the foundation or prerequisite for authentic living, but is what makes us distinctively human. Our anxiety is the cost and the marker of that freedom; we are anxious because we must make choices that are relevant to our ultimate concerns. Existential anxiety signals us of the opportunity to make authentic choice from our freedom. Our freedom is not from oppressive forces that impinge upon us, but "is the potential for discovering, deciding, and actualizing one's existence" (Smith 1985, 654–55). Psychopathology occurs when we retreat from our opportunity to make choices, hide behind our psychological disabilities, and confuse ourselves by hiding behind our problems rather than facing our choices.

Mrs. H's situation is one in which she has the opportunity to become aware of and make choices about the ultimate concerns in her life. Distress causes us to be able to consider new possibilities, but creates temptation to focus attention on more concrete and manageable themes such as the pain we feel (cf. May and Yalom 1989, 380). Mrs. H feels trapped in a marital situation that seems unchangeable. What Mrs. H needs from her existential therapist is a facilitation of her authentic awareness of the freedom she has to make responsible and meaningful choices about what she does in this situation.

Closely allied to the existential valuing of freedom of choice is a valuing of one's autonomy. Existential therapy values the individuality of every person, and stresses the importance of being autonomous. Existential therapy derives this value of autonomy by virtue of its understanding of humankind's individual and ultimate isolation. As May and Yalom (1989, 378) write:

> Existential isolation cuts beneath other forms of isolation. No matter how closely we relate to another individual, there remains a final unbridgeable gap. Each of us enters existence alone and must depart from it alone. Each individual in the dawn of consciousness created a primary self (transcendent ego) by permitting consciousness to curl back upon itself and to differentiate a self from the remainder of the world. Only after that does the individual, now "self conscious," begin to constitute other selves. Beneath this act . . . there is a fundamental loneliness; the individual cannot escape

the knowledge that (1) he constitutes others and (2) he can never fully share his consciousness with others.

Therefore, regardless of how disturbing or tension-producing it may be, each one is ultimately responsible for his or her own choices and decisions in life. Control of one's life may be given to others, but responsibility belongs to each individual and cannot be given away. Some forms of existentialism embrace a "defiant" autonomy where people are solely responsible to themselves. The individualism of these theories is stressed to the point of justifying virtually all actions, as long as they are the result of authentic choice. This is because we are all in the process of "becoming"—trying to discover and make sense out of our individual existences and create our own realities. Personal struggles result from the failure to recognize the fundamental need to exercise one's autonomy in the present situation. Persons become depressed and anxious over their present life circumstances because they believe that they are "victims" of life's circumstances. What these individuals must realize is that they cannot rely on externals (other persons, rules, or institutions) to provide meaning; this inevitably leads to inauthentic living. Human beings have the individual power to choose for themselves what is most important to them. But whatever the outcome of our choices, the important element is the free exercise of our personal autonomy in the face of our individual isolation.

If we are truly autonomous, what do we rely on? What is the marker of our authentic selves? It is our emotional experiencing. In existential terms this means that human beings need to experience the emotional conflicts that are occurring within us. Contrary to many psychologies, this experiencing of emotions will not lead to more difficulties, but will enhance our understanding of authentic living and allow us to feel more genuine. Existential therapy distinguishes itself by wrestling with core issues such as death, aloneness, choice, meaning, growth, responsibility, guilt, and faith. All of these topics can evoke strong emotional responses that are a vital part of our basic humanness and cannot be ignored or minimized. One existentialist, Viktor Frankl, emphasized the subtle but important difference between internalizing an appropriate global willingness to be responsible for all of one's experiences and choices, and not just taking responsibility behaviorally when circumstances so demand (Welter 1987). A major part of becoming responsible is choosing to experience one's emotions regardless of the anxiety those emotions may produce. In summary, then, human beings discover that the road to authenticity starts with experiencing the genuine, anxiety-producing concerns of life.

Christians will no doubt agree that existential therapy struggles with the same aspects of existence that they find to be most significant: life, death, meaning, guilt, responsibility, and choice. But some existential therapies carry the aforementioned values of freedom, autonomy, and experiencing too far. There is no question that human beings have freedom, which they continually exercise; this is one, but only one, of the ways in which we manifest the image of God. The debate comes at the point of how much freedom an individual actually has. First, human freedom is contained within and constrained by the absolute sovereignty of God. As such, this freedom is not the premier value, but one among many that we possess as created persons. Second, the emphasis upon freedom can grow to the point of denying our human finitude. Christianity, while emphasizing the importance of human freedom, also recognizes the degree to which we are shaped by forces beyond our control; "the emphasis upon the creatureliness and finitude of humans in Judeo-Christian anthropology leaves ample room to acknowledge this conditionedness" (Browning 1987, 112). Existential therapy does not seem to balance these competing realities of freedom and conditionedness as well as possible.

Further, Christians will take issue with the existential view of human autonomy. We are relational beings who exist in interdependence and community with God and other humans (cf. Gen. 2:18). Christians and existentialists would agree that autonomy as individuality and limited freedom are "givens" of the human condition; Christians would attribute this to God's sovereign creational intent. We are made in his image, but we are not a part of God or an emanation of God. Because human beings are "made by God out of nothing, then we are different from and separate from God, though we are continually dependent on him as the ultimate ground of our very being" (Jones and Butman 1991, 43). The kind of autonomy found in existential therapy, however, at times denies or minimizes our relational connectedness to God and others, as if persons exist in a relational vacuum. Much of Scripture is a prescriptive account on how human beings are to interrelate. Indeed, part of what it means to have the image of God is to exist in healthy relationships with others. And thus the existential value of autonomy can be imbalanced.

Existential understandings of freedom and autonomy emphasize the courageous act of making choices, but give little attention to the nature of the actual choices made. However, Christianity teaches that neither choosing nor choice is more "valuable" than the other. Choosing is pivotal, as it is a mark of our bearing God's image. The choices made are pivotal because we live in a universe with objective, created meaning and our choices determine whether we are in accord with or at war with those purposes. As Tweedie (1961, 165) noted, we are meant to "ground life in the realm of objective [external] values," not simply to make brute assertions to define ourselves. Christianity teaches that we each are ultimately responsible before God for our actions and choices on earth. In contrast to ultimate autonomy, we are dependent upon a supernatural order which we ought to acknowledge. Christianity also teaches us that we are a community of people who have been chosen by God to relate to one another, to assist one another, to love one another, and to grow with one another in the faith—struggling along the way with issues and problems that come when two or more people commit to common goals and ideals.

Finally, emotional experiencing can be a significant value in life, but only if properly contextualized in the overall understanding of life. For the existentialist, this experiencing is usually elevated to the level of "highest guide" where what one experiences becomes the guiding light to authentic genuine living. As one allows his or her freedom and autonomy to produce his or her emotional experience, he or she can make authentic decisions about life. This seems to us to be nothing short of idolatry—the placing of human autonomy above the commands of God. For Christians, our "being in touch" with our emotional experiences is valuable for several reasons. First, our responsiveness is a created capacity which, like all gifts, should be enjoyed in and for itself. Second, this type of experiencing is indispensable to good decision making. If a Christian leader only has an intellectual understanding of the "don'ts" for living, but does not allow himself or herself to experience the warring emotions that wage within (cf. Rom. 7:15–16, 18, 21–23), then unfortunately he or she is probably going to experience the "don'ts" first hand. Third, this emotional experiencing is a prerequisite for living an authentic Christian life. Repentance, grace, salvation, restoration, and sanctification are all based in part on our emotional understanding of what God has done and continues to do for us through the gift of his Son. The joy and thankfulness of the Christian is not based on his or her intellectual understanding of God's grace alone, but is based on a holistic understanding that includes our head, our heart, and our hands.

Conclusion

Theories of psychotherapy are founded upon metaphysical and ethical assumptions of a religious nature, or that intersect with religious belief. "Values" in various forms pervade these systems of thought. Is this a regrettable state of affairs we should strive to alter? No. Rather, all science is a human activity that is colored by the worldviews, the ideologies, the presuppositions we embrace. Psychology, and particularly psychotherapy theory, is particularly laden with "extra-scientific" beliefs and commitments. This is partially due to the applied nature of the enterprise that demands we transcend the "is" and engage the world of "ought." It is partially due to the sheer enormity of human reality that must be grasped to help a hurting person; it is too much reality to be encompassed by empirical investigation. It is partially due to the slippery, ever-changing, reflexive, ambiguous nature of human reality that allows for an infinite number of explanations. All of these reasons and more force us back upon the presumptions we bring to the study of persons.

How should we respond to this reality? We would argue for two complementary responses. First, this reality calls for an open examination and critique of therapy systems on this basis. The most proper way to deal with this inevitable valuing is explicitly and knowingly. All appraisal of therapy systems will inevitably use one value or presumptive system to critique the other, suggesting the need for openness both about the foundations of a theory and of the standards by which it is being evaluated. Christians should confidently use Christian standards to evaluate psychotherapy approaches. On the other hand, we feel it vital to emphasize that while therapy systems are value systems, they are not *just* value systems. From the ideological foundations, constructs and hypotheses of increasing specificity are generated from which scientifically testable propositions emerge. While we maintain fidelity to our faith commitments, this leads us to treat psychotherapy systems with respect as systems of hypotheses about various facets of human experience, and to have a spirit of humility that while our faith framework is nonnegotiable, the hypotheses we generate from it are not infallible and need to be tested empirically and conceptually.

There seem numerous ways in which the values of counseling theories might influence the values of psychotherapy students and teachers. We probably respond initially to different theories with different levels of credibility given our different starting assumptions, different needs, different ways of evaluating ideas, and so forth. We choose to expose ourselves to some theories more than to others by the training programs and experiences we immerse ourselves in. Training programs are socialization programs that reward conformity to the "correct" point of view. Human beings are likely to seek out confirming information for their preconceived notions and disregard or reinterpret disconfirming evidence, thus allowing us to leave our prejudices only lightly challenged. For instance, clients for therapists in training may be screened to provide optimal training experiences, resulting in confirmatory experiences, while clients that do not fit the paradigm are explained away as "bad clients" (resistant, inauthentic, or maladaptively conditioned). In these and countless other ways, we are shaped by the theories we study. This reality heightens the need for careful evaluation of the values in these theories.

We close with a thought. Therapists and clients have values, which are studied in many of the chapters in this collection. Theories, as we have seen here, embody values. We would argue that the mental health field itself, as an institution created by people, also embodies values in the way it is organized and functions. These values seem infrequently discussed. While ostensibly organized as a service to humanity (since it is a human service), the presence of interdisciplinary rivalries, competition and distrust, unreasonable cost-containment pressures, profit motives, differential status, ideological campaigns, and many other flaws in the mental health field suggest that the Christian practitioner is engaging values alien to the kingdom not only in studying theories but in becoming part of the mental health field as well. How then can we be in the world but not of the world (after John 17:14–16) when we have so little critical understanding as Christian pilgrims in this alien world? This may be another frontier of study for us.

References

Arlow, J. 1989. "Psychoanalysis." In *Current psychotherapies*, ed. R. Corsini and D. Wedding, 19–62. 4th ed. Itasca, Ill.: F. E. Peacock.

Bandura, A. 1986. *Social foundations of thought and action.* Englewood Cliffs, N.J.: Prentice-Hall.

Barbour, I. 1974. *Myths, models, and paradigms.* New York: Harper and Row.

Baucom, D., and S. Epstein. 1990. *Cognitive-behavioral marital therapy.* New York: Brunner/Mazel.

Beck, A. 1988. *Love is never enough.* New York: Harper and Row.

Bevan, W. 1991. Contemporary psychology: A tour inside the onion. *American Psychologist* 46: 475–83.

Brown, H. 1977. *Theory, perception, and commitment: The new philosophy of science.* Chicago: Univ. of Chicago Press.

Browning, D. 1987. *Religious thought and the modern psychologies.* Philadelphia: Fortress.

Evans, C. S. 1982. *Preserving the person: A look at the human sciences.* Grand Rapids: Baker.

_____. 1989. *Wisdom and humanness in psychology: Prospects for a Christian approach.* Grand Rapids: Baker.

Fine, R. 1990. *Love and work: The value system of psychoanalysis.* New York: Continuum.

Gay, P. 1989. *The Freud reader.* New York: Norton.

Gholson, B., and P. Barker. 1985. Kuhn, Lakatos, and Laudan. *American Psychologist* 40: 755–69.

Howard, G. 1985. The role of values in the science of psychology. *American Psychologist* 40: 255–65.

Hurding, R. 1985. *The tree of healing.* Grand Rapids: Zondervan.

Jacobson, N., K. Dobson, A. Fruzzetti, K. Schmaling, and S. Saluska. 1991. Marital therapy as a treatment for depression. *Journal of Consulting and Clinical Psychology* 59: 547–57.

Jacobson, N., and G. Margolin. 1979. *Marital therapy.* New York: Brunner/Mazel.

Jones, S. 1986. "Relating the Christian faith to psychology." In *Psychology and the Christian faith: An introductory reader*, ed. S. Jones, 15–33. Grand Rapids: Baker.

_____. 1988. "A religious critique of behavior therapy." In *Behavior therapy and religion*, ed. W. Miller and J. Martin, 139–70. Newbury Park, Calif.: Sage.

Jones, S., and R. Butman. 1991. *Modern psychotherapies: A comprehensive Christian appraisal.* Downers Grove, Ill.: InterVarsity.

Katz, D., and R. L. Kahn. 1966. *The social psychology of organizations.* New York: Wiley.

Koch, S. 1981. The nature and limits of psychological knowledge. *American Psychologist* 36: 257–69.

Kuhn, T. 1962/1970. *The structure of scientific revolutions.* 2d ed. Chicago: Univ. of Chicago Press.

Mahoney, M. 1976. *Scientist as subject.* Cambridge, Mass.: Ballinger.

Manicas, P., and P. Secord. 1983. Implications for psychology of the new philosophy of science. *American Psychologist* 38: 399–412.

May, R., and I. Yalom. 1989. "Existential therapy." In *Current psychotherapies*, ed. R. Corsini and D. Wedding, 363–404. 4th ed. Itasca, Ill.: F. E. Peacock.

McFall, R. 1982. A review and reformulation of the concept of social skill. *Behavioral Assessment* 4: 1–33.

O'Donohue, W. 1989. The (even) Bolder model: The clinical psychologist as metaphysician-scientist-practitioner. *American Psychologist* 44: 1460–68.

Roberts, R. C. 1987. Psychotherapeutic virtues and the grammar of faith. *Journal of Psychology and Theology* 15: 191–203.

_____. 1991. Mental health and the virtues of community: Christian reflections on contextual therapy. *Journal of Psychology and Theology* 19: 319–33.

Skinner, B. F. 1972. *Beyond freedom and dignity.* New York: Bantam.

Smith, D. 1985. Logotherapy. In *Baker encyclopedia of psychology*, ed. D. Benner, 654–55. Grand Rapids: Baker.

Stuart, R. B. 1980. *Helping couples change.* New York: Guilford.

Toulmin, S., and D. Leary. 1985. "The cult of empiricism in psychology and beyond." In *A century of psychology as science*, ed. S. Koch and D. Leary, 594–617. New York: McGraw-Hill.

Tweedie, D. 1961. *Logotherapy: An evaluation of Frankl's existential approach to psychotherapy from a Christian standpoint.* Grand Rapids: Baker.

Welter, P. 1987. *Counseling and the search for meaning.* Waco: Word.

Wolterstorff, N. 1984. *Reason within the bounds of religion.* 2d ed. Grand Rapids: Eerdmans.

Woolfolk, R. L., and F. C. Richardson. 1984. Behavior therapy and the ideology of modernity. *American Psychologist* 39: 777–86.

Part 2

Before Counseling Begins

Introduction to Part 2

Counseling begins before the helpee contacts the counselor. The expectations of helpee and counselor prepare the participants for counseling, making change more or less likely.

Once counseling begins, the relationship and the information passed between counselor and helpee during the early phases interact with initial expectations to shape the usefulness of counseling.

Expectations Prior to Counseling

Research on expectations prior to counseling has generally established that a client's religiosity affects preference for a counselor of similar religiosity. However, similarity of religiosity of counselor and client has never been shown to affect outcome of counseling.

Most studies of ways that value similarity has affected preferences for counselors have used analogue research. In analogue research, the researcher uses an analogy to counseling. Typically, people who are not seeking counseling are asked to read about a counselor, listen to an audiotape or view a videotape of a counselor, or even interact with a counselor whom they are led to believe has some attitude or belief about religion. Those nonclients then rate the counselor on their preference for, evaluation of, likelihood of referral to, and degree of anticipated change for a client who went to the counselor.

Typically, the more that a participant in such analogue research actually observes a therapist counsel, the less effect initial religious value similarity has on ratings of the counselor. This is not always true. Most analogue studies show counselors to be neutral in their treatment of religious issues. When counselors are shown to treat religious issues by challenging the client's religious values, supporting the client's religious values, or behaving neutrally, then highly religious people evaluate coun-

selors differently than do less religious people (McCullough and Worthington 1992; Morrow, Worthington, and McCullough 1992).

In the following chapter, Ann Hohmann and David Larson investigate
another variable concerning client expectations about counseling—professional identification of the counselor. They use a large national study
of usage of mental health workers to determine some of the factors that
predict who chooses to attend counseling with a clergy versus with a professional mental health worker. Their survey research methodology represents another way that investigators typically study preferences for and
expectations about counseling.

Helpees are not the only participants in counseling who have expectations about counseling. Counselors enter each relationship with a
background that can dramatically shape their counseling. Typically, at
the beginning of their counseling careers, counselors are quite optimistic
about their ability to help people. Although they may not have great confidence in their skill, they look at counseling as potentially curative.
When some helpees do not improve as much as the counselor antici-
pates, the helper usually attributes the failure to himself or herself,
which motivates the counselor to continue to improve his or her counseling skill.

After years of counseling, the counselor may conclude that he or she
is competent, yet the clients still do not improve at an acceptable rate.
Reactions to such realization might prompt the counselor toward one of
several avenues. The counselor might become disillusioned and even bit-
ter about counseling, which will undoubtedly affect his or her counseling
performance. Or, the counselor might change theoretical orientations,
either adopting an already articulated theory of counseling or creating a
variant that fits with the counselor's experience and beliefs. Or, the counselor might change his or her expectations about counseling and try to
stimulate more modest changes than he or she had previously striven to
produce. Regardless of the way that a counselor resolves the confrontation with the finding that not everyone can be helped, the counselor's
expectations about counseling will likely be affected. Unfortunately, no
research has ever investigated the impact of counselors' expectations on
the process or outcome of counseling with Christian counselors—either
clergy or professional mental health workers.

Expectations after Counseling Has Begun

Once the helpee has contacted the counselor, the counselor must
decide whether his or her religious values are to be revealed to the
client, and if so, how, under what circumstances, and with what degree
of importance.

Answers to such questions depend in part on the counselor's theoretical orientation. Freud (1965) and psychodynamic theorists following

Freud recommended that the counselor not reveal his or her values to the client—trying to remain value-free, a "blank screen." Many helpees still regard this as appropriate for counseling and if the counselor reveals his or her religious values, the client is disillusioned or believes the counselor to be unethical or at best ineffective.

Carl Rogers (1951) advocated that the counselor set aside his or her values in favor of exploring the client's values. This was considered a value-neutral position in that the counselor was expected to refrain from making any value judgments about the client's values, accepting them as legitimate regardless of the content of the value.

Many Christians have rejected Rogers's position as being not consistent with Scripture, which proclaims that some values are superior to others. More Christians probably adhere to Freud's position, which recognizes that some values may be less desirable than others but seeks to understand how those values came about psychodynamically. Presumably, if the therapist remains value-free within counseling (though not within his or her personal life), the client will be aided in understanding the psychodynamic forces that have shaped his or her values and in determining whether he or she wishes to modify those values in light of more enlightened understanding that arises from counseling.

Still many modern counselors advocate a value-informed position (Dienhart 1982), in which the counselor exposes his or her values (perhaps including religious values if those seem pertinent to counseling) without imposing the values on the client. Presumably, revealing the counselor's values will help the client make better informed choices than will keeping the counselor's values secret from the client. The value-informed position is most consistent with cognitive, behavioral, and cognitive-behavioral approaches to counseling because of the emphasis on helping clients make rational choices about their psychological functioning.

To date, no research has investigated the effects on clients, values, counseling outcomes, or the process of counseling of counselors' value-free, value-neutral, and value-informed positions.

If a counselor adopts a value-informed position, the counselor is confronted with the problem of how much information to reveal and in what form to reveal it. The research by Katherine Lewis and Douglas Epperson in the present book explores this question by studying pretherapy written information about a Christian counselor. Lewis and Epperson's research is also noteworthy because it is part of a program of research on the topic. Few researchers in religious psychology have pursued systematic programs of research, yet science is built by such systematic efforts. Lewis and Epperson's chapter provides a good model of a careful study that contributes to knowledge about an interesting topic.

Another part of shaping expectations early in counseling is careful assessment. Assessment is guided by theory. The content of what is assessed is dependent on one's understanding of the treatable causes of the client's problems. The method of assessment is dependent on the theory about the nature of therapeutic change.

One potential treatable cause of difficulties is dysfunction within a client's spiritual or religious life. Counselors who are explicitly identified as religious—such as clergy or explicitly identified religious mental health professionals—may directly assess the client's spiritual and religious maturity and its relationship to the person's psychological functioning. Other religious counselors, whose religious beliefs or values may not be known to the client, might be more reluctant to employ direct assessment of religious functioning.

No investigations have studied the effects of explicit versus direct religious assessment on psychological treatment for clients of differing religious orientations. This deficiency must be seen within the context of a general dearth of research on the process of religious counseling.

Newton Malony is another scholar who has pursued a systematic study of one aspect of religious counseling—spiritual and religious assessment. Malony's contributions to the psychology of religion far exceed the bounds of religious assessment, but he has been untiring in his efforts to develop reliable and valid measures of religious maturity. Those efforts are discussed in his chapter.

Whether assessment occurs formally using refined and psychometrically sound instruments at the beginning of counseling or occurs throughout counseling mainly through clinical observations depends on one's theory of therapeutic change. Again, systematic preliminary assessment is usually associated with the rational therapies, such as cognitive, behavioral, and cognitive-behavioral therapies. Ongoing clinical assessment has traditionally been favored by therapists who highly value Freud's clinical methodology. No investigations exist concerning which form of assessment might match best for different client attributes.

The three chapters in part 2 reflect an effort to determine ways to foster positive expectations of counseling that will aid both helpee and helper to affect change that will benefit the religious helpee.

References

Dienhart, J. W. 1982. *A cognitive approach to the ethics of counseling psychology*. Washington, D.C.: Univ. Press of America.

Freud, S. 1965. *Introductory lectures on psychoanalysis*, ed. and trans. J. Strachey. New York: Norton. (Originally published 1933.)

McCullough, M. E., and E. L. Worthington, Jr. 1992. Observers' perceptions of a counselor's treatment of a religious issue: Replication and extension. *Journal of Counseling and Development*, in press.

Morrow, D., E. L. Worthington, Jr., and E. M. McCullough. 1991. Observers' perceptions of a counselor's treatment of a religious issue. *Journal of Counseling and Development,* in press.

Rogers, C. R. 1951. *Client-centered therapy.* Boston: Houghton-Mifflin.

2

Psychiatric Factors Predicting Use of Clergy

ANN A. HOHMANN
AND DAVID B. LARSON

Over a nearly 20-year period (1957–1976), the percentage of Americans who reported seeking help from a professional for a personal problem rose from 14 to 26% (Veroff, Kulka, and Douvan 1981). Of those who sought help, the majority went to clergy, a nonmental health physician, or a mental health professional. Over those two decades, Americans' reliance on all other professional groups decreased.

While the percentage of Americans seeking help from the three groups has increased, notable shifts have occurred in the relative shares in two of the three groups. More Americans report using mental health professionals than they did in the 1950s (31 to 57%), and fewer report consulting physicians (29 to 21%). The percentage seeking guidance from clergy, however, has decreased only slightly (42 to 39%) (Veroff et al. 1981).

This small decrease in the use of clergy is misleading. It would appear that involvement by clergy in the provision of mental health services is waning. However, since the proportion of the population seeking help has risen, the absolute number of people seeking help from clergy in the mid-1970s increased by approximately 50%. Over this same period, the percentage of individuals the clergy refer to mental health professionals has remained virtually unchanged (Gottlieb and Olfson 1987). This is particularly disturbing since there is evidence that clergy are attempting to treat individuals with major mental disorders (Lieberman and Mullan

1978; Wagner and Dobbins 1967). Thus the clergy in this country are taking a substantial role in the provision of care to individuals seeking mental health treatment and are attempting to do so in isolation from trained mental health professionals. The accumulating evidence suggests they are not adequately prepared for the task (Arnold and Schick 1979).

Several studies in the past 10 years have investigated the involvement of clergy in the provision of mental health services. Though the denominational affiliation of the clergy surveyed covers most Christian denominations, the results of the surveys are remarkably similar. Clergy report spending, on average, 10–20% of their time (6–8 hours) each week providing counseling. The topics most frequently addressed are marital or premarital problems, depression and anxiety, adjustment to life, and guilt and salvation (Abramczyk 1981; Arnold and Schick 1979; Gilbert 1981; Lowe 1986; Mollica, Streets, Boscarino, and Redlich 1986; Virkler 1979). However, in a sample of traditional clergy (including Roman Catholic and Jewish), 46% reported they spent most or some of their counseling time with individuals with diagnosed mental illness (Mollica et al. 1986).

Despite this evidence that clergy acknowledge psychopathology among counseled parishioners, clergy report referring fewer than 10% of those they counsel to mental health professionals (Gilbert 1981; Lowe 1986; Mollica et al. 1986; Virkler 1979). Thus they are treating, without assistance, at least 90% of those seeking their help. There is no existing evidence to suggest this lack of referral is due to differences in the severity of disorder or in the demographic characteristics of patients clergy and mental health professionals counsel. In fact, it is primarily clergy, not patient, characteristics that predict likelihood of referral and style and message of counseling (Gottlieb and Olfson 1987; Meylink and Gorsuch 1988). Formal education in counseling or psychology, a low level of religious orthodoxy, and frequent interaction with other clergy in the community are positively associated with the likelihood of referring to mental health specialists and with the perceived value of counseling (Clark and Thomas 1979; Gilbert 1981; Pattison 1969; Rumberger and Rogers 1982); low education and a high level of religious orthodoxy are associated with reluctance to refer and use of religious instruction (Larson 1968; Lowe 1986).

In light of the overall reluctance by clergy to refer, it is notable that all studies measuring clergy perception of training adequacy found a majority believed their counseling training was deficient (Arnold and Schick 1979; Linebaugh and Devivo 1981). Fifty to 81% of the clergy studied believe they were inadequately prepared by seminary and postseminary education to cope with mental or emotional problems (Kaseman and Anderson 1977; Lowe 1986; Virkler 1979; Winett, Majors, and Stewart 1979; Wylie 1984), particularly depression and feelings of inadequacy. In a survey of a wide variety of Protestant clergy, 45% stated they had received no training regarding criteria that would indicate when a parishioner could benefit from mental health specialist treatment, 55% received no training on mental health specialist referral, and 56% received no training in how to assist parishioners in making the transition to a mental health specialist (Virkler 1979). Thus it is no surprise that in a sample of Church of Christ clergy 96% thought training programs in mental health issues should be required in seminary.

Clearly, the clergy themselves recognize a problem exists. Their training fails to provide them with information to diagnose, treat, or refer. However, the types of psychiatric disorders they are called upon to treat, and do so largely without assistance, have never been specifically identified. In this chapter, we will identify those diagnostic categories and explore the patient characteristics that predict who will seek help for mental health problems from clergy and from mental health professionals.

Method

Data for these analyses come from the combined, five-site, first wave of the Epidemiological Catchment Area (ECA) study, the contents and methods of which have been described in detail elsewhere (Burnam, Hough, Escobar et al. 1987; Eaton, Holzer, Von Korff et al. 1984; Eaton and Kessler 1985; Regier, Myers, Kramer et al. 1984; Robins, Helzer, Weissman et al. 1984). The core data set includes responses from a multistage probability sample of adults in New Haven County, eastern Baltimore, St. Louis, five counties in the Durham area, and the Venice and East Los Angeles areas of Los Angeles County. The overall response rate was approximately 78%, with 3000 to 5000 respondents per site, for a total of 18,572 interviews. Interviews included information on demographic variables, use of health and mental health services, and psychiatric diagnosis. All analyses were weighted to the original demographics of the areas sampled.

Measures

Psychiatric status was determined through use of the Diagnostic Interview Schedule (DIS), a diagnostic algorithm based on DSM-III criteria (Robins, Helzer, Croughan et al. 1981; Robins, Helzer, Ratcliff et al. 1982). To be compatible with the services questions, which ask for lifetime use of clergy or outpatient mental health specialists, lifetime DIS diagnoses and symptom counts were used.

The present analyses focus on two subgroups from the ECA: individuals who report having sought help from clergy for problems with emotions, nerves, drugs, alcohol, or mental health at any time in their lives but not from outpatient mental health specialists (n=526); individuals who report having sought help from outpatient mental health specialists at any time in their lives but not from clergy (n=2,059). The group of individuals who sought help from both sources (n=519) was eliminated from the analyses because of the ambiguity inherent in the service use experiences of this group. There is no way of knowing if visits to clergy constituted 1% or 99% of service use. Thus the group seeking help from both sources was too heterogeneous to produce easily interpretable results and was eliminated.

Treatment by an outpatient mental health specialist was defined as that received from outpatient public or private psychiatrists, mental health centers, psychiatric outpatient clinics in general, or psychiatric hospitals, Veterans Administration outpatient clinics, and drug or alcohol clinics.

A caveat in interpreting the results is important. Because we are using lifetime diagnoses and estimates of lifetime service use, there is no way of knowing if symptoms preceded service use, how close in time use followed an individual's recognition of symptoms (if indeed that was the time sequence), how often a source of care was used, or to what degree individuals forgot or concealed certain types of service use. Thus these results should be considered as indicative of trends, not definitive patterns.

Statistical Methods

The complex, nonrandom sampling of the ECA project requires sophisticated estimation of variance. Standard statistical packages assume random sampling and can greatly underestimate the variance and overestimate the statistical significance of variables included in the analyses. Thus, the SESUDAAN (Shah 1981) and RTI Logit (Shah, Folsom, Harrell et al. 1984) programs, which use the Taylor series linearization method to provide estimates of variance, were used to obtain appropriate standard errors for determination of statistical significance.

Since many demographic and diagnostic characteristics are correlated, logistic regression was used to separate out the independent effects of the various characteristics. Logistic regression also provides a more powerful test of trends than do bivariate analyses.

The statistic presented in a logistic regression is the odds ratio. In the case of this analysis, a statistically significant odds ratio greater than 1 signifies a greater than average probability of seeking help from a mental health professional. A statistically significant odds ratio less than 1 (and greater than zero) signifies a greater than average probability of seeking help from clergy. An odds ratio equal to 1 (or statistically nonsignificant) signifies that a person with that characteristic is no more likely to seek help from a mental health professional than from the clergy; thus, that characteristic does not predict help seeking.

Table 2.1
Sociodemographic Characteristics of ECA Respondents Who Have Sought Mental Health Care from Clergy and Mental Health Specialists During Their Lifetimes

	N	*Clergy* (n = 526) Weighted Percent	(se)	N	*Mental Health Specialists* (n = 2,059) Weighted Percent	(se)
Gender						
**Female	375	65.65	(2.41)	1206	53.96	(1.36)
Race						
American Indian	5	1.31	(0.58)	18	0.92	(0.22)
Asian	1	0.25	(0.25)	1	0.46	(0.16)
Black	105	15.63	(1.67)	365	14.16	(0.86)
Hispanic	42	10.02	(1.72)	133	6.86	(0.77)
White	367	72.78	(2.23)	1489	77.60	(0.91)
Marital Status						
Married	236	54.15	(2.57)	798	48.03	(1.16)
**Widowed	88	9.06	(1.11)	162	4.18	(0.44)
Separated	42	6.20	(1.14)	165	5.70	(0.52)
*Divorced	76	11.40	(1.39)	414	16.20	(0.86)
Never Married	83	19.19	(2.35)	517	25.89	(1.09)
Age						
18–24	68	19.27	(2.54)	268	16.43	(1.07)
**25–45	225	45.51	(2.19)	1121	54.53	(1.31)
46–64	121	25.31	(2.45)	417	23.15	(1.34)
**65+	112	9.91	(1.21)	253	5.89	(0.54)
Education						
***Professional Degree	25	4.48	(0.82)	210	10.00	(0.82)
Socioeconomic Status Quartiles						
First (lowest)	102	12.70	(1.39)	330	12.28	(0.97)
Second	181	35.22	(2.89)	584	27.90	(1.08)
Third	164	35.47	(2.47)	674	34.67	(1.16)
**Fourth (highest)	76	16.61	(1.83)	460	25.15	(1.30)

Differences between individuals seeking help from clergy or mental health specialists significant at:

*p < .05
** p < .01
*** p < .001

Results

As would be expected from the literature on use of psychiatrists and clergy (Gurin, Veroff, and Feld, 1960; Kadushin 1969; Marx and Spray 1973), certain demographic groups are more likely to seek help from one source than the other (see table 2.1). Women are more likely to seek help, in general, and are more likely to go to clergy than are men. The widowed and the elderly are more likely to seek help from clergy than from mental health specialists; the divorced, the young working-age group, those with a profes-sional degree, and those in the highest socioeconomic class are more likely to seek professional help from mental health specialists than from clergy. No significant racial differences exist.

Examination of the relationship between source of help and psychiatric symptomatology reveals differences not reported in previous studies. There were no statistically significant differences between the two groups in the total number of psychiatric symptoms reported on the DIS or in the number of lifetime diagnoses computed by the algorithm. More detailed information on these diagnostic results is reported in table 2.2.

Without adjusting for possible confounding variables and effect modifying factors, significant differences between those who seek help from clergy and those who seek help from mental health professionals exist in three diagnostic categories. Alcohol abuse, drug abuse, and panic disorder are seen predominantly by mental health specialists.

To control for the effects of associated diagnostic and demographic categories, multiple logistic regression was used to build models to predict use of clergy and mental health specialists. Results of the DSM-III diagnostic, subject characteristic, and best fit models are presented in table 2.3.

In model 1, the predictive power of sociodemographic, health, and social services information in the use of either clergy or mental health

Table 2.2

Lifetime Psychiatric Diagnoses of ECA Respondents Who Have Sought Mental Health Care from Clergy and Mental Health Specialists During Their Lifetimes

	Clergy Weighted Percent	(se)	Mental Health Specialists Weighted Percent	(se)
Cognitive Impairment	1.94	(0.69)	2.56	(0.45)
Bipolar Disorder	2.42	(0.79)	3.09	(0.47)
Major Depressive Episode	15.68	(2.06)	18.18	(1.08)
Major Depressive Episode, Grief	17.50	(2.13)	19.26	(1.11)
Dysthymia	10.68	(1.88)	10.36	(0.92)
Single Episode, Depression	5.72	(1.25)	5.17	(0.47)
Recurrent Episode, Depression	9.18	(1.72)	12.00	(0.91)
Atypical Bipolar	1.67	(0.60)	1.92	(0.30)
**** Alcohol Abuse or Dependence	12.64	(1.87)	28.03	(1.24)
**** Drug Abuse or Dependence	6.63	(1.53)	17.62	(0.99)
Schizophrenia	4.97	(1.84)	5.27	(0.62)
Schizophreniform	2.76	(1.64)	1.16	(0.30)
Obsessive Compulsive	7.75	(1.41)	7.49	(0.68)
Phobia	25.75	(2.65)	23.63	(1.00)
Somatization	0.39	(0.25)	1.14	(0.25)
*** Panic Disorder	1.65	(0.56)	5.92	(0.65)
Antisocial Personality	5.03	(1.19)	8.77	(0.78)

Diagnostic differences between percent of individuals who seek care from clergy vs. mental health speciality sector significant at:

*** $p < .001$
**** $p < .0001$

specialists is presented. When diagnosis is not taken into account but the intercorrelations between the nondiagnostic variables are, women, the widowed, and persons 65 years of age and older were significantly more likely to seek help from clergy than from mental health specialists. Those with a professional education, receiving disability payments from Social Security, the Veterans Administration, state government or other source, or who received health (not mental health) care from a professional in the six months prior to interview were significantly more likely to seek help from a mental health specialist than from clergy.

In model 2, relationships between the diagnostic categories and help source are presented. Results are similar to the bivariate analysis, with one addition. An association between schizophreniform disorder and use of the clergy was significant in the multivariate analysis. Individuals who receive DIS diagnoses of schizophreniform disorder are six times more likely to seek help from the clergy than from mental health specialists.

Model 3 represents the most parsimonious predictive model of help seeking, including only those diagnostic and descriptive variables that have a statistically significant association with choice of help sought. The statistically significant diagnoses remain unchanged when controlling for respondent characteristics. When controlling for statistically significant diagnoses, age and gender are no longer significant predictors, though the odds of choosing clergy or mental health professionals remained virtually unchanged.

Discussion

The ECA data confirm the results of previous research on the characteristics of individuals who choose mental health professionals and clergy for help with emotional or substance abuse problems. Those with higher education and those who have preestablished connections to the health and welfare systems of this country are more likely to choose mental health professionals; women, the elderly, and the widowed are more likely to seek care from the clergy.

The ECA data do not confirm the results of previous research concerning the higher use of clergy for mental health problems; unlike previous research, in this community sample, more people reported consulting mental health professionals than clergy. The increased use of mental health professionals might be explained by methodological differences between the two studies. First, previous studies typically compare use of clergy with use of one other mental health professional; this study compared use of clergy with use of all other mental health professionals, including psychiatrists, psychologists, social workers, and counselors. Second, previous studies have compared use of clergy with mental health professionals for treatment of a small range of emotional or mental health problems. The ECA question regarding need for care covers a

Table 2.3
Logistic Regression Model of Source of Consultation for Problems with Emotions, Nerves, Drugs, Alcohol, or Mental Health

	Model 1 n = 2,526			Model 2 n = 2,856			Model 3 n = 2,546		
	Odds Ratio	Beta	(se)	Odds Ratio	Beta	(se)	Odds Ratio	Beta	(se)
Intercept		-1.23	(1.15)		1.24	(0.09)		-0.18	(0.31)
Subject Characteristics									
Female	0.62***	-0.47	(0.13)						
Professional Education	2.16***	0.77	(0.24)				2.75****	1.01	(0.24)
Black	0.77	-0.26	(0.16)						
Hispanic/American Indian	0.70	-0.36	(0.21)						
Receiving Unemployment $	0.82	-0.20	(0.32)						
Receiving Disability $	3.11****	1.14	(0.28)				2.95****	1.08	(0.27)
Receiving Social Security $	1.61	0.48	(0.28)						
Receiving Welfare $	1.50	0.40	(0.22)						
Highest SES Classification	3.72	1.31	(0.87)						
Widowed	0.51***	-0.67	(0.21)				0.41****	-0.90	(0.19)
Age									
25–45 years old	1.32	0.28	(0.19)						
46–64 years old	0.97	-0.03	(0.23)						
65+ years old	0.47*	-0.76	(0.33)						
Received health care from professional in past 6 months	1.33*	0.29	(0.12)				1.35**	0.30	(0.12)
Used general medical system for mental health care	0.82	-0.20	(0.22)						

	Model 1 n = 2,526			Model 2 n = 2,856			Model 3 n = 2,546		
	Odds Ratio	Beta	(se)	Odds Ratio	Beta	(se)	Odds Ratio	Beta	(se)
Lifetime Diagnoses									
Cognitive Impairment				1.31	0.27	(0.57)			
Major Depression				1.35	0.30	(0.63)			
Major Depression, Grief				0.73	-0.32	(0.40)			
Dysthymic Disorder				0.84	-0.18	(0.25)			
Bipolar Disorder				0.86	-0.15	(0.54)			
Single Depression				1.01	0.01	(0.54)			
Recurrent Depression				1.36	0.31	(0.54)			
Atypical Bipolar				0.94	-0.06	(0.56)			
Alcohol Dependency				2.38****	0.87	(0.19)	2.42****	0.88	(0.19)
Drug Dependency				2.60***	0.96	(0.28)	2.54***	0.93	(0.27)
Schizophrenia				1.18	0.16	(0.37)			
Schizophreniform				0.16**	-1.84	(0.68)	0.13**	-2.05	(0.65)
Obsessive Compulsive				0.73	-0.32	(0.26)			
Phobic Disorder				0.79	-0.23	(0.14)			
Somatization Disorder				1.66	0.51	(0.85)			
Panic Disorder				3.61***	1.28	(0.40)	3.40***	1.22	(0.38)
Antisocial Personality				1.01	0.01	(0.32)			

* Significant p < .05
** Significant p < .01
*** Significant p < .001
**** Significant p < .0001

Note: Mental health specialists include private or public psychiatrists and professionals at mental health centers, general hospital psychiatric outpatient clinics, psychiatric hospital clinics, Veterans Administration outpatient clinics, drug clinics, and alcohol clinics. Odds ratios greater than one are associated with seeking help from mental health professionals; odds ratios less than one are associated with seeking help from clergy.

much broader range of problems, including "problems with emotions, nerves, drugs, alcohol, or their mental health." The addition of drug and alcohol problems to an already broad list is likely to further increase the prevalence of use of mental health professionals.

The ECA data allowed us to explore the association between particular DSM-III diagnostic categories and choice of care. The strong association between alcohol dependency, drug dependency, and panic disorder and use of mental health specialists suggests that those who are most likely to use the professional mental health care system have prior linkages to the health and welfare systems which, in turn, give them easier access to outpatient mental health treatment. This inference is reinforced by two of the three subject characteristic variables that predict use of mental health professionals: receiving disability funds and receiving general medical care in the six months prior to interview.

Interpretation of the diagnostic category predicting use of clergy is more problematic. Schizophreniform disorder, as defined by the DIS algorithm, is a disorder in which an individual has a sufficient number of symptoms to be diagnosed as schizophrenic, but the time duration is less than six months. Thus in operational terms, schizophreniform disorder can be considered short-term schizophrenia.

The schizophrenia questions pose a problem in defining schizophreniform disorder. Many of the questions in the DIS used to make the diagnosis do not necessarily have single interpretations. Questions about thought control, receipt of special messages, special visions, hearing voices others cannot hear, and being touched when nothing and no one is present are likely to elicit affirmative responses from an individual who believes strongly in the importance of faith experiences and is naive about psychiatric diagnostic nosology (Barnhouse 1986). And since, for most religious individuals, such experiences would be of short duration and readily recalled, they could then receive a DIS diagnosis of schizophreniform disorder.

The ECA interviewers were required to record any delusions volunteered by the subjects, decide whether they sounded plausible, and record the reasons for the decision. They were told to base their determination on the cultural context of the response. The records were reviewed by data editors and psychiatrists, if necessary, to evaluate interviewers' decisions. This determination can be difficult in clinical practice. It would have been even more difficult in a field survey since the clinician evaluating an interviewer's decision would have had no therapeutic relationship with the subject and thus not know his or her religious and cultural history.

Thus the statistically significant relationship between schizophreniform disorder and use of clergy should be interpreted with caution. However, this does not mean the diagnosis itself should be discounted. The prevalence of the disorder is extremely low (0.1%) (Robins, Helzer, Weissman et al. 1984) and little is known about those with the diagnosis. Since the disorder may be a clue to the course of certain types of schizophrenia, it is critical that this diagnostic population receive careful, in-depth, clinical examination, with sensitivity to the potential effect of religious beliefs on diagnosis.

The most important finding of this study is the lack of statistical significance in the association between the more serious psychiatric diagnoses and use of mental health professionals. Clergy are equally likely to see individuals seeking help with emotional problems who have diagnoses of major depression, bipolar disorder, atypical bipolar disorder, schizophrenia, obsessive compulsive disorder, and antisocial personality. The absence of a statistically significant association between these major psychiatric diagnoses and seeking mental health specialty care is contrary to what we expected to find. In a few cases (e.g., major depression), this may be due to large standard errors or to the fact that one would expect only 5% of the variables to be statistically significant by chance alone anyway. However, due to the counterintuitive nature of these results, we feel that further work needs to be done to determine the degree to which clergy in this country are attempting to treat, without assistance, individuals who could probably benefit from treatment by skilled mental health professionals using state-of-the-art treatment regimens.

The ECA data can indicate a problem in referral exists but not the cause of the problem. We do not know if clergy attempted to refer any of these individuals or if referrals were rejected. There are many types of access barriers for clergy referring parishioners and for individuals seeking care from psychiatric professionals. These access barriers may, in large part, account for our findings.

The simple fact is that clergy are more accessible. While in the late 1970s there were approximately 500,000 clergy (Jacquet 1980), there were only 40,000 psychiatrists, psychologists, and social workers (Manderscheid, Witkin, and Rosenstein 1985). Many small towns and rural areas have no mental health professionals or facilities and travel over long distances is necessary to reach care. Even if care is physically accessible, it may be neither financially nor culturally accessible (Lee 1976; Virkler 1979). An important additional barrier for very religious clergy and parishioners is a fear or distrust of secular mental health professionals (King 1978; Worthington 1986). Clergy, on the other hand, are plentiful, accessible to rural populations, likely to be part of the cultural milieu of an area, available on a drop-in basis, and free.

Thus the clergy have significant advantages over mental health services system professionals in gaining access to individuals in need of mental health treatment. Since the ECA data suggest that clergy are caring for disorders just as serious and potentially disabling as are those treated by mental health professionals and lack the training to do so, it would seem appropriate for mental health professionals to seek ways to encourage clergy to link their counseling efforts with the professional system.

Clergy have clearly indicated their lack of understanding of both mental disorders and the mental health delivery system (for example, Arnold and Schick 1979). Many have also expressed a distrust of the secular mental health care establishment, as evidenced by their reluctance to refer and the source of referral when they do (Kadushin 1969; Marx and Spray 1973). Therefore, it would be in the best interests of those individuals with diagnosable psychiatric disorders if mental health professionals worked to improve community links with clergy and sought to communicate to church leaders the importance of incorporating mental health training into seminary education. With community links and training in psychiatric nosology and appropriate avenues of referral, clergy might feel less threatened by the secular mental health profession and be more likely to refer parishioners with serious mental disorders. In this way, clergy could provide a valuable complementary role to that of mental health professionals in the treatment of mental disorder.

References

Abramczyk, L. W. 1981. The counseling function of pastors: A study in practice and preparation. *Journal of Psychology and Theology* 9: 257–65.

Arnold, J. D., and C. Schick. 1979. Counseling by clergy: A review of empirical research. *Journal of Pastoral Counseling* 14: 76–101.

Barnhouse, R. T. 1986. How to evaluate patients' religious ideation. In *Psychiatry and religion: Overlapping concerns*, ed. L. H. Robinson, 89–105. Washington, D.C.: American Psychiatric Press.

Burnam, M. A., R. L. Hough, J. I. Escobar, M. Karno, D. M. Timbers, C. A. Telles, and B. Z. Locke. 1987. Six-month prevalence of specific psychiatric disorders among Mexican Americans and non-Hispanic whites in Los Angeles. *Archives of General Psychiatry* 44: 687–94.

Clark, S. A., and A. H. Thomas. 1979. Counseling and the clergy: Perceptions of roles. *Journal of Psychology and Theology* 7: 48–56.

Eaton, W. W., C. E. Holzer, M. Von Korff, J. C. Anthony, J. E. Helzer, L. George, A. Burnam, J. H. Boyd, L. G. Kessler, and B. Z. Locke. 1984. The design of the epidemiologic catchment area surveys: The control and measurement of error. *Archives of General Psychiatry* 41: 942–48.

Eaton, W. W., and L. G. Kessler, eds. 1985. *Epidemiologic field methods in psychiatry: The NIMH Epidemiologic Catchment Area Program.* New York: Academic.

Gilbert, M. G. 1981. Characteristics of pastors related to pastoral counseling and referral. *Journal of Pastoral Counseling* 16: 30–38.

Gottlieb, J. F., and M. Olfson. 1987. Current referral practices of mental health care providers. *Hospital and Community Psychiatry* 38: 1171–81.

Gurin, G., J. Veroff, and S. Feld. 1960. *Americans view their mental health.* New York: Basic.

Jacquet, C. H. 1980. *Yearbook of American churches,* 1979. Nashville: Abingdon.

Kadushin, C. 1969. *Why people go to psychiatrists.* New York: Atherton.

Kaseman, C. M., and R. G. Anderson. 1977. Clergy consultation as a community mental health program. *Community Mental Health Journal* 13: 84–91.

King, R. R. 1978. Evangelical Christians and professional counselors: A conflict of values? *Journal of Psychology and Theology* 6: 276–81.

Larson, R. F. 1968. The clergyman's role in the therapeutic process: Disagreement between clergymen and psychiatrists. *Psychiatry* 31: 250–60.

Lee, R. R. 1976. Referral as an act of pastoral care. *Journal of Pastoral Care* 30: 186–97.

Lieberman, M. A., and J. T. Mullan. 1978. Does help help? The adaptive consequences of obtaining help from professionals and social networks. *American Journal of Community Psychology* 6: 499–517.

Linebaugh, D. E., and P. Devivo. 1981. The growing emphasis on training pastor-counselors in Protestant seminaries. *Journal of Psychology and Theology* 9: 266–68.

Lowe, D. W. 1986. Counseling activities and referral practices of ministers. *Journal of Psychology and Christianity* 5: 22–29.

Manderscheid, R. W., M. J. Witkin, and M. J. Rosenstein. 1985. Specialty mental health services: System and patient characteristics— United States. In *Mental health, United States 1985,* ed. C. A. Taube and S. A Barrett, 7–69, (DHHS Publication No. ADM 85–1378). Washington, D.C.: U.S. Government Printing Office.

Marx, J. H., and S. L. Spray. 1973. Psychotherapeutic "birds of a feather": Social-class status and religio-cultural value homophily in the mental health field. *Journal of Health and Social Behavior* 13: 413–28.

Meylink, W. D., and R. L. Gorsuch. 1988. Relationship between clergy and psychologists: The empirical data. *Journal of Psychology and Christianity* 7: 56–72.

Mollica, R. F., F. J. Streets, J. Boscarino, and F. C. Redlich. 1986. A community study of formal pastoral counseling activities of the clergy. *American Journal of Psychiatry* 143: 323–28.

Pattison, E. M. 1969. *Clinical psychiatry and religion.* Boston: Little, Brown.

Regier, D. A., J. K. Myers, M. Kramer, L. N. Robins, D. G. Blazer, R. L. Hough, W. W. Eaton, and B. Z. Locke. 1984. The NIMH epidemiologic catchment area program. *Archives of General Psychiatry* 41: 934–41.

Robins, L. N., J. E. Helzer, J. Croughan, and K. S. Ratcliff. 1981. National Institute of Mental Health Diagnostic Interview Schedule: Its history, characteristics and validity. *Archives of General Psychiatry* 38: 381–89.

Robins, L. N., J. E. Helzer, K. S. Ratcliff, and W. Seyfreid. 1982. Validity of the Diagnostic Interview Schedule, Version II: DSM-III diagnoses. *Psychological Medicine* 12: 855–70.

Robins, L. N., J. E. Helzer, M. M. Weissman, H. Orvaschel, E. Gruenberg, J. D. Burke, and D. A. Regier. 1984. Lifetime prevalence of specific psychiatric disorders in three sites. *Archives of General Psychiatry* 41: 949–58.

Rumberger, D. J., and M. L. Rogers. 1982. Pastoral openness to interaction with a private Christian counseling service. *Journal of Psychology and Theology* 10: 337–45.

Shah, B. V. 1981. *SESUDAAN: Standard errors program for computing of standardized rates from sample survey data.* Research Triangle Park, N.C. : Research Triangle Institute.

Shah, B. V., R. E. Folsom, F. E. Harrell, et al. 1984. *Survey data analysis software for logistic regression.* Research Triangle Park, N.C.: Research Triangle Institute.

Veroff, J., R. A. Kulka, and E. Douvan. 1981. *Mental health in America: Patterns of help-seeking from 1957 to 1976.* New York: Basic.

Virkler, H. A. 1979. Counseling demands, procedures, and preparation of parish ministers: A descriptive study. *Journal of Psychology and Theology* 7: 271–80.

Wagner, E. E., and R. D. Dobbins. 1967. MMPI profiles of parishioners seeking pastoral counseling. *Journal of Consulting Psychology* 31: 83–84.

Winett, R. A., J. S. Majors, and G. Stewart. 1979. Mental health treatment and referral practices of clergy and physician care-givers. *Journal of Community Psychology* 7: 318–23.

Worthington, E. L., Jr. 1986. Religious counseling: A review of published empirical research. *Journal of Counseling and Development* 64: 421–31.

Wylie, W. E. 1984. Health counseling competencies needed by the minister. *Journal of Religion and Health* 23: 237–49.

3

Values, Pretherapy Information, and Informed Consent in Christian Counseling

**KATHLEEN N. LEWIS AND
DOUGLAS L. EPPERSON**

It is widely accepted that values play an integral role in the therapeutic process and that therapists' values affect the values of their clients (e.g., Beutler 1981; McMinn 1984; Strupp 1980). Due to the potential for value persuasion and influence during therapy, the issue of informed consent in conjunction with the delivery of psychological services has received increasing attention. Several authors have suggested that psychologists must provide "full disclosure" concerning their values, goals, and procedures prior to commencing any therapeutic relationship (e.g., Bergin 1980; Smith 1981; McMinn 1984; Neumann 1986). These writers believe that full disclosure allows clients to take responsibility for the choice to participate in a potentially value-changing experience. Not only does full disclosure enhance clients' awareness of the potential for and direction of value persuasion, but research reveals that such pretherapy information may also increase clients' ability to detect subtle influence attempts when they do occur (Lewis and Lewis 1985).

Although the issue of informed consent is largely an ethical and legal one, some relevant questions can be empirically explored. A recent series of studies has investigated whether pretherapy disclosure of a counselor's values and techniques affects perceptions of the counselor and willingness to see the counselor (Enns and Hackett 1990; Epperson and Lewis 1987; Lewis, Davis, and Lesmeister 1983; Lewis, Epperson, and Foley 1989; Lewis and Lewis 1985; Schneider 1985). Most of these studies have compared participants' reactions to a limited amount of pretherapy information (e.g., a phone book advertisement with or without the label *feminist therapist*) to an explicit statement outlining the therapist's values and approach to therapy (either feminist or humanistic). With the exception of Enns and Hackett (1990), these studies suggested that the explicit disclosure of values by a counselor prior to the beginning of therapy increased participants' ability to identify correctly her value orientation. However, explicit information about the values of a feminist therapist created negative perceptions of that counselor and a reluctance to see her. This was true for both feminist and traditional participants. In contrast, the Enns and Hackett study, which used videotape as the medium of exchange for information, found that feminist participants preferred a feminist counselor who made an explicit value statement over one who only implied her values.

Only the Lewis and Lewis (1985) study examined the effects of pretherapy information on participants' reactions to a Christian counselor. However, in that study, counselor-client value similarity was manipulated using a specific value stand on the single issue of premarital sex. Thus, dissimilarity of global values may have been partly responsible for participants' negative reactions to the explicit Christian counselor. Furthermore, the explicit Christian approach was presented in the third person and merely described the counselor as a "committed Christian" with "beliefs and values based on the Bible."

The present study was designed to determine if the effects found in the line of research already described generalizes to disclosure of controversial values other than feminist values. Furthermore, in investigating the disclosure of Christian values, this study improves upon the earlier work of Lewis and Lewis (1985) by generating and empirically validating a narrative description of a Christian counselor, incorporating a description of a "traditional" counselor parallel to the Christian counselor description in form but substantially different in content, and using a validated measure of fundamentalist Christian belief to differentiate between evangelical Christian and other participants, providing a means for determining client-counselor value similarity. On the basis of previous research, we hypothesized that pretherapy descriptions, compared with a simple label, would produce more complete and accurate perceptions of the counselor's values, orientation, and goals, and that this information would affect perceptions of and preferences for counselors.

Method

Participants

Participants were 360 students, 179 men and 181 women, who volunteered to participate in the study for extra credit in their introductory psychology courses at Iowa State University. Participants ranged in age from 17 to 47 years, with a mean of 19.5 years. Approximately 17% of the participants reported having previously received counseling. The total N is slightly different in some analyses due to missing data.

Design and Experimental Manipulations

This study used a 2 x 2 x 2 x 2 factorial design: Counselor's Orientation (Christian or traditional/humanistic) x Participants' Religious Orientation (evangelical Christian, nonevangelical Christian) x Explicitness of Information (label, description) x Participant's Sex (male, female). The factorial combination of the two levels of counselor's orientation and the two levels of explicitness of information defined the four experimental conditions. These four conditions were manipulated through the use of four types of written material. Thus, participants read either an advertisement or a description of a traditional or a Christian counselor.

Both the traditional label and traditional description conditions were identical to those used in previous studies of pretherapy information (Epperson and Lewis 1987; Lewis et al. 1989). In the traditional label condition, participants received a copy of an advertisement from a midwestern telephone book in which a female psychologist was advertised as a licensed psychologist who did individual and marriage counseling.

The traditional description included information from the traditional advertisement as well as a description of generally humanistic and nondirective values and procedures, written in the first person. The traditional counselor describes herself as viewing counseling as a learning and growing experience and states a need to know the client and to understand his or her feelings and experiences. The counselor indicates that she would listen to the client and help clarify thoughts and feelings as the client begins to gain a new understanding of himself or herself. The counselor claims to try to use methods and techniques best suited to the client's problem and indicates that goals and methods will be mutually agreed upon. This description was intended to reflect consensus values (Bergin 1985) rather than a specific approach to counseling. Although this description was not formally validated, several colleagues and graduate students all agreed that the description was nondirective and communicated respect for autonomy.

In the Christian label condition, participants read an advertisement identical to that used for the traditional label counselor, with the addition of the words *Christian counselor*. The Christian description provided an explanation of the values, assumptions, and procedures of the counselor as well as the information from the advertisement. The Christian description was written in paragraph form and summarized the central values and procedures agreed upon by numerous experts in the field of Christian counseling (e.g., Crabb 1977; Collins 1981; Narramore 1960; Ward 1977).

In the Christian counselor description, the counselor communicates her belief that value-free counseling is both unwise and impossible to achieve. Thus, her desire is that potential clients understand her values, beliefs, and approach to counseling. These include her belief that, among other factors (e.g., physiological, social, psychological) spiritual issues may be involved in personal problems. The counselor also relates that the main goal of Christian counseling is to enable clients to take steps toward greater emotional and spiritual health and, in the process, become more like Jesus Christ. The counseling relationship is described as one in which the counselor encourages clients to depend upon God for forgiveness, comfort, hope, and change. The counselor states her intent to attempt to offer unconditional love as would Jesus Christ. Consistent with her values, the counselor mentions that in addition to psychological techniques, counseling may involve prayer and the use of the Bible.

The Christian description was sent to 60 psychologists who were contributors and editors of the *Journal of Psychology and Christianity* from 1987–1989. These individuals were asked to provide information about themselves and rate the representativeness and accuracy of the Christian description. Forty-six individuals completed this questionnaire, 44 of whom reported that they were at least moderately knowledgeable about Christian counseling ($m = 6.30$ on the 7-point scale described below). The ratings of the two who reported less than moderate knowledge were deleted. The resulting group included 39 males and 5 females, with 43 having a Ph.D. in psychology (98%) and one having a Ph.D. in counseling and guidance. Eighty-six percent of respondents had some type of license or certification (32 licensed psychologists, 3 AAMFT certified marriage and family therapists, 3 other certificates). Raters' ages ranged from 30–62 ($m = 43.78$). All had published work on Christian counseling (median = 8), 28 had taught a course on Christian counseling, and 39 had provided supervision in Christian counseling. All 44 raters identified themselves as Christians, and 30 (68%) identified themselves as Christian counselors.

Using a 7-point scale, anchored by *not at all* (1) and *very* (7), raters reported that the beliefs in the description clearly were Christian beliefs ($m = 6.11$), that those beliefs generally were central to Christianity ($m = 5.41$), and that the description presented a representative view of Christian counseling within the limitations of length ($m = 5.02$). For the subset of 30 individuals who identified themselves as Christian counselors, the means were even higher (6.20, 5.73 and 5.37, respectively).

Instruments

Shepherd Scale. A modified version of the Shepherd Scale (Bassett et al. 1981) was used to assess participants' identification with evangelical Christian beliefs and practices. The Shepherd Scale was designed specifically for use in research to differentiate evangelical Christians from others, utilizing the Bible to operationally define evangelical Christianity. The original scale contained 38 items that assessed the theological beliefs and religious practices of respondents. Substantial reliabilities have been reported for the Shepherd Scale, and this scale also correlates significantly with other instruments measuring Christian beliefs (Bassett et al. 1981).

A factor analysis of the Shepherd Scale (Pecnik and Epperson 1985) provided strong evidence for a general factor (religious beliefs) which accounted for 68% of the common variance in the scale. Twenty-three of the 38 Shepherd Scale items loaded substantially (> .40) on the general factor. Moreover, the correlation between scores on the general factor and total Shepherd Scale scores was .97. The 23 items loading on the general factor also were highly intercorrelated; Cronbach's coefficient alpha for the 23 items was .95. Finally, correlations between the scores on the general factor and indices of religion were equivalent to those obtained when the total scale was employed (Pecnik and Epperson 1985).

Based on the data, the 13 items with the highest loadings on the general factor (loading > .62) were selected for the modified Shepherd Scale. The items were responded to on a 4-point scale (1 = not true; 4 = true) allowing a range of possible score of 13 to 52. Scores for participants ranged from 13 to 52. Based on a median split, participants scoring 40 or greater were considered evangelical Christians (n = 182, m = 46.78). Those scoring less than 41 were considered to be more liberal Christians or non-Christians (n = 178, m = 29.20). For ease of labeling, these two groups are referred to, respectively, as evangelical Christians and non-evangelical Christians in the remainder of this chapter.

Impressions of the Counselor Questionnaire (ICQ). The ICQ consisted of 15 statements. Participants indicated their degree of agreement with each statement using a 5-point scale, with the points labeled *do not agree at all* (1), *slightly agree* (2), *moderately agree* (3), *strongly agree* (4), and *completely agree* (5). Two items on the ICQ served as checks on participants' carefulness in reading the counselor descriptions and awareness of the manipulation of counselor's orientation. Item 4 of the ICQ described the counselor as a licensed psychologist and should have been endorsed by all participants. Item 7 described the counselor as a Christian counselor and should have been endorsed most strongly by those participants who read the Christian advertisement or the Christian description.

Of the remaining 13 statements, 5 were drawn from the Christian description and 4 were drawn from the traditional description.

Responses to these statements by participants reading one of the two descriptions provided additional data regarding participants' carefulness in reading the counselor descriptions. More importantly, the responses of participants receiving the advertisements were expected to provide data relevant to the assumptions participants made on the basis of a label alone.

Four other statements on the ICQ were designed to elicit inferences about the counselor. Two items addressed the likelihood of the counselor attempting to influence the thoughts, values, or behavior of clients; one item elicited perceptions of participant-counselor value similarity; and one item elicited information about participants' willingness to refer a friend to the counselor.

Counselor Preference Questionnaire (CPQ). The CPQ was used to assess confidence in a counselor's potential helpfulness with several personal problems. For each of 13 problem areas, participants were asked to indicate how likely they would be to choose to see the counselor described in their materials from a large number of counselors. The 13 problem areas included anxiety, drug or alcohol abuse, depression, sexual problems, eating problems, conflicts with parents, marital or relationship problems, academic problems, career choice, lack of assertiveness, homosexuality, unwanted pregnancy, and clarification/exploration of self and values. Participants indicated on a 5-point scale whether they would *definitely not choose the counselor* (1), be *somewhat likely to choose the counselor* (2), be *moderately likely to choose the counselor* (3), be *very likely to choose the counselor* (4), or *definitely choose the counselor* (5).

Procedure

Participants were given a packet of information containing a description of the study, a consent form, one of the four counselor advertisements/descriptions, the ICQ, the CPQ, two "dummy" instruments, and the Shepherd Scale. Participants were told that the present research involved the completion of several sets of unrelated materials. They were told that they would first read a counselor description and then answer questions related to that counselor. Second, they would fill out several unrelated questionnaires concerning their attitudes and values. To enhance the impression that the "counselor study" and attitude surveys were unrelated, two "dummy" instruments were included in participants' packets before the Shepherd Scale. These questionnaires were titled "Personal Values Scale" and "Attitudes Toward Self Scale." Following completion of these scales, participants were debriefed.

Analyses

In summary, the design included 16 groups defined by the factorial combination of counselor's orientation (Christian vs. traditional), participant's religious orientation (evangelical Christian vs. nonevangelical Christian), explicitness of information (label vs. description), and sex of participant (male vs. female). Data from the two manipulation checks were analyzed with 2 x 2 x 2 x 2 analyses of variance (ANOVAs). To capitalize on expected correlations and preserve the established level of alpha (.05), we analyzed the remaining 13 items of the ICQ with a Multivariate Analysis of Variance (MANOVA). Multivariate F-ratios were based on Pillai's trace. Significant multivariate effects were explored with ANOVAs. Data from the CPQ were analyzed in an identical manner.

In all but the analyses of the two manipulation check items, the Counselor's Orientation x Explicitness of Information interaction and the main effect for counselor's orientation were of greatest interest. The emergence of the preceding interaction effect would confirm the results of other studies regarding the importance of explicit information for participants to be accurately and fully informed, thus basing resulting preferences in reality rather than on assumptions.

Results

Manipulation Checks

For the statement, "This counselor is a Christian counselor," the 2 x 2 x 2 x 2 ANOVA produced the expected significant effect for Counselor's Orientation, $F(1,359) = 429.19$, $p < .0001$. The significant difference for counselor's orientation was in the appropriate direction, with participants in the Christian counselor conditions (4.38) agreeing more strongly with the statement than participants in the traditional counselor conditions (2.03).

As reflected in the overall mean of 4.62, virtually all participants agreed with the item, "This counselor is a licensed psychologist." There was no difference for counselor's orientation on this statement.

Impressions of Counselor Questionnaire

The MANOVA on the responses of participants to the remaining 13 items of the ICQ revealed significant multivariate main effects for counselor's orientation, multivariate $F(13,318) = 33.14$, $p = .0001$; participant's orientation, multivariate $F(13,318) = 5.76$, $p = .0001$; and explicitness of information, multivariate $F(13,138) = 8.74$, $p = .0001$. In addition, significant multivariate effects were found for the Counselor's Orientation x Explicitness of Information interaction, multivariate $F(13,318) = 8.84$, $p = .0001$, and the Counselor's Orientation x Participant's Orientation interaction, multivariate $F(13,318) = 2.30$, $p = .007$.

As indicated in table 3.1, exploration of the significant multivariate effect for counselor's orientation revealed significant univariate main effects for counselor's orientation on eight of the nine statements drawn

Table 3.1

Means and F-Ratios for Participants' Impressions of Counselors Reported by Counselor's Orientation and the Interaction of Counselor's Orientation X Explicitness of Information

Items	Counselor's Orientation			Counselor's Orientation X Explicitness of Information[a]				
				Traditional		Christian		
This counselor:	Traditional	Christian	F^b	Labeled	Described	Labeled	Described	F^b
1. believes that personal problems are sometimes the result of sinful behavior.	1.73	3.02	127.99**	1.91$_C$	1.57$_D$	2.35$_B$	3.78$_A$	49.25**
2. would encourage me to look in the Bible for scriptural solutions to my problems.	1.67	3.53	296.28**	1.59$_C$	1.75$_C$	2.92$_B$	4.20$_A$	24.17**
3. might invite me to pray with her.	1.56	3.20	228.11**	1.47$_C$	1.65$_C$	2.50$_B$	4.00$_A$	34.14**
4. would want me to accept Jesus Christ as my personal Savior.	1.54	3.31	252.91**	1.53$_C$	1.55$_C$	2.47$_B$	4.24$_A$	54.97**
5. believes that the counseling process can be an opportunity to experience God's love and forgiveness.	1.75	3.30	178.36**	1.74$_C$	1.75$_C$	2.78$_B$	3.88$_A$	18.81**
6. views counseling as a process to help me understand myself.	3.77	3.37	14.33**	3.51$_B$	4.02$_A$	3.52$_B$	3.23$_B$	15.42**
7. would be flexible in finding ways to help me solve my problems.	3.40	3.21	47.80**	3.83$_{AB}$	3.98$_A$	3.62$_B$	2.76$_C$	19.43**
8. would not do anything in counseling that I didn't agree to.	3.67	3.31	8.39**	3.48$_A$	3.85$_A$	3.56$_A$	3.04$_B$	8.82**
9. would focus on my "inner worlds" to help me better understand myself.	3.20	3.20	0.05	2.99	3.40	2.99	3.43	0.00
10. would try to influence my thoughts and behavior.	2.36	3.17	47.85**	2.52$_{BC}$	2.22$_C$	2.83$_B$	3.54$_A$	18.55**
11. would hold values and opinions similar to mine.	2.68	2.83	3.33	2.48	2.87	2.82	2.85	2.44
12. would encourage me to accept her values.	1.87	2.91	88.88**	1.81$_C$	1.92$_C$	2.34$_B$	3.54$_A$	23.23**
13. would be someone to whom I would willingly refer a friend.	3.34	2.74	11.48**	2.79$_B$	3.46$_A$	2.84$_B$	2.63$_B$	13.52**

Note: The first five items were drawn from the explicit Christian counselor description, and the next four items were drawn from the explicit traditional counselor description. The remaining four items were included to tap perceptions of influence, value similarity, and willingness to refer. The items were ordered randomly on the questionnaire completed by participants. Degree of agreement with items was indicated on a 5-point scale, with higher scores indicating greater agreement.

[a] Means in the same row with different subscripts are significantly different, $p \leq .05$.

[b] $df = 1,330$ *$p \leq .05$ ** $p < .01$

from the counselor descriptions. Significant main effects of explicitness of description were also found on seven of the nine statements. More important, in terms of the questions posed in this research, was the finding that all but one of these significant univariate main effects were modified by significant univariate Counselor's Orientation x Explicitness of Information interactions. Thus, the main effects are presented only in tables 3.1 and 3.2, while the significant univariate interaction effects for Counselor's Orientation x Explicitness of Information are presented in table 3.1 and also briefly discussed below.

All five of the statements drawn from the Christian counselor description produced significant interaction effects. As indicated in table 3.1, means for participants reading the Christian counselor description revealed agreement with the statements drawn from that description. To isolate significant differences, the data were collapsed across counselor's orientation and explicitness of information, allowing us to use Duncan's Multiple Range Test, corrected for unequal n as a post hoc test. Post hoc tests indicated that the described Christian counselor was perceived as more likely than the other three counselors to view problems as a result of sin, look to the Bible for solutions, invite clients to pray, want clients to accept Christ as Savior, and see counseling as an opportunity to experience God's love and forgiveness. The labeled Christian counselor was also seen as significantly more likely to have a Christian perspective on all of the items than either of the traditional counselors, who differed significantly from one another on only one of the statements drawn from the Christian description. Participants in the traditional description condition saw the counselor as less likely to view problems as a result of sin than did participants in the traditional label condition. However, the means indicate that both groups disagreed with this statement.

Three of the four statements drawn from the traditional counselor description produced significant univariate Counselor's Orientation x Explicitness of Information interaction effects. As indicated in table 3.1, means for participants reading the traditional counselor description were at the extreme and in the appropriate direction, again providing evidence that participants attended to and gained accurate information from the counselor description. Post hoc tests indicated that the described traditional counselor was perceived as more likely than all other counselors to view counseling as a process of self-understanding. This counselor was also seen as more likely than both Christian counselors to be flexible in treating problems. Furthermore, the described Christian counselor was seen as less flexible in treating problems than either of the labeled counselors. Finally, the described Christian counselor was seen as less likely than all other counselors to do only things that the client had agreed to.

Significant univariate Counselor's Orientation x Explicitness of Information interaction effects were obtained on three of the four remaining

Table 3.2

Means and F-Ratios for Participants' Impressions of Counselors Reported by Participant's Orientation and the Interaction of Counselor's Orientation X Participant's Orientation

Items	Explicitness of Information			Participant's Orientation[a]			Counselor's Orientation X Participant's Orientation[b]				
							Traditional		Christian		
This counselor:	Labeled	Described	F^c	Non-E	E	F^c	Non-E	E	Non-E	E	F^c
1. believes that personal problems are sometimes the result of sinful behavior.	2.13	2.60	20.34**	2.38	2.35	0.04	1.74	1.73	3.03	3.01	0.09
2. would encourage me to look in the Bible for scriptural solutions to my problems.	2.26	2.90	44.90**	2.58	2.57	0.12	1.65	1.68	3.54	3.52	0.05
3. might invite me to pray with her.	1.99	2.77	56.34**	2.32	2.40	1.29	1.56	1.56	3.11	3.31	1.24
4. would want me to accept Jesus Christ as my personal Savior.	2.01	2.81	63.07**	2.31	2.50	4.95*	1.49	1.59	3.14	3.47	1.10
5. believes that the counseling process can be an opportunity to experience God's love and forgiveness.	2.27	2.74	22.45**	2.36	2.64	7.03**	1.58	1.91	3.15	3.44	0.07
6. views counseling as a process to help me understand myself.	3.51	3.65	1.56	3.39	3.76	13.57**	3.60	3.93	3.18	3.58	0.11
7. would be flexible in finding ways to help me solve my problems.	3.72	3.41	10.83**	3.44	3.69	5.23*	3.92A	3.90A	2.94C	3.48B	8.11**
8. would not do anything in counseling that I didn't agree to.	3.52	3.47	0.29	3.43	3.56	0.32	3.71	3.63	3.14	3.48	2.80
9. would focus on my "inner worlds" to help me better understand myself.	2.99	3.41	13.08**	3.05	3.34	8.10**	3.14	3.25	2.95	3.44	2.65
10. would try to influence my thoughts and behavior.	2.68	2.84	3.78	2.73	2.78	0.41	2.29	2.44	3.18	3.15	0.48
11. would hold values & opinions similar to mine.	2.65	2.86	5.25*	2.42	3.08	42.73**	2.56BC	2.79B	2.27C	3.39A	18.46**
12. would encourage me to accept her values.	2.08	2.68	31.01**	2.41	2.35	0.08	1.94	1.80	2.89	2.93	0.77
13. would be someone to whom I would willingly refer a friend.	2.82	3.07	4.59*	2.64	3.24	28.28**	2.97A	3.30A	2.30B	3.18A	6.87**

Note: The first five items were drawn from the explicit Christian counselor description, and the next four items were drawn from the explicit traditional description. The remaining four items were included to tap perceptions of influence, value similarity, and willingness to refer. The items were ordered randomly on the questionnaire completed by the participants. Degree of agreement with items was indicated on a 5-point scale, with higher scores indicating greater agreement.

[a] E = evangelical Christian participants, non-E = nonevangelical Christian participants.

[b] Means in the same row with different subscripts are significantly different, $p \leq .05$.

[c] df = 1,330 *$p \leq .05$ **$p \leq .01$

statements on the ICQ. As indicated in table 3.1, post hoc tests revealed that participants viewed the described Christian counselor as more likely than the other three counselors to influence clients' thoughts or behavior and to encourage clients to accept her values. Participants also viewed the labeled Christian counselor as more likely than either of the traditional counselors to encourage clients to accept her values and as more likely than the described traditional counselor to influence clients' thoughts and behaviors. Participants were more willing to refer a friend to the described traditional counselor than to any of the other three counselors, who did not differ significantly from each other on this variable.

Significant univariate main effects for participant's orientation were found on two of the four statements taken from the traditional description and two taken from the Christian description. As indicated in table 3.2, evangelical Christian participants rated all counselors as more likely to view counseling as a process of self-understanding, focus on the client's inner world, want clients to accept Jesus as their Savior, and view counseling as an opportunity to experience God's love and forgiveness. Examination of the means reveals that the main effects generally were caused by the elevated ratings given by the evangelical participants to the Christian counselors or to the depressed ratings given by nonevangelical participants to the Christian counselor.

One of the main effects for participant's orientation was modified by a significant Counselor's Orientation x Participant's Orientation interaction. Post hoc tests, collapsing across counselor's orientation and participant's orientation, indicated that evangelical and nonevangelical participants perceived the traditional counselors as more flexible in solving problems than either of the Christian counselors. Evangelical participants also saw the Christian counselors as significantly more flexible than did nonevangelical participants.

Significant Counselor's Orientation x Participants' Orientation interactions were obtained for two of the statements on the ICQ not tied to the counselor descriptions. Post hoc tests revealed that perceived value similarity was highest between evangelical Christians and the Christian counselor, significantly greater than that between any other client-counselor pairing. Evangelical Christians also rated their values as significantly more similar to the traditional counselor than did nonevangelical Christian participants to the Christian counselor. However, the mean values for all groups except the evangelical Christian participant–Christian counselor pair revealed only slight to moderate agreement with the statement that "this counselor's values are similar to mine." Post hoc tests also indicated that nonevangelical participants were clearly not likely to refer a friend to the Christian counselor. The other client-counselor pairs showed no differences in willingness to refer.

Table 3.3

Means and F-Ratios for Participants' Likelihood of Choosing to See the Described Counselor Reported by Counselor's Orientation and the Interaction of Counselor's Orientation with Explicitness of Information

| | Counselor's Orientation | | | Counselor's Orientation X Explicitness of Information[a] | | | | |
| | | | | Traditional | | Christian | | |
Type of Problem:	Traditional	Christian	F^b	Labeled	Described	Labeled	Described	F^b
1. Anxiety or nervousness	3.29	2.60	40.84**	3.09_B	3.48_A	2.80_B	2.36_C	13.45**
2. Drug or alcohol abuse	2.70	2.59	0.63	2.50	2.90	2.47	2.71	0.53
3. Depression	3.53	3.05	18.91**	3.37_B	3.70_A	3.18_{BC}	2.90_C	6.67**
4. Sexual	2.78	2.14	27.26**	2.73	2.82	2.30	1.95	2.66
5. Eating	2.78	2.29	13.41**	2.57_B	2.99_A	2.42_{BC}	2.14_C	9.00**
6. Conflicts with parents	3.42	3.04	10.93**	3.17_B	3.68_A	3.09_B	2.99_B	7.26**
7. Marital or relationship	3.88	3.34	19.65**	3.91	3.85	3.60	3.05	1.85
8. Academic	2.77	2.39	8.66**	2.49_B	3.05_A	2.49_B	2.29_B	10.57**
9. Career selection	2.27	2.06	2.38	2.00_B	2.54_A	2.07_B	2.04_B	5.60*
10. Lack of assertiveness	2.86	2.57	6.21*	2.58_B	3.14_A	2.68_B	2.44_B	12.03**
11. Homosexuality	2.45	2.03	10.72**	2.31	2.59	1.99	2.08	0.09
12. Unwanted pregnancy	2.54	2.20	7.40**	2.22	2.89	2.16	2.24	2.97*
13. Clarification of self/values	3.60	3.26	8.98**	3.33_A	3.88_B	3.41_B	3.10_B	11.38**

Note. The likelihood of a participant choosing to see the counselor described for each of the 13 problem areas listed above was self-reported on a 5-point scale, with 1 = definitely would not, 2 = somewhat likely, 3 = moderately likely, 4 = very likely, and 5 = definitely would.
[a] Means in the same row with different subscripts are significantly different, $p \leq .05$.
[b] $df = 1,120$ $*p \leq .05$ $**p \leq .01$

Counselor Preferences

The MANOVA on responses to the 13 items of the CPQ revealed significant multivariate main effects for counselor's orientation, multivariate $F(13,324) = 4.80$, $p = .001$; explicitness of information, multivariate $F(13,324) = 2.32$, $p = .0059$; and participant's orientation, multivariate $F(13,324) = 2.90$, $p = .0005$. Significant multivariate effects were also found for the Counselor's Orientation x Explicitness of Information interaction, multivariate $F(13,324) = 2.06$, $p = .0161$, and the Counselor's Orientation x Participant's Orientation interaction, multivariate $F(13,324) = 2.08$, $p = .0152$.

As indicated in table 3.3, exploration of the significant multivariate effect for counselor's orientation revealed significant univariate main effects on 11 of the 13 items of the CPQ. Significant univariate main effects for explicitness of information were found on 3 of the 13 CPQ items. More importantly, significant univariate Counselor's Orientation x Explicitness of Information interactions modified all but 4 of the Counselor Orientation main effects as well as one of the main effects for Explicitness of Information. Thus, the main effects are presented in tables 3.3 and 3.4, while the significant univariate interaction effects are presented in table 3.3 and summarized below.

Eight of the CPQ items produced significant Counselor's Orientation x Explicitness of Information interactions. Post hoc tests revealed that the described traditional counselor was preferred over all other counselors for each of the problems: anxiety, depression, eating disorders, conflicts with parents, academics, career choice, lack of assertiveness, and self-exploration. Post hoc tests indicated differences among the other three counselors on only three of the CPQ problems. The labeled traditional counselor was preferred to the described Christian counselor for problems with depression and eating disorders. Both labeled counselors were preferred over the described Christian counselor for difficulties with anxiety. Unmodified main effects for counselor's orientation revealed that traditional counselors were preferred to Christian counselors for relationship, sexual, and homosexual issues.

Significant univariate main effects for participant's orientation were found on 12 of the 13 preference items, as indicated in table 3.4. In each case, evangelical Christian participants rated counselors more favorably than did nonevangelical Christian participants. Five of these main effects were modified by significant univariate Counselor's Orientation x Participant's Orientation interactions, as shown in table 3.4. Post hoc tests revealed that for all of the interaction effects there was a general disinclination on the part of nonevangelical Christian participants to work with the Christian counselors. The data also suggested that many of the effects for participant's orientation were largely due to the extremely low ratings given by nonevangelical Christian participants to the Christian coun-

Table 3.4

Means and F-Ratios for Participants' Likelihood of Choosing to See the Described Counselor Reported by Explicitness of Information, Participant's Orientation, and the Interaction of Counselor's Orientation with Participant's Orientation

| | Explicitness of Information | | | Participant's Orientation[a] | | | Counselor's Orientation X Participant's Orientation[b] | | | | |
| | | | | | | | Traditional | | Christian | | |
Problem:	Labeled	Described	F^c	Non-E	E	F^c	Non-E	E	Non-E	E	F^c
1. Anxiety or nervousness	2.95	2.94	0.08	2.78	3.10	8.62**	3.16	3.41	2.40	2.78	0.57
2. Drug or alcohol abuse	2.48	2.81	8.44**	2.48	2.80	7.84**	2.71$_A$	2.70$_A$	2.25$_B$	2.91$_A$	6.44*
3. Depression	3.27	3.31	0.07	3.10	3.48	12.18**	3.43	3.64	2.77	3.31	2.81
4. Sexual	2.52	2.40	0.98	2.27	2.64	9.96**	2.74$_A$	2.81$_A$	1.79$_B$	2.47$_A$	5.66*
5. Eating	2.49	2.59	0.43	2.43	2.65	4.55*	2.68	2.87	2.16	2.42	0.12
6. Conflicts with parents	3.13	3.35	3.26	2.98	3.48	18.92**	3.27	3.57	2.68	3.39	2.47
7. Marital or relationship	3.75	3.47	4.64*	3.34	3.87	17.01**	3.87$_A$	3.89$_A$	2.80$_B$	3.85$_A$	15.30**
8. Academic	2.49	2.69	2.69	2.40	2.76	9.50**	2.71	2.84	2.09	2.69	2.86
9. Career selection	2.04	2.30	3.78	1.97	2.36	9.94**	2.09	2.45	1.84	2.27	0.13
10. Lack of assertiveness	2.63	2.81	2.31	2.57	2.86	6.96**	2.72	3.00	2.43	2.71	0.02
11. Homosexuality	2.15	2.35	2.30	2.19	2.30	0.95	2.54$_A$	2.37$_A$	1.83$_B$	2.24$_A$	4.57*
12. Unwanted pregnancy	2.19	2.56	7.53**	2.11	2.63	16.28**	2.44$_A$	2.65$_A$	1.78$_B$	2.61$_A$	5.77*
13. Clarification of self/values	3.37	3.50	0.58	3.21	3.65	14.51**	3.45	3.75	2.95	3.55	2.22

a E = evangelical Christian participants, non-E = nonevangelical Christian participants.
a Means in the same row with different subscripts are significantly different, $p \leq .05$.
b df = 1,120 * $p \leq .05$ **$p \leq .01$

selors, while evangelical and nonevangelical participants rated the traditional counselors more similarly.

Discussion

The results of the current investigation are largely consistent with those obtained in previous studies in this line of research (Epperson and Lewis 1987; Lewis et al. 1983; Lewis et al. 1989; Lewis and Lewis 1985; Schneider 1985). This consistency demonstrates the generalizability of earlier studies conducted using the feminist therapy approach to Christian counseling, another counseling approach with a very explicit value orientation. Together, these studies provide empirical support for the suggestion that the provision of pretherapy information about a counselor's values, goals, and techniques enhances potential clients' ability to make informed choices regarding a counseling relationship. However, the results of all these studies must be interpreted with the caution appropriate to an analog design.

One of the central questions asked in this research line, including the present study, has involved the sufficiency of a label (e.g., Christian counselor or feminist counselor), as opposed to more explicit information for ensuring potential clients' informed consent. The emergence of 11 significant Counselor's Orientation x Explicitness of Information interactions on the 13 items of the ICQ was consistent with previous studies and clearly supported the crucial role of explicit pretherapy information in informing potential clients about the values and assumptions underlying a counseling label. Participants receiving only the Christian advertisement showed significantly less confidence in their inferences about the counselor's beliefs, techniques, and orientation than did those receiving explicit descriptions. However, as opposed to previous studies in which a labeled feminist counselor was perceived as similar to the two traditional counselors and quite different from the described feminist counselor, in this study the labeled Christian counselor was seen as more likely to use Christian counseling techniques than either of the traditional counselors. The ratings for the labeled Christian counselor on the items drawn from the Christian description were significantly lower than those given to the described counselor, but significantly higher than those given to both traditional counselors. Thus, it appears that participants were able to correctly extrapolate from the label *Christian* to the assumptions underlying the label, but they had less confidence about their inferences than the explicitly informed participants. The fact that a label alone can give *some* general indication of a therapist's values supports calls such as Neumann (1986) for reform in APA's ethical standards. Neumann suggests that "Principle 10 should be amended to require a brief identification of therapist's values in public listings and other service announcements" (191). More research is needed to clarify which labels convey generally accurate impressions to potential clients. Based upon current studies, it appears that the label *Christian counselor* is more widely understood than *feminist therapist*.

While it is encouraging to find that the label *Christian counselor* implies to potential clients some degree of adherence to certain beliefs and practices, these same findings may be problematic to practitioners. According to Worthington and Gascoyne (1985), "there is more diversity in counseling style and theory among counselors who are Christians than there is unity of style and theory" (29–30). Christian counselors may vary a great deal in their approach to religious issues as well as in their use or rejection of psychological theories and techniques (e.g., Adams 1970 vs. Bustanoby 1976 vs. Crabb 1977 vs. Narramore 1960). However, potential clients may be unaware of the range of Christian beliefs and even potential incompatibility of particular Christian approaches with their own beliefs and values. Furthermore, potential clients may be somewhat rebuffed by Christian approaches due to the erroneous assumption that they represent a rigid adherence to a narrow range of "Christian" therapy techniques. As evidence for this assumption, both described and labeled Christian counselors were viewed as being less flexible in dealing with clients' problems than the described traditional counselors. Moreover, labeled and described Christian counselors were viewed as significantly more likely than traditional counselors to encourage clients to accept their values and attempt to influence clients' thoughts and behaviors. In previous articles, we have discussed clients' expectation of value-neutrality on the part of counselors (see Lewis et al. 1989). The presentation of controversial values (e.g., Christian or feminist) violates clients' expectations and often conveys inflexibility and rigidity. On the other hand, the presentation of consensus values, such as those found in the traditional description, confirms expectations and enhances perceptions of tolerance and flexibility. It appears that in order for potential clients to be informed and confident about their assumptions regarding a counselor, explicit pretherapy information detailing both the counselor's controversial beliefs and the range of typical psychological and religious practices would be preferable to a label alone.

In previous research (Epperson and Lewis 1987; Lewis et al. 1989) explicit pretherapy information of a controversial nature has generally decreased willingness to see a counselor except in areas deemed relevant to the counselor's values (e.g., career concerns with explicit feminist counselors). However, the opposite effect occurs when participants are exposed to the explicit traditional description containing largely consensus values (Bergin 1985).

In the present study, presentation of explicit information about the traditional counselor enhanced participants' willingness to see that counselor or to refer a friend, as it has in previous studies. However, the provision of explicit information about the Christian counselor did not result in an overall decreased willingness to see that counselor, as was the case for an explicitly described feminist therapist in previous studies. This is evident in the fact that willingness to see the labeled vs. the described Christian counselor was different in only one of the seven significant Counselor's Orientation x Explicitness of Information interactions reported in table 3.3. Of the remaining four unmodified main effects for counselor's orientation, differences in willingness to see the labeled vs. described Christian counselor appear to have substantially contributed to only two.

The reason for explicit information about the Christian counselor not resulting in an overall disinclination to see that counselor appears to be the significant Counselor's Orientation x Participant's Orientation interaction effects. As indicated in table 3.4, these interaction effects are due to the nonevangelical Christian participants' decreased willingness to see the Christian counselors. In each of these interactions, evangelical Christian participants were equally willing to see the Christian or traditional counselors. Of the remaining unmodified main effects for counselor's orientation, about 50% appear to be due to the generally more dramatic differences in nonevangelical participants' willingness to see the traditional vs. Christian counselors.

Thus, in this study, there appeared to be some effect for value similarity. It is interesting to note that evangelical Christian participants indicated significantly greater belief than nonevangelical Christian participants that *all* counselors would view counseling as an opportunity to experience God's love and forgiveness, want them to accept Jesus as Savior, and hold values similar to theirs. Thus, the effect of value similarity may have been attenuated by questionable assumptions about the traditional counselors on the part of evangelical Christians.

Overall, the results of this study are largely consistent with past research in pointing to the importance of explicit pretherapy information for informed consent. Additionally, the results suggest that this can be done without alienating the population most likely to utilize Christian counseling services. We can only assume that the inclusion of consensus values in descriptions of Christian counseling would make such services even more attractive to potential Christian clients. This may be even further enhanced when pretherapy information is provided in person, as suggested in research by Enns and Hackett (1990).

Counselors should always meet their ethical obligations. The present study begins to identify ways that this can be done responsibly and without decreasing utilization by likely users, and further research will help refine these methods. We would encourage Christian counselors to be in the vanguard in establishing and encouraging such practices.

References

Adams, J. E. 1970. *Competent to counsel.* Phillipsburg, N.J.: Presbyterian and Reformed.

Bassett, R. L., R. D. Sadler, E. E. Kobischen, D. M. Skiff, I. J. Merrill, B. J. Atwater, and D. W. Livermore. 1981. The Shepherd Scale: Separating the sheep from the goats. *Journal of Psychology and Theology* 9: 335–51.

Bergin, A. E. 1980. Psychotherapy and religious values. *Journal of Consulting and Clinical Psychology* 48: 95–105.

Bergin, A. E. 1985. Proposed values for guiding and evaluating counseling and psychotherapy. *Counseling and Values* 29: 99–116.

Beutler, L. E. 1981. Convergence in counseling and psychotherapy: A current look. *Clinical Psychology Review* 1: 79–101.

Bustanoby, A. 1976. *You can change your personality: Make it a spiritual asset.* Grand Rapids: Zondervan.

Collins, G. 1981. *Helping people grow: Practical approaches to Christian counseling.* Santa Ana, Calif.: Vision House.

Crabb, L. J., Jr. 1977. *Effective biblical counseling.* Grand Rapids: Zondervan.

Enns, C. Z., and G. Hackett. 1990. Comparison of feminist and non-feminist women's reactions to variants of nonsexist and feminist counseling. *Journal of Counseling Psychology* 37: 33–40.

Epperson, D. L., and K. N. Lewis. 1987. Issue of informed entry into counseling: Perceptions and preferences resulting from different types and amounts of pretherapy information. *Journal of Counseling Psychology* 34: 266–75.

Lewis, K. N., C. S. Davis, and R. Lesmeister. 1983. Pretherapy information: An investigation of client response. *Journal of Counseling Psychology* 30: 108–12.

Lewis, K. N., D. L. Epperson, and J. Foley. 1989. Informed entry into counseling: Client's perceptions and preferences resulting from different types and amounts of pretherapy information. *Journal of Counseling Psychology* 36: 279–85.

Lewis, K. N., and D. A. Lewis. 1985. Pretherapy information, counselor influence, and value similarity: Impact on female clients' reactions. *Counseling and Value* 29: 151–63.

McMinn, M. R. 1984. Religious values and client-therapist matching in psychotherapy. *Journal of Psychology and Theology* 12: 24–33.

Narramore, C. M. 1960. *The psychology of counseling.* Grand Rapids: Zondervan.

Neumann, J. K. 1986. The American Psychological Association and value pluralism. *Journal of Psychology and Theology* 14: 185–93.

Pecnik, J. A., and D. L. Epperson. 1985. A factor analysis and further validation of the Shepherd Scale. *Journal of Psychology and Theology* 13: 42–49.

Schneider, L. J. 1985. Feminist values in announcements of professional services. *Journal of Counseling Psychology* 32: 637–40.

Smith, D. 1981. Unfinished business with informed consent procedures. *American Psychologist* 36: 22–26.

Strupp, H. H. 1980. Humanism and psychotherapy: A personal statement of the therapist's essential values. *Psychotherapy: Theory, Research, and Practice* 17: 396–400.

Ward, W. O. 1977. *The Bible in counseling.* Chicago: Moody.

Worthington, E. L., Jr., and S. R. Gascoyne. 1985. Preferences of Christians and non-Christians for five Christian counselors' treatment plans: A partial replication and extension. *Journal of Psychology and Theology* 13: 29–41.

4

The Relevance of "Religious Diagnosis" for Counseling

H. Newton Malony

I trust the reader will tolerate my beginning this essay with a whimsical reference to the Morris Motorcar Company of Great Britain. Four of its products provide a helpful framework around which to organize these thoughts about the relevance of making a "religious diagnosis" in counseling. I first became aware of the Morris line of cars when I saw a strange, undersized, blunt-nosed, wood-paneled station wagon on the streets of Los Angeles. Close inspection revealed this to be the Morris "Minor"—an English import, which had attracted a semi-cult following in the United States. The Morris Minor provides a construct around which to debate the salience or importance of religion in the lives of those who come to counselors for help.

Prior to discussing the importance of religion in contemporary life, I would like to mention three other cars produced by the Morris company. Their names provide constructs around which the remainder of this essay is organized. In addition to the Minor line, Morris also produces "Mini," "Midi," and "Maxi" automobiles. I first became aware of the Mini when I discovered it was the cheapest car my wife and I could rent for a circle trip to and from some reconditioned castles outside Lisbon, Portugal. I did not realize when making these arrangements that the two-door Mini was just what the name implied—a diminutive car with minimal space and comfort for a six-foot-tall person like myself! It took a sabbatical year in Oxford, the home of Morris Motors, for me to realize that the company also produced the Midi, a medium-sized sedan with tolerable space, and the Maxi, a large car with luxurious accommodations. Using the names of these three autos, I intend to describe a set of diagnostic procedures that have been developed to minimally, moderately, and maximally incorporate religion into the counseling process.

Thus, the outline of this essay will be as follows. First, under the "Minor" heading, I will consider the thesis that religion plays only a minor role in human experience and, therefore, is not a factor in emotional disturbance or mental health. If this is so, time spent by counselors in evaluating religion may be of little value. This thesis must be considered, if not countered, by those who would attach any importance to dealing with religious issues in counseling.

Second, under the "Mini, Midi, and Maxi" heading I will describe and evaluate the following:

   the attempts that have been made to diagnose religious status in counselees

   the uses of religious assessment in the diagnostic process as conceived
   within the five axes of the DSM-III R

   the several functions of religion in human life

   some definitions of religious maturity.

In discussion of these issues, the mini-midi-maxi continuum will be applied in several ways: from good to bad, from small to large, from one to many, and from minimal to maximal.

Religion: Of Minor or Major Importance in Life?

In determining the relevance of making religious diagnoses in counseling, an initial question must be answered, namely, How important is religion to the mental health of the average person? The rationale for addressing such a question is this. If religion is an important dimension of human experience, then counselors should not neglect to evaluate its status. If, however, religion plays an insignificant role in the emotional adjustment of the average person, then counseling time might be better spent in other ways than in making a religious diagnosis. After all, counseling time is limited and counselors are always making judgments about what aspects of life to emphasize and what aspects to ignore.

There is some warrant for contending religion is a pervasive fact of human life. Sociology has long stated that every human society has three basic institutions—family, state, and religion. Surveys of American culture support this presumption. They have concluded that 90% of Americans say they believe in God, over 50% belong to some religious group, and about 30% participate in weekly religious activity. A recent study by sociologist Barry Kosmin supports these statistics (O'Guinn 1991). Only

7.5% of the population reported they had no religion, while 80% claimed to be Christian. Assuming that self-identification and attendance are synonymous with importance, it seems logical to assume that religion would have import for the life adjustment of most persons and that some form of religious diagnosis should be included in the standard battery of tests administered by counselors (Malony 1985). Along with social histories and family dynamics, religion might be assumed to be one of the more crucial factors influencing emotional disturbance and mental health.

In even stronger support for this presumption, I reaffirmed, in an earlier essay (Malony 1983), the model of the social psychologist Theodore Sarbin that adjustment to the "transcendent" is an essential ingredient of social identity. Sarbin (1970) asserted that every individual must adjust to transcendental reality and must accommodate to the physical, situational, interpersonal, and idealistic environments of life. Transcendental reality is understood to mean that province of life usually ascribed to religion. It includes the supernatural, transempirical reality in terms of which people find ultimate meaning to their existence. I agreed with Sarbin concerning the absolute necessity that persons come to terms with this transcendent dimension at the same time that they adjust themselves to their bodies, their cultures, their associates, and their values.

I went one step beyond Sarbin, however, in suggesting that this transcendent reality is the most important of the five life-environments. Social identity, from this point of view, is not determined by adding up adjustments across all of the environments but is a function of multiplying the sum of the other four by the individual's adjustment to the transcendent (Malony 1983). If my contention about the primacy of adjustment to transcendent reality is correct, religion is not only one of the important life dimensions that should be assessed by counselors, it would probably be the most important. If this is true, then making a religious diagnosis becomes a necessity, not an option.

However, my views about the importance of religion in contemporary life are not universally shared. There is a widespread contention that religion has become irrelevant to daily life. I am convinced that many counselors have shared this view in the past; else why have there been only rare attempts to assess religious status along with evaluations of personality, social history, family background, intelligence, and cognitive functioning? Management theorist Peter Drucker speaks for many such theorists in his reported statement, "Religion lives off the excess of society." By this Drucker means that religion, like hobbies and recreations, has become, for most people, what they do with their spare time. It is no longer central to their lives, if indeed, it ever was. Society's main thrust, according to this analysis, has become irreligious, or secular. Religion is passe—no longer central to society's life. According to this view, some persons continue to be religious, most do not. Religion is a private affair that is becoming less and less viable for the great majority of the public, quite apart from their identification of themselves as "Christian" and quite apart from their cultural accommodation to church attendance in their spare time.

Lesslie Newbigin (1986) sums up this point of view in a penetrating account of cultural developments since the Enlightenment. He notes how ludicrous it is for churches in societies that have become secularized and almost irreligious to continue to send missionaries into cultures that have become self-consciously religious and where the church is growing at a fast rate. Newbigin (1986) sees this transition from the sacred to the secular as a result of the influence of modern science and, especially, the work of Isaac Newton. He states, "The effect of the work of the new scientists, and above all the brilliant vision of Newton, was to replace this [divine purpose] explanatory framework with another. The real world disclosed by the work of science was one governed not by purpose but by natural laws of cause and effect" (24).

The way in which these scientific changes came to affect individual existence and the importance of religion for daily life is critical to note. The central conviction of scientists that reason, rather than faith, is the essential rule by which their research is to be undertaken, became the basis for everyday interaction with the world. Reason meant those "analytical and mathematical powers by which human beings could attain (at least in principle) to a complete understanding of, and thus a full mastery of nature—of reality in all its forms . . . no alleged divine revelation, no tradition however ancient, and no dogma however hallowed has the right to veto its exercise" (Newbigin 1986, 25). The rational individual became the norm from the 18th century to the present.

"Rational individuals" were presumed to have the potential as well as the right to exercise their reason in search for reality. From this presumption came the ideas of the human right to life, liberty, and the pursuit of happiness, according to Newbigin. Since teleology, or final purpose, had been obliterated from human understanding by the advent of the age of reason, happiness was no longer defined by life after death or even pleasing God here and now. Happiness became defined in this-worldly terms by all rational individuals by themselves alone. According to Newbigin, medieval people did not expect to find full happiness on earth, but rational persons did. "The methods of modern science provide no grounds for belief that there is something beyond death. Hence the whole freight of human happiness has to be carried in a few short and uncertain years that are allowed us before death ends it all. The quest for happiness becomes that much more hectic, more fraught with anxiety than it was to the people of the Middle Ages" (Newbigin 1986, 27).

This analysis of the cultural situation in the western world challenges the view that religion still has much import for the average individual.

In contrast to the view that all individuals have to deal with transcendent reality and/or that their adjustment to this dimension of life colors the rest of their existence, this analysis implies that religion is, indeed, as Drucker suggested, an "excess" elective, not a requirement, of life. Religion is thus thought to be a private option rather than a public mandate.

In an innovative follow-up study of students in the Sierra Project, Day (1991) reported conclusions that support this view that there is a lack of religious concerns in many young adults. The Sierra Project was a living/learning project initiated by the University of California to raise the level of moral development in college students. In interviews some years later, Day (1991) was surprised to note the lack of religious influence and involvement among these students who, by the time of the interviews, were almost 30 years old. According to Day, the inference that there is still a "religious factor" to which counselors need to attend may be more a "guild" issue of professionals who define themselves as students of religion than a social reality. There may be no religious influence to measure among most adults. Those who want to study religion may be talking to themselves.

In spite of Day's conclusion that the day of religion may have passed, the fact remains that a significant percentage of the American public still consider themselves to be religious and they continue to participate in organized religious groups. One has to admit that there is an element of cultural conformity to these statistics in that participation is twice as high in the south than in the west. Certainly the data on American religion is duplicated nowhere in the western world. Religious participation in Britain and Europe is very slight. It also has to be acknowledged, however, that there are innovative ways to express religious interest, as can be seen in the appeal of the new religions and New Age movements. Nevertheless, the messages communicated by leaders in these religious experiences do not fall on completely deaf ears. Some people are still being influenced by transempirical, transcendent ideas, and it would appear prudent to assess whether and how religion is impacting their lives, be they ever so few.

In a survey of California psychologists, a majority of those surveyed indicated that their clients presented spiritual problems to them in counseling (Shafranske and Malony 1985). These results were later replicated in a national sample (Shafranske and Malony 1990). It would seem as if religious issues are still arising in counseling even if the larger society seems to be becoming more secular. While we may admit that counselees are a societal subgroup and/or that religion has become a private, subcultural affair, it would seem a strategic move to determine its importance among specific individuals in the face of clear mandates in the helping professions to consider cross-cultural influences in emotional disturbances. The rest of this essay is based on this judgment that religion is, indeed, at least a minor, if not a major, influence in some, if not all, persons' lives.

Mini, Midi, and Maxi Issues Regarding Religious Diagnosis

Attempts to Diagnose Religion

The first of the mini, midi, and maxi issues regarding religious diagnosis pertains to previous attempts to undertake religious diagnoses among counselees. Chief among these were the early efforts of psychiatrist Edgar Draper and his colleagues at the University of Mississippi Medical School (Draper, Meyer, Parzen, and Samuelson 1965). They concluded that they could classify patients into valid psychiatric categories on the basis of patients' responses to the simple prompt, "Tell me about your religion." This could be termed a mini attempt because it asked only one question and because it only inferred the import of religion for psychopathology and made no judgments about the maturity of patient's faith itself.

However, this effort (Draper et al. 1965) illustrates the basic difference between diagnosis and research. Draper and his colleagues functioned in a medical school where the emphasis was more on treatment than on research. In diagnosis, treatment is the prime concern. In research, understanding is the prime goal. While it is true that the conclusions reached in research can be applied, in diagnosis the results are primarily directed to remediation. Thus, the critical aspect of diagnosis is that all assessments are brought together in a combined report designed to help counselors do a better job of helping people. Typically, research investigations are undertaken for their own sake—the advancement of knowledge rather than the betterment of one individual. While the literature is replete with research studies of religion (e.g., Batson and Ventis 1982; Spilka, Hood, and Gorsuch 1985), the examples of diagnostic approaches have been fewer (Draper et al. 1965; Malony 1988; Pruyser 1965).

Although many of us who have worked in mental hospitals know how seductive diagnosing can be and how rare are those occasions when counseling is truly based on diagnosis, we also know that this is not how it should be. Diagnosing is not an end in itself. Where the meaning of diagnosis is taken seriously, information about persons is always used in their treatment.

Uses of Religious Diagnosis

There are a variety of ways that counselors can use the information they obtain in making religious diagnoses (Malony 1991). The first option is to disregard the data. This may sound contradictory to the idea that all information obtained in the diagnostic process is to be used or not gathered in the first place. However, disregarding counselees' religion may be appropriate if they simply reported themselves to be religious out of cultural conformity. Further, if counselees' religion is very weak and unformed, the counselor may choose to disregard it and work instead with stronger determinants of behavior. After all, time is critical in treatment and no counselor is able to attend to every aspect of his or her counselees' lives. Religion is only one of the life-dimensions being evaluated, and there may be other more viable areas that need to be considered.

An even more radical option for counselors is to annihilate the religion of their counselees on the basis of their diagnostic conclusions. Without doubt, most counselors would argue against those types of religion where clients reported God telling them to commit violent acts or where they claimed to be Jesus Christ or the devil.

Sometimes the situation is less clear, however. Here is where a standard of good religion must be brought into consideration. Many counselors might shy away from trying to annihilate another person's faith because they either didn't know enough about a given religion or feared that they might be imposing their interpretations or values into the situation. I recall a psychiatrist who sought my counsel as to whether a hospitalized nun who wanted to pray every hour for the sins of the world—she felt personally responsible—was being pathologically religious. The psychiatrist asked whether this is normal behavior for nuns. I was able to help him assess her religious behavior as pathological by concluding that she did not come from a cloistered convent, nor was the order to which she belonged one that emphasized solitary prayer. The psychiatrist lacked a standard by which to judge her behavior and was hesitant to confront it.

Illustrative of this reluctance are the findings in the aforementioned study of the relationships between spiritual/religious orientations and the practice of psychotherapy (Shafranske and Malony 1990). While over half of the psychologists in this survey felt it was appropriate to know the religious background of their clients and to use religious language, metaphors, and concepts in counseling, they nevertheless disapproved of praying or using the Bible or other scripture. While most of the psychologists felt they could handle religious issues, they readily admitted their knowledge had its limits.

In an effort to provide counselors with a diagnostic tool that had built-in criteria for judging the validity of clients' religion, we sought the counsel of theologians. Taking our cues from Paul Pruyser's (1976) challenge to psychologists to take the content of faith seriously, we designed an 8-category, 33-question interview that a group of theological scholars judged to be a comprehensive survey of the basic dimensions of optimal religious functioning (Malony 1988). This Religious Status Interview is thought to be a scale that counselors, with proper training, can use to make diagnostic judgments without feeling they lack knowledge or are imposing their idiosyncrasies onto their clients. It should be noted, however, that this interview is designed to be used exclusively with Christian clients and is not applicable to persons who profess other religions. There is a need for psychologists and theologians from other traditions to work together to produce reliable and valid measures for diagnosing religious status from their points of view.

Continuing a discussion on the uses of diagnoses, the next option available to counselors is to correct the religion of their clients. Like annihilation, correction should be undertaken on the basis of informed criteria rather than on biased judgments. For example, consider the case of Laura, a character in the novel *Men and Angels* (Gordon 1986) who became overly religious in reaction to a disapproving and rejecting mother. She assumed a quiet, self-deprecating, masochistic role in which she imagined God had chosen her for some profoundly important role. She eventually committed self-sacrificing suicide, convinced that God was calling her to spill her blood to save her employer.

Had the Religious Status Interview (Malony 1988) been used by Laura's counselor, her religion would have been identified as needing correction. The RSI includes a dimension "Experiencing Fellowship" in which one of the questions is, What does being part of the family of God mean to you? Persons who claim a self-righteous exclusive relationship with God and a judgmental attitude toward others are rated as less mature in their Christian faith. Another question included in a dimension called "Knowing God's Leadership and Direction" is, How does your faith relate to your various roles in your family, occupation, and community? Here having a sense of positive role-identity that is related to religion is rated as more mature. Both of these judgments are based on criteria for optimal religious functioning determined by Christian theologians. Laura would have been judged as correct in relating her vocation to God's will for her life, but as incorrect in assuming that she was destined to sacrifice herself in that endeavor. She was not purer than her employer, nor did God intend that she sacrifice her life in a Joan-of-Arc fashion.

Counselors can use such a scale as the RS Interview and/or the RS Inventory, which has also been developed, to correct the religion of their counselees, confident that their counsel represents valid professional judgments. This is the same confidence that counselors express when they administer standardized measures of intelligence, brain damage, and personality. Counselors need such criterion-based measures so that they can assist clients to better conform to the norms of their religious traditions. Counselors can assume that such conformity will lead to higher personal satisfaction, less internal conflict, greater social approval, and more effective adjustment.

The last possible use of religious diagnoses by counselors is to encourage clients to apply their faiths to their lives. Where religion appears to be effective and valid, as judged by such measures as the RSI, counselors can offer support and reassurance. Clients can be reminded of the way the faith they have affirmed in the diagnostic interview should work in their lives. Clients can be encouraged to apply their faith to the problems for which they came to counseling. Of course, such encouragement should be based on the counselor's judgment that the individual's religion is important and mature.

In summary, this first section of the mini-midi-maxi issues has considered efforts to diagnose religious status in clients. After a distinction was made between diagnosis and research, several uses of information gleaned from religious evaluation were described. The Religious Status Interview (Malony 1988) was used as an illustration of a measure that was grounded in the opinions of theologians that the scale adequately covered the dimensions they considered important in the Christian experience of life. The next issue to be discussed is how religious diagnosis is related to the axes of the DSM III-R (American Psychiatric Association 1987).

Religious Diagnosis and the DSM III-R

Since the five-axis method of diagnosis recommended in the American Psychiatric Association's *Diagnostic and Statistical Manual of Mental Disorders, 3d edition, Revised* (1987) has become the norm among mental health counselors, it would seem important to envision how religious diagnoses with such measures as the RSI (Malony 1988) can be interrelated with these concerns. The five axes of the DSM III-R are as follows:

Axis 1—the symptom pattern as it can be observed in the client's present functioning. Two examples might be a former atheist who suddenly becomes convinced that everything painted red symbolizes the blood of Christ and a missionary child who becomes depressed six weeks after coming to the United States to attend college. A religious diagnosis would help determine whether religion was or was not an explicit part of the pathological symptoms that brought a given individual for counseling. On the surface, pathological religion does seem to be an aspect of the first case of the atheist but not an aspect of the second case of the missionary child. However, this last inference would need to be checked out via some measure such as the RSI in order to ascertain to what extent the youth interpreted his depression in terms of rejection by Christian parents and/or felt guilty at his own weakness and loneliness in the face of a new environment. Making a religious diagnosis can have much import for Axis 1 decisions. The prime question to be answered is whether religion is or is not an overt or covert part of the observed symptoms. Religion's presence or absence among the symptoms is the issue.

Axis 2—the underlying mental status of the client prior to the outbreak of the symptoms. Two examples might be an older pastor with a long history of church ministry who suddenly becomes hyperanxious about the quality of his sermons and cannot sleep and a mother who had reared her children apart from any organized religious involvement who becomes depressed after her daughter marries. Along with evaluations of the personality patterns and intellectual abilities that existed prior to either of these breakdowns, a religious diagnosis could be used to determine the maturity or immaturity of the pastor's and the mother's religious functioning before they became upset. Here the questions would be, Is his or her religious faith a personality strength or weakness? Did his or her religion keep him or her from becoming more seriously disturbed or was it a vulnerable part of the personality adjustment? What was the status of religious functioning before he or she became sick?

Axis 3—the physical state of the person. Two examples might be a 55-year-old arthritic man who suddenly becomes manic and withdraws all his money to invest in a high-risk scheme and a slightly overweight young adult nurse who is trying to adjust to a divorce. The explicit question to be asked is, What are the confounding biological conditions that exist in these persons that might be affecting their emotional or mental state? Religious functioning would not seem to apply here. Yet, the interaction between physical maladies and faith could be extremely important. A religious diagnosis might conclude that although the 55-year-old man suffered from a chronic physical condition, he had accepted it as part of the creative process in which physical deterioration was part of God's plan. In the case of the nurse, her overweight might be perceived as due to her overindulgence and her failure to take care of her body as God intended. In Axis 3, the interaction between faith and physical condition is the prime issue that might be considered in a religious diagnosis.

Axis 4—stress during the past year as rated on a five-point scale. Two examples might be an adolescent whose parents divorced and who had to change schools three months ago and an elderly woman whose husband of 60 years had to be hospitalized for respiratory infection. Here the interaction between stress and faith could be explored through religious diagnosis. A religious history might be undertaken so that the way in which clients handled stress could be better understood. In one study utilizing the Religious Status Interview (Atkinson 1986), elderly women who were more mature in their Christian faith tended to experience less distress (lower anxiety, depression, hostility) than did those who were less mature, quite apart from the amount of stress they had experienced in their lives. This illustrates how Axis 4 considerations can include information from religious diagnoses.

Axis 5—overall level of adjustment in the past year. Two examples might be a college junior who had failed to be elected to a music honor society in the fall, who had difficulty sleeping during the winter, and who became suicidal after not being chosen for a senior jazz band in the spring, and a businesswoman whose outstanding sales record over the past 12 months resulted in a promotion to district manager over which she became extremely agitated. In the one case the level of past adjustment was very low while in the other case it was extremely high. Of critical import in Axis 5 would be the role religion played in these differing levels of adjustment. It might be found that the adolescent had simply accommodated himself to the religious patterns of his parents and had never applied his faith to any real-life problems while the businesswoman might have previously utilized her faith in a number of life-crises. Here religious diagnosis might give insight into the "trait" as opposed to the "state" of religion in the lives of clients. The subtle and not-so-subtle manner in which religious faith affected adjustment is the prime issue here.

As can be seen, religious diagnosis can play a critical role in decisions made on all five of the axes of the DSM III-R. These include symptoms (Axis 1), mental status (Axis 2), reactions to physical condition (Axis 3), handling of stress (Axis 4), and religious trait effects on overall adjustment (Axis 5). In all these ways, religion can function minimally, moderately, or maximally. The next mini-midi-maxi issue to be discussed pertains to the several functions of religion in human life.

The Function of Religion in Life

Much has been written about what religion does for people. Milton Yinger (1970) exemplifies this literature in his conclusion that religion is the way people handle life's basic enigmas, tragedies, and mysteries. In a previous comment on this definition, I suggested that "enigmas are the incongruities and injustices that result from breakdowns in the give and take of the social contract. Tragedies are unexpected disruptions, losses, injuries, and deaths that occur prematurely in life. Mysteries are the ultimate imponderables about purpose, meaning, and destiny that plague the human consciousness" (Malony 1991, 4). I would like to expand Yinger's definition and my elaboration into a taxonomy of ways in which religion can contribute positively to human adjustment. I see this as an extension to my previous essay on "The case *for* religion: A counter to Albert Ellis" (1985). In that essay, I argued that mature religion did much good for people. This argument is in contrast to Ellis's contention that religion did bad things *to* people.

The taxonomy of the functions of religion in life clearly illustrates the mini-midi-maxi continuum. The functions start with the least and end with the most religion can do for persons. It should be noted that this list is uniquely applicable to the tenets of the Christian tradition. They are separated into Defensive, Coping, and Transforming groups (see table 4.1).

The list in table 4.1 is a first attempt to arrange the functions of religion along a continuum from a defensive to a coping to a transforming dimension. I conceive all of these functions as positive. I do not agree with James (1904) that the ethical "fruits" of religion are any more intrin-

Table 4.1
Functions of Religion in Life

Positive Defensive Functions of Religion
   1—comforts persons in the face of disaster.
   2—promises ultimate recompense to persons in the presence of injustice.
   3—security for persons in the midst of uncertainty.
   4—assures persons there will be relief from drudgery and pain.
   5—assists persons in accepting harsh realities.

Positive Coping Functions of Religion
   6—encourages hope in the face of failure and tragedy.
   7—helps persons adjust to the demands of life.
   8—defines a reality in which persons feel treasured and needed.
   9—offers salvation through which persons can align themselves with a
        divine plan.
   10—promises forgiveness and restoration into community when persons
        do wrong.
   11—stimulates courage, which leads to attempts to try again in the face of
        failure and disappointment.
   12—offers persons a sense of joy and fulfillment in life.
   13—gives persons a fellowship to which to belong.
   14—provides a framework for understanding life as having purpose and
        meaning.

Positive Transforming Functions of Religion
   15—provides persons with a perspective by which to judge right from wrong,
        good from bad.
   16—calls persons to live by ideals above the level of selfish desire.
   17—furnishes persons a transforming perspective by which to make judgments
        and with which to identify.

sically valuable than religion's "roots," which promise compensation for the tragedies and enigmas of life. While we might all agree with the biblical writer of the Book of James that faith should be followed by work (James 2:14–26), the prime way in which religion functions for most counselees, at least initially, is in a defensive, compensatory manner. In the midst of stress, religion provides security and that is as it should be.

Initially, diagnosis will find, almost always, religion serving a self-centered need. This is good. It is the very least that religion can do. Counselors should applaud, not discount, this religious function because they are interested, first and foremost, in helping persons readjust to life. While there may always be need to probe this defensive function of religion in order to see that persons do not deny reality or withdraw from life, there is also the need to honor rather than disapprove of this basic positive role for religion. We scholars might prefer that persons go beyond defensive and coping to transforming faith but we need to remind ourselves of the caution expressed by James Dittes (1971) that such preferences may be an elitist scholarly bias that is unrealistic for most persons.

I turn next to the final mini-midi-maxi issue, namely, a statement of religious maturity based on these comments about positive religious functions.

Definitions of Religious Maturity

There have been numerous definitions of religious maturity (Allport 1954; Elkins, Hedstrom, Hughes, Leaf, and Saunders 1988; Propst 1988). However, no one of these takes seriously that religion can be mature when it functions to enhance everyday adjustment nor are they specifically construed within the Christian tradition. In regard to everyday religious functioning, it is important for counselors who utilize religious diagnosis to remember that maturity, like health, can be defined in three ways: negatively, normally, and idealistically. Persons can be healthy if they are no longer sick (a negative definition), if they are as well as other persons their age (a normal definition), or if they are "weller" than well (an idealistic definition). Similarly, persons can be religiously mature if they are not religiously immature (negative definition) or if their religion is functioning for them as well as for others (normal definition).

Counselors should honor these negative and normal levels of religious functioning and not judge religious functioning idealistically by applying a standard in this area they would hesitate to apply in family relations, intelligence, or personality traits. In the terms I have been using in this essay, counselors should not discredit mini and midi criteria of religious functioning in their application of religious diagnoses.

The definition of maturity we have used in the development and use of the Religious Status Interview and Inventory (Malony 1988) takes these comments about levels of maturity into account. It also assumes that most persons are religious in terms of the major traditions provided by their culture (Sunden 1974) and is therefore grounded in the affirmations of the Christian tradition.

"Mature Christians are those who have identity, integrity, and inspiration. They have 'identity' in that their self-understanding is as children of God, created by him and destined by him to live according to a divine plan. They have 'integrity' in that their daily lives are lived in the awareness that they have been saved by God's grace from the guilt of sin and that they can freely respond to God's will in the present. They have 'inspiration' in that they live with the sense that God is available to sustain, comfort, encourage, and direct their lives on a daily basis. These dimensions of maturity relate to belief in God the Father, God the Son, and God the Holy Spirit. They pertain to the Christian doctrines of creation, redemption, and sanctification. They provide the foundation for practical daily living" (Malony 1985, 28). It is my conviction that such a definition as this can serve the minimal, the moderate, and the maximal (mini-midi-maxi) understandings for counselors to make judgments about what they find in religious diagnoses.

As noted earlier, at given times in people's lives religion can function in defensive, in coping, and in transformative ways. While counselors might hope for transformative functioning, they should honor defensive and coping religious functioning when it is appropriate. After all, the goals of counseling can themselves be conceived in this manner. Most of the time, counselors are concerned to restore persons to normal adjustment. Only rarely do counselors have the privilege of assisting persons in living up to their potential.

Conclusion

This essay has considered the relevance of making religious diagnoses in counseling. After a discussion of importance of religion for contemporary life, it was suggested that religion still played a crucial role in the lives of a significant part of the population. Although there seems to be increasing secularization in the western world, religion plays more than a minor role in life according to counselor surveys. Under the rubric of mini-midi-maxi, several issues pertaining to making religious diagnoses were discussed: the difference between diagnosis and research; the uses of religious diagnosis in counseling; the relationship of religious diagnosis to DSM III-R axes; the positive functions of religion in life; and definitions of religious maturity. It was proposed that the development of the Religious Status Interview and Inventory (Malony 1988) met the need for a scale with valid theological criteria, normal maturity assumptions and questions appropriate for making religious diagnoses among Christians.

References

Allport, G. W. 1954. *The individual and his religion.* New York: Macmillan.

Batson, C. D., and W. L. Ventis. 1982. *The religious experience: A social-psychological perspective.* New York: Oxford Univ. Press.

Day, J. M. 1991. *Moral development, belief, and unbelief? Young adult accounts of religion in the process of moral growth.* Paper presented at the 5th European Congress on Psychology of Religion, Leuven, Belgium, August.

Dittes, J. E. 1971. Typing the typologies: Some parallels in the career of church-sect and extrinsic-intrinsic. *Journal for the Scientific Study of Religion* 10: 375–83.

Draper, E., G. E. Meyer, Z. Parzen, and G. Samuelson. 1965. On the diagnostic value of religious ideation. *Archives of General Psychiatry* 13 (September): 202–7.

Elkins, D. N., J. Hedstrom, L. L. Hughes, A. Leaf, and C. Saunders. 1988. Toward a humanistic-phenomenological spirituality: Definition, description, and measurement. *Journal of Humanistic Psychology* 28(4): 5–18.

Gordon, M. 1986. *Men and angels.* Hammondsworth, Middlesex, England: Penguin.

James, W. 1904. *The varieties of religious experience.* New York: Longmans Green.

Malony, H. N. 1985. The case for religion: A counter to Albert Ellis. Unpublished manuscript, Graduate School of Psychology, Fuller Theological Seminary, Pasadena, California.

_____. 1985. Assessing religious maturity. In *Psychotherapy and the religiously committed patient,* ed. M. Stern, 25–33. New York: Haworth.

_____.1988. The clinical assessment of optimal religious functioning. *Review of Religious Research* 30(1): 3–15.

_____. 1991. The place of religious diagnosis in evaluations of mental health. In *Religion and mental health,* ed. F. W. Schumaker. New York: Oxford Univ. Press.

_____. 1991. The use of religious assessment in counseling. In *Religion, personality and mental health,* ed. L. B. Brown, 41–69. New York: Springer-Verlag.

_____. 1992. How counselors can help people become more spiritual through religious assessment. In *Religion, mental health and mental pathology,* ed. H. Grzymala-Moszcaynska. Amsterdam: Rodolpi.

Malony, H. N., ed. 1983. *Wholeness and holiness: Readings in the psychology/theology of mental health.* Grand Rapids: Baker.

Newbigin, L. 1986. *Foolishness to the Greeks: The gospel and western culture.* Grand Rapids: Eerdmans.

O'Guinn, G. 1991. 8 of 10 Americans claim to be Christian. *The United Methodist Reporter* April 12, 3.

Propst, L. R. 1988. *Psychotherapy in a religious framework: Spirituality in the emotional healing process.* New York: Human Sciences.

Pruyser, P. W. 1976. *The minister as diagnostician.* Philadelphia: Westminster.

Shafranske, E. P., and H. N. Malony. 1985. Religion, spirituality, and psychotherapy: A study of California psychologists. Paper presented at the meeting of the California Psychological Association, San Francisco, February.

_____. 1990. Clinical psychologists' religious and spiritual orientations and their practice of psychotherapy. *Psychotherapy* 27(1): 111–20.

Spilka, B., R. W. Hood, and R. L. Gorsuch. 1985. *The psychology of religion: An empirical approach.* Englewood Cliffs, N.J.: Prentice-Hall.

Yinger, M. 1970. *The scientific study of religion.* New York: Macmillan.

Part **3**

During Counseling and Psychotherapy

Introduction to Part 3

Roughly speaking, religious beliefs consist of propositional statements about what one believes to be true concerning God, people, the cosmos, and the relationships among them. Religious beliefs can be general or discrete. They can pertain to devotional practices and to mundane activities. They can guide behavior in a large segment of life or be relegated to a life-proof compartment. Beliefs can include adherence to doctrines of a church or can be idiosyncratic.

Religious values are aspects of religion a person believes to be important. Religious values may be global, which is usually what is meant by religious commitment. Or religious values can be more discrete. How global religious commitment should be assessed is unclear. Should it involve church attendance, attachment to one's religious beliefs, the level of one's integration of religiosity into the daily life, the level of adherence to creedal statements, loyalty to one's religious group, or subjective feelings of religiosity?

Clearly one can find discrete religious beliefs, behaviors, and feelings of differential value. Which discrete religious values, then, most affect a person's behavior? Many scholars have attempted to identify important religious values throughout the ages. Recently, Worthington (1988) proposed a theory about discrete values that are important to religious people. He applied the theory to counseling, and since its proposal, it has received modest support from independent investigators such as Keating and Fretz (1990) as well as from Worthington's own additional research (McCullough and Worthington 1992; Worthington, Hsu, Gowda, and Bleach 1988; Worthington, Hsu, Berry, Gowda, and Bleach 1989).

In the following chapter, Worthington summarizes the current state of scholarship on religious values in counseling, including a brief summary of his theoretical speculations. Goldsmith and Hansen critically examine his theory and extend and modify it with a metaphor concerning which values might be affected in counseling or psychotherapy.

These papers are quite different in their approach. Worthington gives a broad summary of an entire field, suggesting a new way to conceptualize research on religious values. Goldsmith and Hansen offer a scholarly critique and illustrate their points using case studies.

One of the main deficiencies with scholarship on religious values is a lack of instrumentation to measure important religious values reliably and validly. Rokeach (1967) developed the Rokeach Value Survey, which requires people to rank order terminal and instrumental values. Because it employs rank order, though, a person who is indifferent to life might rank order the values similarly to a person whose life is strongly driven by his or her values.

Finding or creating measures of religious beliefs, values, and commitment is essential to determining potential benefits of religious counseling. Evidence mounts that suggests that religious psychotherapy has no different mental health outcomes with religious clients than does secular psychotherapy. However, religious therapy may have more positive outcomes at strengthening clients' spiritual resources than does secular therapy. Without good measures of religious values, such a proposition cannot be reliably investigated.

It is incumbent on religious researchers to determine the effects of religious counseling and psychotherapy. It may well be that religious counseling or psychotherapy makes no actual difference. Until good instrumentation is developed, shown to be psychometrically sound, and employed with clinical populations, this worthwhileness of religious psychotherapy cannot be determined.

References

Keating, A. M., and B. R. Fretz. 1990. Christians' anticipations about counselors in response to counselor descriptions. *Journal of Counseling Psychology* 37: 293–96.

McCullough, M. E., and E. L. Worthington, Jr. 1992. Observers' perceptions of a counselor's treatment of a religious issue: Replication and extension. *Journal of Counseling and Development,* in press.

Rokeach, M. 1967. *Value survey.* Sunnyvale, Calif.: Halgren Tests.

Worthington, E. L., Jr. 1988. Understanding the values of religious clients: A model and its application to counseling. *Journal of Counseling Psychology* 35: 166–74.

Worthington, E. L., Jr., K. Hsu, K. K. Gowda, and E. Bleach. 1988. *Preliminary tests of Worthington's (1988) theory of important values in religious counseling.* Paper presented at the First International Congress on Christian Counseling, Atlanta, November.

Worthington, E. L., Jr., J. T. Berry, K. Hsu, K. K. Gowda, and E. Bleach. 1989. *Factor analytic study of the Religious Values Survey.* Paper presented at the meeting of the Virginia Psychological Association, Richmond, October.

5

Psychotherapy and Religious Values: An Update

EVERETT L. WORTHINGTON, JR.

Over the last century, psychotherapists have been alternately hot and cold toward religion (see Bergin 1983). In the future, though, psychotherapists will increasingly be forced to deal with religious issues in psychotherapy, at least during the next 30 or so years. There are four primary reasons for this.

First, within the United States in the past two decades, religious people have become more vocal about their religious beliefs and practices. While mainline Christian denominations have decreased in size, many religious people—notably Jews and conservative Christians—have demanded explicitly religious counselors of their own religious persuasion.

Second, the number of religious cults has increased (see Bromley and Hammond 1987). While few cult members seek counseling from practicing psychotherapists, many cult members leave their cult and are reintegrated into society, so the future is likely to bring many of them to counselors' offices.

Third, the influx of immigrants into the United States has resulted in an importation of significant communities of diverse religious beliefs. The United States, always a melting pot for cultures and religions, is continually shifting toward increased ethnic and religious multiplicity. Mex-

This chapter is a modification of a paper presented as an invited address for Division 36, Psychologists Interested in Religious Issues, at the meeting of the American Psychological Association, 1989, New Orleans.

ican-Americans and Cubans (primarily Roman Catholic), Indo-Chinese immigrants from Vietnam, Thailand, and Cambodia (primarily Buddhist), and immigrants from Africa and Middle Eastern countries (primarily Muslim) have flooded the United States. Further, the higher education system in the United States has attracted foreign students of a variety of religions to the United States, and many will either stay in the United States or return later.

Fourth, with the increasing cultural diversity and with dramatic breakthroughs in telecommunications and other communication technologies comes more pressure for people to understand and tolerate alternative philosophies, religious and otherwise, from east and west. This has led to a rapid rise in personal humanistic religions, such as the New Age religion, and in other humanistic religions (see Sperry 1988).

These forces will increasingly impel psychotherapists, including Christian psychotherapists, to deal with clients of different religious beliefs and values. We must anticipate this and define clear positions about and reasons for our treatment of religion in psychotherapy.

Psychologists who value an empirical approach to knowing naturally turn to research to help decide how to deal with religious issues in psychotherapy. In the following sections, I briefly summarize research and outline some issues that must be addressed to cope with a 21st-century clientele for psychotherapists.

A Brief Summary of Research

Several scholars have reviewed research on religious values in psychotherapy (e.g., Beutler 1979, 1981, 1989; Beutler, Crago, and Arizmendi 1986; London 1986; Miller and Martin 1988; Quackenbos, Privette, and Klentz 1985, 1986; Strupp, Hadley, and Gomez-Schwartz 1977). For example, Beutler (1979) conceptualized psychotherapy as an instance of interpersonal persuasion. He suggested that therapists may transmit specific values and beliefs, especially religious values, to clients in successful psychotherapy. Substantial research has supported this suggestion.

In 1981, Beutler examined value convergence in psychotherapy. He reviewed studies in three areas. First, reviewing 16 studies, Beutler found that especially for individual therapy, value convergence was usually related to positive outcomes in therapy (in 12 of the 16 studies). Second, reviewing 7 studies, he concluded that initial *dis*similarity was more conducive to patient-therapist convergence than was initial value similarity. Third, Beutler (1981) reviewed 22 studies investigating the relationship between initial client-therapist similarity and improvement in therapy. Twelve studies showed a positive relationship between value similarity and improvement, 5 showed a negative relationship, 2 found no relationship, and 3 demonstrated either a curvilinear relationship or mediation by some other variable. With this hodge-podge of findings, he hypothesized (on the basis of Beutler, Pollack, and Jobe 1978) that change in sexual and religious values but not in other values might promote successful therapy. He concluded that the precise relationship between initial value similarity and therapy outcome was unclear, but it certainly did not support Bergin's (1980) suggestion that initial similarity of religious values would be likely to be salutary for clients.

In 1986, Beutler, Crago, and Arizmendi evaluated the extant research as showing little support that therapists or clients preferred therapy with individuals who had similar religious beliefs and values. They concluded that improvement was more dependent on the therapists' ability to accept patients' preferred beliefs than vice versa. In contrast, patients usually felt more positively toward therapists who *rejected* some of their beliefs, and patients tended to acquire some of their therapist's values during therapy. Beutler et al. acknowledged that their samples were constricted because religious patients might seek therapy from clergy and religious therapists.

Worthington (1986) reviewed the empirical literature from 1974 to 1984 on religious counseling. He suggested that highly religious clients have been said to have two fears about psychotherapy with nonreligious therapists: having their values changed and being misunderstood or misdiagnosed.

Regarding the fear of having their values changed, Worthington concluded that the fear was founded. Therapists often promote value change in clients partially by guiding the clients' goal selection and partially by other less well explicated mechanisms. On the other hand, evidence did not support the fears of religious people who believed that they might be misdiagnosed by a psychotherapist whose religious beliefs differed from the client's (see research by Houts and Graham 1986; Lewis and Lewis 1985; Margolis and Elifson 1979, 1983; Wadsworth and Checketts 1980; Worthington and Scott 1983). Therapists have generally been able to set aside considerations of their own religious beliefs and make assessments that are consensually validated by other therapists. Since Worthington's (1986) review, Gartner, Harmatz, Hohmann, Larson, and Gartner (1990) found evidence that religiously and politically extreme patients were assigned psychiatric diagnoses more frequently than were patients whose religious and political views were unknown. Further, clinicians expressed less empathy but no different ratings of pathology, internal stress, or client maturity for patients politically and religiously different from themselves than for patients similar to themselves. Extreme political and religious positions taken by therapists did not affect clinical judgments. Generally, Gartner et al.'s work supported most previous findings (see also Shafranske and Malony 1990) with the additional insight that extreme positions by clients suggest a higher likelihood of client psychopathology to most therapists.

There are some differences between the conclusions drawn by Beutler (1981) and Worthington (1986). Importantly, they drew from different data bases. Beutler gave most importance to clinical studies of secular psychotherapy. Clinical research typically administers a questionnaire assessing values of both therapists and clients before and after therapy and relates these values to measures of outcome, such as clients' evaluation of therapy, therapists' and clients' evaluations of improvement in therapy, and post-therapy religious and other values. As Beutler, Crago, and Arizmendi suggested in 1986, however, highly religious clients are often selected out of this sampling of psychotherapy patients. They often do not attend secular psychotherapy. Next to physicians, clergy are the most consulted mental health professionals and they refer only about 10% of their clients to secular mental health professionals (Meylink and Gorsuch 1988). (Of course, referrals from secular therapists to clergy almost never happen.) In studies of religious values in secular psychotherapy, with most highly committed religious people systematically purged—albeit the purging is done by the client, not the therapist—those clients who are sampled have a wide range of religious values, and many are lukewarm on religion if they care at all. This clientele makes for modest correlations between religious value similarity and measures of therapy outcome.

This parallels research on personality summarized by Mischel (1973; see Kenrick and Funder 1988, for an update). Mischel found only modest correlations between personality measures such as aggressiveness and aggressive behavior. Mischel pointed out that, usually, the personality trait that was being measured was the trait that was important to the *researcher* and not necessarily to the person being measured. Bem and Allen (1974) and Bem and Funder (1978) demonstrated that much more variance could be accounted for if respondents selected personality traits that were important to *them*.

Beutler, Jobe, and Elkins (1974) recognized this weakness in research on values in therapy. They measured values they thought to be of high, medium, or low centrality to clients. For example, they identified the need for approval, the threatening nature of the world, and the belief in God as being of high centrality to patients; reactions to Jesus Christ and Karl Marx as being of medium centrality; attitudes towards premarital sex and the need for laws as being of low centrality to clients. In their sample, they found that medium centrality values were most affected by psychotherapy.

The problem is that clients might not have agreed with this value structure. For instance, the disinterested agnostic does not find a reaction to Jesus Christ as worth even considering. However, the committed

Southern Baptist fundamentalist might profess a belief in Jesus to be at the very center of his or her value structure. While the agnostic might easily modify his or her views about Jesus—since it doesn't matter to him or her anyway—the fundamentalist would probably rather switch therapists.

A More Specialized Theory

It is therefore suggested that theories are needed that apply strictly to highly committed religious clients. There is recent evidence that clients' values can make an enormous difference in predicting outcomes of psychotherapy. Nugent and Constantine (1988) analyzed 103 cases in marital therapy using data collected over a two-year period. The therapist explained in easily understandable terms four descriptions of marital paradigms to troubled couples. Couples selected which paradigm they most identified with. The therapist attempted to match treatment to the couple's preferred paradigm. In cases where the partners agreed on the paradigm, the success rate was 92%! True, this study was uncontrolled, by an author who was also the therapist, and who studied marital therapy, not religious therapy. Yet, it suggests that matching treatment to the client's central values might result in extremely successful therapy.

Which religious values are typically important to highly committed religious clients? Worthington (1988) proposed a theory about important religious values in counseling. Three propositions compose the corpus of the theory. First, *highly religious people* find three value dimensions important for evaluating therapy. These three value dimensions have gained salience due to the historical controversies in western religions, which have polarized people on the values. The dimensions are the authority the person affords Scripture or other sacred writings; the authority the person affords (especially) ecclesiastical leaders (but potentially the authority the person affords other leaders, such as government officials, parents, or even employers); and the degree with which the person identifies with the norms of his or her religious group. Nonreligious or antireligious people might find these value dimensions irrelevant to their perception of therapy. According to the second proposition, people can be located at roughly a "point" in a hypothetical three-dimensional value space. The third proposition recognizes the interpersonal nature of therapy. Each person is thought to tolerate a range of different opinions in others for each of the three important value dimensions. This defines a "zone of toleration" about the person's individual value position. If the client detects the counselor's values to be within the client's zone of toleration, counseling will have a good chance of favorable outcomes—generally dependent on other extrareligious factors. However, if the counselor's values are detected to be outside the client's zone of toleration, then some potentially unfavorable outcomes—such as premature termination, resistance, or failure to heed suggestions by the therapist—may occur. Of course, the therapist might also find the client's values to be outside his or her zone of toleration. In such an event, the probability of referral would be high and the therapist's subjective feelings toward the client might be less positive than otherwise. Shafranske and Malony (1990) found some support for Worthington's (1988) theory.

Religious values in highly religious clients are thought to be activated more by explicitly religious situations than by religiously neutral situations. For example, the client's values should be expected to come to the fore more in pastoral counseling, counseling with a cleric, or counseling with an explicitly religious therapist than with a therapist in some secular setting. Further, particular counseling sessions and interventions might activate the values of highly religious clients, even if the setting and therapist are explicitly religiously neutral. For example, if the client (or therapist) brings up a religious issue, then the client will employ his or her religious values.

Worthington reported preliminary investigations of this theory (Worthington, Hsu, Gowda, and Bleach 1988). The three scales used to measure the constructs proposed in the theory were found to possess acceptable psychometric properties. Weaker psychometric support was found for measurement of a person's zone of toleration (see Goldsmith and Hansen 1991, for a theoretical critique of that concept). Support was found for the proposition that highly religious people employed the evaluative dimensions more than medium or low religiously committed people. Additionally, religious situations evoked religious value evaluations more than did nonreligious situations.

In an independent test of Worthington's theory, Keating and Fretz (1990) found that Christians with higher religious commitment held more negative anticipations for counseling than did people with lower religious commitment. Counselors described as Christian were the most accepted by highly religious people, whereas counselors described as being empathic with Christian concerns and those described as secular prompted more negative anticipations. For non-Christians, no differentiation was made between counselors described as empathic to religion and those described as Christian, but secular counselors were not expected to deal as well with religious issues as the other counselors.

A Framework for Organizing Research

The Framework

To avoid confusion, such as the differences in findings reported by Beutler and by Worthington in their various reviews, research on religious beliefs and values in psychotherapy should consider three independent factors: religiosity of the client (high religiosity versus no, low, or medium religiosity); religiosity of the therapist (religious or not); and content of therapy (religious or not). Conceivably, more variables might be important and finer discriminations might be necessary among therapists and among types of content during therapy, but the state of the science currently does not justify such distinctions. (See Kelly 1990, for an eight-category system.) These three variables are arrayed into a 2 x 2 x 2 design for ease of conceptualization (see fig. 5.1).

Figure 5.1

A Proposed Taxonomy for Structuring Research in Psychotherapy and Religious Values

Non-highly Religious Clients

Therapist

		Religious	Not Religious
Content	Religious	Clients become more religious	Clients become less religious
	Not Religious	Client religion not affected	Client religion not affected

Highly Religious Clients

Therapist

		Religious	Not Religious
Content	Religious	Clients satisfied; religion supported	Clients may terminate early
	Not Religious	Effects on client are uncertain	Clients' religion decreases or unchanged

Non-highly Religious Clients

First, considering the top half of figure 5.1—concerned with clients who are not highly committed to religion—Beutler's research and theorizing largely applies to those four boxes. In the top two boxes of the 2 x 2 grid, religious content in therapy is likely to result in clients changing their values to be more in accord with their therapist. When the therapist is more religious than the client, the client will likely become more religious than his or her present status; when the therapist is less religious than the client, the client will likely become less religious than his or her present status.

On the bottom of that grid, little effect on client religion is anticipated. If the therapist is religious but religious content is never addressed in therapy, little effect will occur; if both therapist and client are not religious and religious content is never addressed in therapy, thoroughly secular therapy will occur.

The future of research in psychotherapy and religious values with non-highly religious clients must entail modifications from our present course. The paradigm used successfully by Beutler and others have unearthed useful findings, but is unlikely to yield much more of great value.

1. Rather, we must identify instances of specific discussions of religious values and examine what happens in and what results from those conversations.

2. We must determine the *mechanisms* of religious value influence when the content of the session does not involve explicitly religious counseling techniques.

3. We must investigate the effects of different theories of psychotherapy on the values of clients who are antagonistic to religion and on those who are tenuously or moderately committed to religion. Beutler and Bergan (1991) have recently proposed a theoretical framework for directing these investigations. They suggest five fundamental dimensions on which therapeutic systems, cultures, client groups, or therapists can be evaluated: time (past, present, or future), activity (doing or feeling), relational (individaulism or group identity), humans' relationship to existence (dominant over natural forces or submissive to God or nature), and the nature of humans (basically evil, neutral, or good). They propose that scholars investigate clashes in values on those fundamental dimensions.

4. We must continue to investigate the effect of thoroughly secular therapy on clients whose religious values (and especially religious beliefs) do not match their therapists' (see Bergin 1980, 1983, 1988; Bergin and Jensen 1990; Tjeltveit 1986; Shafranske and Malony 1990).

5. We must investigate the effects of therapeutic techniques that are at least connotative of religion when used by religious or nonreligious therapists in secular therapy. For example, interventions promoting forgiveness have received attention recently (see DiBlasio and Benda 1991; Fitzgibbons 1986; Hope 1987; Worthington and DiBlasio 1990).

6. We must attend more to the ethics of counseling the religious client. A number of therapists have recently suggested that, as a minimum, knowledge of a client's specific religious beliefs is invaluable in counseling the religious client (e.g., Koltko 1990; Lovinger 1984; Moyers 1990).

Highly Religious Clients

Returning to figure 5.1, the bottom 2 x 2 box applies to highly religious clients. Religious therapists dealing with religious issues with highly religious clients (upper left quadrant) requires additional investigation. Several recent articles have begun to examine the prevalence of the use of religious counseling techniques, but little has been done to determine how effective the techniques are in alleviating psychological symptoms and in promoting religious or spiritual growth (see Ball and Goodyear 1991; Moon, Bailey, Kwasny, and Willis 1991; Worthington, Dupont, Berry, and Duncan 1988). A variety of studies suggest that the client-therapist match in religious values might influence expectations about therapy and quality of therapeutic relationship (see Worthington 1988 for a review; see also Wyatt and Johnson 1990 for a recent example with "clients" who are not highly committed to religion).

Beutler (1989), though, suggests that the clients might be too similar to their therapists to experience much change in psychological functioning. No inpatient or outpatient clinical research supports the hypothesis that better outcomes are found in religious psychotherapy than when the match is less exact. To the contrary, Propst, Ostrum, Watkins, and Morris (1984) found, in a preliminary investigation of religious psychotherapy, that *nonreligious* therapists had better outcomes using religious counseling with religiously committed clients than did religious therapists.

When highly religious clients discuss their religious beliefs and values with nonreligious therapists, poor counseling outcomes are anticipated (Worthington 1988). This proposition has received little direct testing. In Propst et al.'s (1984) study, nonreligious therapists followed a carefully prepared and controlled religious protocol and were effective. Most nonreligious therapists will not follow such a protocol; their values will likely be introduced into therapy and their clients will likely detect those values.

Additional research is needed measuring the effects on highly religious clients of secular psychotherapy (nonreligious therapist dealing with nonreligious content in therapy). Researchers need to consider the effects on both psychological and religious domains.

Similarly, research is needed measuring the effects on highly religious clients *and their therapists* when religious therapists conduct therapy that does not deal with religious issues. Of additional interest, do clients receiving therapy that does not deal with religion from a therapist whom the client knows to be religious experience more sense of violation of expectations than if the therapist is not known to be religious?

A variety of topics concerning research with highly religious clients must be addressed. I have identified six.

1. The scholarly study of religious values in therapy must investigate extant theories and propose new theories about religious therapy with highly religious clients from a variety of faiths. Theories dealing with Christian clients are especially needed, but based on the expected shift in types and numbers of religious clients in future decades, other theories about dealing with clients of eastern and Chinese religions are needed as well (see Beck 1990; Hesselgrave 1984). Christian therapists must wrestle even more explicitly with the morals and ethics of when and how to appropriately share the Christian faith with nonreligious clients and with clients who espouse a different religion (Tjeltveit 1986).

2. We must develop or apply more theories that explain and undergird our empirical understanding of values, both in psychotherapy and outside of psychotherapy. Social psychology might be a fruitful place to look for such theories (see Kelley and Thibault 1978, for example).

3. Therapists need to broaden their horizons to other literatures in understanding the uses and abuses of religious values in psychotherapy. For example, there is a substantial literature about how black people form racial identities and how blacks with different levels of racial identities prefer counselors with different characteristics (Parham and Helms 1981). By analogy, religious clients—especially those highly involved in religious subcultures that prescribe much of the behavior of their members—might go through similar stages in the development of their religious identities. Those stages might affect their relationships with counselors.

Another potentially fertile literature is the literature on feminist therapy. For example, Lewis, Davis, and Lesmeister (1983) investigated pretherapy information about the feminist views of potential counselors. They told feminist subjects that their counselor was either a traditional nonfeminist counselor, a feminist counselor, or a feminist counselor with certain explicit values about feminism. The feminist subjects essentially rejected the feminist counselor who had stated specific value positions. They preferred the counselor who was labeled "feminist" but whose values were not made explicit. Lewis et al. (1983) suggest that feminist clients might "project" their own notions of feminism onto the counselor if the counselor is not explicit with his or her views.

By analogy, one might expect the same thing for "Christian" or "Jewish" clients with a "Christian" or "Jewish" therapist, respectively. Giving too much information about one's religious beliefs to a highly religious client might be as countertherapeutic as giving no information. There is a need to evaluate exactly what the optimum quantity and quality of values to share with clients at the outset of therapy—even with the very religious client. Lewis and Epperson (1991) have investigated this recently. The pattern of results differed from that of "feminist" counseling. Disclosure of oneself as a Christian therapist did not lead to rejection by clients who did not share those beliefs. Lewis and Epperson's research exemplifies how heuristic other literatures can be for research in Christian counseling.

4. We need to investigate theories using the full range of methodologies within the mature science of psychotherapy research. That means we need to do more empirical investigations on real clients with real therapists. We need to control our samples so that we investigate meaningful samples. In all investigations, at a minimum, we must use degree of religious commitment as a blocking variable in our investigations of religion in therapy.

Further, we must realize that religious people often make distinctions that are emotionally important to them and their religious reference group. Conservative and liberal Christians do not often behave similarly in religious matters—even those who are equally religiously committed. It is as if we were studying psychotherapists and indiscriminantly lumped psychoanalysts, behavior therapists, and Gestalt therapists together and tried to discover what was common across psychotherapies. We could identify some broad characteristics—as the research on the common factors hypothesis shows—but how useful is that finding to the practicing psychoanalyst? If we are to understand more than the veneer of religious values in therapy, we must adopt a modified insider perspective in which we examine the differences in religion perceived by the highly religious.

5. Science is value-laden, but scientists have evolved methodologies for limiting the intrusion of values in the practice of science. Both religious and nonreligious therapists have also evolved procedures that protect clients from unwarranted value intrusion by therapists—either pro- or antireligion—and allow for the free inclusion in therapy of religious values for people who are highly committed to religion. As researchers, we must make explicit these rules of thumb that have evolved in many therapists' and clerics' practices, and we must put them to the test in our laboratories and clinics to determine that the rules do indeed work and

accomplish the goals wanted by the client, the therapist, and important representatives of society (see Strupp, Handley, and Gomez-Schwartz 1977). As of now, these rules have not been made explicit within the mainstream literature of psychology.

I would suggest that procedures for dealing with religious beliefs and values be specified in at least three areas. First, procedures for structuring initial expectations for therapy must be specified. For example, is it helpful for clients to be offered an explicit choice between "Christian-oriented therapy," in which Christian concepts and explicit interventions are used, versus "secular therapy," in which such an explicitly Christian orientation will not be undertaken unless the client later requests it explicitly? How much pretherapy information is maximally helpful? Is too little or too much information inhibitory, and for which types of clients?

Second, procedures should be outlined for dealing with religious content during a counseling session. This might take the form of a series of questions that the therapist asks himself or herself. Some answers will route the counselor toward continuing the interview without discussing religion. Other answers will lead to new questions. (a) Is religious involvement mentioned, implied, or is the question begged (such as description of blatant sin or satanic involvement)? (b) If yes, how much would changes in religious beliefs or values affect the client's life? (c) If religious content is mentioned by the client, how much would *not* talking about religion affect the client's life? (d) If religious changes would affect the client substantially or if not discussing religion would similarly affect the client, then ask, Do I as therapist think changes in religious beliefs or values would benefit the client? (e) If yes, would changes in religious beliefs or values likely cause harm to someone in the client's life that would outweigh benefits to the client and to others? (f) If no, the counselor can discuss religion with the client.

The third instance requiring explicit procedures for dealing with religion would be during the discussion of religious issues. As the discussion continued, the therapist would evaluate whether the client's decision-making process was adequate and whether his or her informational base (concerning religion) was adequate. If both were adequate, the therapist would facilitate a client-centered discussion aimed at clarifying the client's thoughts, feelings, and values. If decision making were inadequate, the therapist might give feedback on effective decision making. If the informational base were judged to be inadequate, the therapist would first insure that the client was informed of the therapist's relevant religious beliefs and values, exposing them but not imposing them on the client, then the therapist would tell the client the relevant information, advice, or counsel. This would allow the client to evaluate the information as an informed consumer of psychological information.

Other procedures also need explication. For example, little has been written about how to handle religious values in marriage counseling or family therapy with clients who are unanimous in their beliefs or values and with clients who are divided in their beliefs and values.

6. Finally, natural scientists have recently propounded an approach to science called by some "the science of chaos"—though the "science of free will" might be a more apt name for it.[1] Fundamentally, it argues that some natural processes are best described not by precise cause-and-effect relationships, but by defining *boundary conditions* within which occurs unspecified and unspecifiable interaction.

Adopting the view that the uses of religious values in therapy were phenomena to which this approach to science applied would change the focus of scientists investigating religious values in therapy. Rather than be concerned with discovering exact prediction rules about (for example) the effects of particular therapists' values on their particular clients' values or on outcomes of therapy in particular conditions, we should try to find the boundary rules that apply in various situations and expect considerable variation within each set of boundary conditions (see Howard 1985, 1988, 1989, who arrives at similar conclusions from another direction). Our task is to define appropriate and inappropriate boundary conditions for each instance and then to investigate empirically their effectiveness at delimiting behaviors during different types of therapy.

As an initial attempt to specify some boundary conditions that might define how and when religious values are discussed in therapy, let us use an initial framework proposed by Strupp, Hadley, and Gomez-Schwartz (1977). They suggested that therapy values and goals are due to the interaction of therapist, client, and society.

The therapist will provide input because of his or her *therapy values* and *therapist values* (see Dienhart 1982 for an elaboration of this distinction). Therapy values are those values inherent in the presuppositions of the theory of therapy. Therapist values are those held by the therapist, which may be in congruence or in conflict with therapy values. The therapist will also have an impact on religious values in therapy based on the therapist's *style* once religious issues are mentioned. Styles might be roughly thought of as being the bulldog style—once the therapist gets hold of a religious issue, he or she never lets go until the issue is resolved—or the hit-and-run style—the issue is dealt with only superficially (either because the issue sidetracks the agenda of the session, or the

1. Parenthetically, for people interested in religious issues, the "science of chaos" should immediately call to mind the sometime endless debates about free will versus God's sovereignty. The analogical insight derived from the science of chaos might be that God's sovereignty affixes the boundary conditions and within those, humans operate with relative freedom. In some conditions, the boundary rules are relatively constrained, but in other conditions the boundary rules are lax.

therapist deems the issue of marginal importance to therapy, or the therapist is threatened by the discussion of religious values).

The client's contribution to discussion of religious values in therapy will depend on the client's *religious commitment* and three important *religious values* that I have discussed in this article and elsewhere (Worthington 1988). It will also depend on the client's *patterns of coping with stress* (see Pargament's 1987 research) and the client's *attributional patterns* (see Spilka, Shaver, and Kirkpatrick 1985). More specifically, the place of religious values in therapy might depend on the involvement of religion with the *client's specific problems* and on the client's *interpersonal style*.

Society's influence is the product of influences of interested parties from family, friends, significant others, employers, and social systems such as schools, courts, welfare agencies, and insurance companies.

Within therapy, an inner boundary determining the role of religious values in therapy is dependent on the *relationship* between client and therapist. Trusting long-term relationships and exploratory uncommitted relationships are thought to be more conducive to exploration of religious values in therapy than are moderate-term, weakly bonded relationships.

The *setting of therapy* also will affect whether religious values are dealt with in therapy. Therapeutic settings shape—at least initially—clients' expectations for therapy. For example, when a person seeks counseling from a cleric, the person expects the cleric to address spiritual topics. The implicit therapeutic contract is to deal with problems from a spiritual point of view or perhaps to deal with spiritual causes of psychological problems. On the other hand, when the person seeks help from a mental health professional who is explicitly identified as a Christian, the therapeutic contract is primarily to solve the psychological problem and secondarily to solve it within a Christian framework.

Finally, the *events of therapy* will affect the likelihood of the discussion of religious values in therapy. Conversation is continually new and often surprising in the twists and turns. The explicit mention of religious values—often in nonplanful ways—might affect its impact on therapy.

References

Ball, R. A., and R. K. Goodyear. 1991. Self-reported professional practices of Christian psychologists. *Journal of Psychology and Christianity* 10: 144–53.

Beck, J. R. 1990. Cultural reflection: A necessary task for the Christian psychotherapist. *Journal of Psychology and Theology* 18: 123–30.

Bem, D. J., and A. Allen. 1974. On predicting some of the people some of the time: The search for cross-situational consistencies in behavior. *Psychological Review* 81: 506–20.

Bem, D. J., and D. C. Funder. 1978. Predicting more of the people more of the time: Assessing the personality of situations. *Psychological Review* 85: 485–501.

Bergin, A. E. 1980. Psychotherapy and religious values. *Journal of Consulting and Clinical Psychology* 48: 95–105.

_____. 1983. Religiosity and mental health: A critical reevaluation and meta-analysis. *Professional Psychology: Research and Practice* 14: 170–84.

_____. 1988. Three contributions of a spiritual perspective to counseling. *Counseling and Values* 33: 21–31.

Bergin, A. E., and J. P. Jensen. 1990. Religiosity of psychotherapists: A national survey. *Psychotherapy* 16: 3–7.

Beutler, L. E. 1979. Values, beliefs, religion and the persuasive influence of psychotherapy. *Psychotherapy: Theory, Research and Practice* 16: 432–40.

_____. 1981. Convergence in counseling and psychotherapy: A current look. *Clinical Psychology Review* 1: 79–101.

_____. 1989. *Value change in counseling and psychotherapy: A search for scientific credibility.* Invited paper presented at the meeting of the American Psychological Association, New Orleans, August.

Beutler, L. E., and J. Bergan. 1991. Value change in counseling and psychotherapy: A search for scientific credibility. *Journal of Counseling Psychology* 38: 16–24.

Beutler, L. E., M. Crago, and T. G. Arizmendi. 1986. Research on therapist variables in psychotherapy. In *Handbook of psychotherapy and behavior change*, ed. S. L. Garfield and A. E. Bergin, 3d ed., 257–310. New York: Wiley.

Beutler, L. E., A. M. Jobe, and D. Elkins. 1974. Outcomes in group psychotherapy: Using persuasion theory to increase treatment efficiency. *Journal of Consulting and Clinical Psychology* 42: 547–53.

Beutler, L. E., S. Pollack, and A. M. Jobe. 1978. Acceptance: Values and therapeutic change. *Journal of Consulting and Clinical Psychology* 46: 198–99.

Bromley, D. G., and P. E. Hammond, eds. 1987. *The future of new religious movements.* Macon, Ga.: Mercer Univ. Press.

DiBlasio, F. A., and B. B. Benda. 1991. Practitioners, religion, and the use of forgiveness in the clinical setting. *Journal of Psychology and Christianity* 10: 166–72.

Dienart, J. W. 1982. *A cognitive approach to the ethics of counseling psychology.* Washington, D. C.: Univ. Press of America.

Fitzgibbons, R. P. 1986. The cognitive and emotional uses of forgiveness in the treatment of anger. *Psychotherapy* 23: 629–33.

Gartner, J., M. Harmatz, A. Hohmann, D. Larson, and A. F. Gartner. 1990. The effect of patient and clinician ideology on clinical judgment: A study of ideological countertransference. *Psychotherapy* 27: 98–106.

Goldsmith, W. M., and B. K. Hansen. 1991. Boundary areas of religious clients' values: Impact for therapy. *Journal of Psychology and Christianity* 10: 224–36.

Hesselgrave, D. J. 1984. *Counseling cross culturally: An introduction to theory and practice for Christians.* Grand Rapids: Baker.

Hope, D. 1987. The healing paradox of forgiveness. *Psychotherapy* 24: 240–44.

Houts, A. C., and K. Graham. 1986. Can religion make you crazy? Impact of client and therapist religious values on clinical judgments. *Journal of Consulting and Clinical Psychology* 54: 267–71.

Howard, G. S. 1985. The role of values in the science of psychology. *American Psychologist* 40: 255–65.

_____. 1989. *A tale of two stories: Excursions into a narrative approach to psychology.* Notre Dame, Ind.: Academic Publications.

Keating, A. M., and B. R. Fretz. 1990. Christians' anticipations about counselors in response to counselor descriptions. *Journal of Counseling Psychology* 37: 293–96.

Kelley, H. H., and J. W. Thibaut. 1978. *Interpersonal relations: A theory of interdependence.* New York: Wiley.

Kelly, E. W., Jr. 1990. Counselor responsiveness to client religiousness. *Counseling and Values* 35: 69–72.

Kenrick, D. T., and D. C. Funder. 1988. Profiting from controversy: Lessons from the person-situation debate. *American Psychologist* 43: 23–34.

Koltko, M. E. 1990. How religious beliefs affect psychotherapy: The example of Mormonism. *Psychotherapy* 27: 132–41.

Lewis, K. N., C. S. Davis, and R. Lesmeister. 1983. Pretherapy information: An investigation of client responses. *Journal of Counseling Psychology* 30: 108–12.

Lewis, K. N., and D. L. Epperson. 1991. Values, pretherapy information, and informed consent in Christian counseling. *Journal of Psychology and Christianity* 10: 113–31.

Lewis, K. N., and D. A. Lewis. 1985. Impact of religious affiliation on therapists' judgments of patients. *Journal of Consulting and Clinical Psychology* 53: 926–32.

London, P. 1986. *The modes and morals of psychotherapy.* 2d ed. New York: Hemisphere.

Lovinger, R. J. 1984. *Working with religious issues in therapy*. New York: Jason Aronson.

Margolis, R. D., and K. W. Elifson. 1979. A typology of religious experience. *Journal for the Scientific Study of Religion* 18: 61–67.

_____. 1983. Validation of a typology of religious experience and its relationship to the psychotic experience. *Journal of Psychology and Theology* 11: 135–41.

Meylink, W. D., and R. L. Gorsuch. 1988. Relationship between clergy and psychologist: The empirical data. *Journal for Psychology and Christianity* 7(1): 56–72.

Miller, W. R., and J. E. Martin, eds. 1988. *Behavior therapy and religion: Integrating spiritual and behavioral approaches to change*. Newbury Park, Calif.: Sage.

Mischel, W. 1973. Toward a cognitive social learning reconceptualization of personality. *Psychological Review* 80: 252–83.

Moon, G. W., J. W. Bailey, J. C. Kwasny, and D. E. Willis. 1991. Christian counseling techniques: A new look at some old disciplines. *Journal of Psychology and Christianity* 10: 154–65.

Moyers, J. C. 1990. Religious issues in the psychotherapy of former fundamentalists. *Psychotherapy* 27: 42–45.

Nugent, M. D., and L. L. Constantine. 1988. Marital paradigms: Compatibility, treatment, and outcome in marital therapy. *Journal of Marital and Family Therapy* 14: 351–69.

Parham, T. A., and J. E. Helms. 1981. The influence of Black students' racial identity attitudes on preferences for counselor's race. *Journal of Counseling Psychology* 28: 250–57.

Propst, L. R., R. Ostrum, P. Watkins, and M. Morris. 1984. *Preliminary report of the comparative efficacy of religious and nonreligious cognitive-behavioral therapy for the treatment of clinical depression in religious individuals*. Paper presented at the meeting of the Society for Psychotherapy Research, Banff, Canada, June.

Quackenbos, S., G. Privette, and B. Klentz. 1985. Psychotherapy: Sacred or secular? *Journal of Counseling and Development* 64: 290–93.

_____. 1986. Psychotherapy and religion: Rapprochement or antithesis? *Journal of Counseling and Development* 65: 82–85.

Shafranske, E. P., and H. N. Malony. 1990. Clinical psychologists' religious and spiritual orientations and their practice of psychotherapy. *Psychotherapy* 27: 72–78.

Sperry, R. W. 1988. Psychology's mentalist paradigm and the religion/science tension. *American Psychologist* 43: 607–13.

Spilka, B., P. Shaver, and L. Kirkpatrick. 1985. General attribution for the psychology of religion. *Journal for the Scientific Study of Religion* 24: 1–20.

Strupp, H. J., S. W. Hadley, and B. Gomez-Schwartz. 1977. *Psychotherapy for better or worse*. New York: Jason Aronson.

Tjeltveit, A. C. 1986. The ethics of value conversion in psychotherapy: Appropriate and inappropriate therapist influence on client values. *Clinical Psychology Review* 6: 515–37.

Wadsworth, R. D., and K. T. Checketts. 1980. Influence of religious affiliation on psychodiagnosis. *Journal of Consulting and Clinical Psychology* 48: 234–40.

Worthington, E. L., Jr. 1986. Religious counseling: A review of published empirical research. *Journal of Counseling and Development* 64: 421–31.

_____. 1988. Understanding the values of religious clients: A model and its application to counseling. *Journal of Counseling Psychology* 35: 166–74.

Worthington, E. L., Jr., and F. A. DiBlasio. 1990. Promoting mutual forgiveness within the fractured relationship. *Psychotherapy* 27: 219–23.

Worthington, E. L., Jr., P. A. Dupont, J. T. Berry, and L. A. Duncan. 1988. Therapists' and clients' perceptions of religious psychotherapy in private and agency settings. *Journal of Psychology and Theology* 16: 282–93.

Worthington, E. L., Jr., and G. G. Scott. 1983. Goal selection for counseling with potentially religious clients by professional and student counselors in explicitly Christian or secular settings. *Journal of Psychology and Theology* 11: 318–29.

Worthington, E. L., Jr., K. Hsu, K. K. Gowda, and E. Bleach. 1988. *Preliminary tests of Worthington's (1988) theory of important values in religious counseling*. Paper presented at the International Congress on Christian Counseling, Atlanta, November.

Wyatt, S. C., and R. W. Johnson. 1990. The influence of counselors' religious values on clients' perceptions of the counselor. *Journal of Psychology and Theology* 18: 158–65.

6

Boundary Areas of Religious Clients' Values: Target for Therapy

W. MACK GOLDSMITH
AND BETTY K. HANSEN

Here is a truism: "Values are important in psychotherapy." Originally, therapists were supposed to be value-neutral, but it was already clear when London (1964) wrote his classic book on the subject that clients in psychotherapy are in the process of value change and that therapists are not value-neutral. Thus questions arose: In what ways, if any, do therapist values affect clients' values, and how might these changes affect therapeutic outcomes? Beutler (1981) has named these two issues as the "convergence" of values and the "importance" of values in therapy. Before we review and discuss these issues, we want to detour to clarify some concepts and indicate the goals of this chapter.

We also want to share with you some of our own clinical observations and material from five interviews that Betty Hansen conducted with former clients to explore our notion of mapping value domains. Here is an example of such an interview:

Brad joined a Vietnam veterans' group when he became unable to work because of flashbacks to his war experiences.[1] He said,

1. All names used in these case illustrations have been changed.

An earlier version of this chapter was presented to the Christian Association for Psychological Studies, Western Region (CAPS-West), June 23, 1990, Vancouver, British Columbia.

I used to be pretty conventional—totally out of touch with my feelings. I didn't place much importance on a way of life that is personally fulfilling. But since I got into therapy, that has become really important. Church used to be pretty important. I went most Sundays, even to the evening service, and we were in small Bible-study groups. But when my life started falling apart and I couldn't work, it seemed like the people in church didn't know how to react to me. They were successful and I was a failure. I think I embarrassed them. The pastors were better. They tried to understand about post-traumatic shock, and they even went to the movie *Platoon*, but I got the feeling that after a while, when I kept on being depressed, they didn't know how to help. Maybe they got tired of waiting for me to get better.

I'm working now, our marriage is better, and life is smoother, but I haven't gone back to church. I'm kind of the same way to God. He's there, and I pray to him, but something's missing. Maybe I'll work on my relationship to him someday, but right now I'm just trying to survive emotionally.

Brad's values shifted in therapy from more formal, externally generated ones to more internal, personal ones. His evaluation of himself shifted from concerns with external actions to internal feelings. His beliefs in the importance of participating in his religious community diminished as he perceived the discrepancy between his values and theirs.

"Beliefs" are perceptions of what is true: Brad believes in God; he believes his pastors meant well. "Values" are beliefs about what is "good" or "bad"; that is, right or wrong, valuable or hurtful. They can be my own perceptions of "good" or "bad" or what others communicate that they consider "good" or "bad." For example, Brad now believes that being in touch with his feelings is important but that going to church is less so. The key here is that all beliefs, including values, are perceptions. They are usually perceptions shared, at least in part, with a believing community, be it a church, three guys at a lunch table, or just a therapist.

Value conflicts can have their source in ambivalence; that is, disagreement with myself, in a sense, on whether something is good or bad. However, because values are almost always shared beliefs, the most difficult value conflicts tend to occur when I see myself disagreeing with others in my social reference group. As Worthington (1989) points out, the reference group most salient to highly religious people is often their church or other religious community, and the degree to which these people identify with the norms of their religious group is a powerful determiner of values. Conflicted values lead to inconsistent or oscillating behavior. Worthington (1989) remarks,

Salient situational stimuli often elicit behavior that the person later finds abhorrent to his or her value system. Some people consistently behave in ways dissonant to their values (e.g., people with extraordinary sensitivity to situational cues or with weakly held or conflicting values. . . .) (166).

Our next interview case illustrates dissonance between values and behavior that can result from severely conflicted beliefs, the classic conflict between the urge to be "good" and the urge to be "happy." Karen grew up in a conservative Christian home. Between the ages of 13 and 19 she was sexually molested by three ministers. For several years after her marriage at age 17 she drank heavily and had numerous affairs, while continuing to attend church regularly. Eventually the conflict between her behavior and her values precipitated a crisis and she renewed her Christian commitment.

> I always believed it was important to live a Christian life. When I was drinking and sleeping around, I knew I was sinning. That life seemed the only way I could fill up the emptiness inside but I hated myself the whole time.

Her response indicates how conflicted values become differentiated and then firmer and more coherent in therapy:

> It's funny, but I don't think I've changed my beliefs very much. What has changed since therapy is that I am more understanding of how trapped people can be by sin. I think I'm less legalistic about labeling other people's actions as sin. I know that my drinking was sinful, but I no longer believe that it's wrong for anyone to drink at all. I can see shades of gray now where before therapy I saw everything as black and white.

Values, being perceptions of what is right, good, or significant, are reflected in the goals toward which behavior is directed. Karen's behavior shows that conflicted or ambivalent values lead to inconsistent motives and goals. Much of counseling and psychotherapy[2] is aimed at discovering the goals which determine the client's dysfunctional behaviors, attitudes, and emotions. Our success as therapists depends on our ability to intervene within a client's value system in order to help the client set healthier goals, both for life activities and for the therapy itself.

The focus of this chapter is to suggest that religious clients express their value conflicts in somewhat different ways than nonreligious clients do and that therapists can see value conflicts, especially religious ones, as a way to find fertile ground for therapeutic interventions. In this latter point, we are not proposing a new therapy or even a new intervention strategy. Rather, we hope to suggest some ways to map a client's value system so that the intervention strategy of choice may have maximal effect. We believe the approach we are suggesting is compatible with a wide range of dynamic, cognitive, and systems theories.

---

2. We use the terms *counseling, therapy,* and *psychotherapy* interchangeably in this chapter.

Beutler (1981) reviewed over 50 studies to determine whether clients' and therapists' personalities and belief systems converge during therapy and also whether such convergence was correlated with improvement in the course of therapy. He reports that (a) there was convergence in the form of clients adopting their therapists' belief systems in successful therapy, (b) the more dissimilar the belief systems were at the start of therapy, the more convergence occurred, but (c) no firm conclusions could be made about the complex relationship of convergence and success. Beutler (1981) reports research (Beutler, Pollack, and Jobe 1978) to suggest that changes in some value areas, sexual and religious in particular, correlate with therapeutic improvement. He notes that, though little researched, the possibility for change in religious values has been of special interest to therapists. These opinions range from the assumption that religious values cannot be changed to the view that they should be a main target of change. He concludes:

> It now appears clear both that religious values can be changed and that in some instances, at least, such change is related to criteria of improvement (Beutler et al. 1978, 98).

Bergin (1980) concluded that similarity of values between religious clients and their therapists enhances favorable outcomes, but Beutler (1981) is not so sure. He states: "Clearly if sharing a religious and theistic philosophy is as advantageous as Bergin (1980) claims, it is not in evidence here" (96). Worthington (1986, 1989) has reviewed a large number of studies dealing with values of highly religious clients and concluded that, along with fear of misdiagnosis, religious clients' major fear was that their values would be changed in therapy by nonreligious therapists; they preferred therapists who shared their values. Worthington (1991) has summarized his and his associates' thinking and some empirical studies on the role of religious clients' values. We refer the reader to that article for a review of material that was key to the development of the present chapter.

Based on his earlier research, Beutler (1981) suggests that "attitudes of medium centrality, as defined by Rokeach (1973), may be more relevant both to convergence and to improvement than are attitudes of greater or less centrality" (98). By "centrality," Beutler refers to the relative importance of the value in clients' value systems. However, Worthington (1989) argues that Beutler's conclusions about a broad-based population of clients may not apply to highly religious people. In short, what is "medium"—that is, indifferent—for one person might be strong for another, and that a fundamentalist, for example, "would probably rather switch than fight. Switch therapists, this is" (11).

"Salience" is a key aspect of Worthington's (1986, 1989) values model. Salience is the measure of a value's importance in a person's thinking and feeling, not whether that person is pro or con on the issue. If a value has high salience, one tends to interpret and evaluate oneself, the environment, and social relations in terms of the value. Worthington proposes that highly religious westerners, Christians in particular, hold three salient value dimensions: the role of authority of Scripture, of human religious leaders, and degree of identification with the norms of their religious group. In a similar vein, Koltko (1990) proposes that clients hold "metabeliefs," that is, beliefs about beliefs and notes that highly religious clients, Mormons in his case, hold key metabeliefs that their religion is both very important and very potent. Koltko's "importance" is similar to Worthington's "salience" and Beutler's "centrality": Koltko's "potency" adds the notion that highly religious people feel their religion provides powerful tools for meeting life's challenges.

Worthington holds, in principle, that a person's views on his three dimensions could be represented by a point or, more likely, a region plotted in three-dimensional space. The region representing the person's value position is surrounded by a "zone of toleration" for differing views of others; these zones also differ from believer to believer. The view of those whose values are perceived as falling outside the toleration zone will be rejected, and the holder of those views may be treated with contempt or hostility. It is clear that a secular or antireligious counselor might well be seen as holding views outside a highly religious person's zone of toleration. Worthington (1989) suggests that this kind of value mismatch in therapy will result in such unfavorable outcomes as premature termination or increased resistance. Some research (Worthington 1988; Worthington, Hsu, Gowda, and Bleach 1988), has supported this view.[3]

Worthington (1989) has several hypotheses about how both clients' and therapists' zones of toleration affect therapy. He says that the size of these zones may be affected by contextual pressures, presentational styles, emotional states, and previous communication patterns. He adds, "Enduring psychological pain usually restricts a person's zone of toleration and defines the boundaries of the zone sharply" (1988, 170). He says this restriction can become a rigid defensive pattern in which a hurting client is open only to ideas that do not challenge existing beliefs. Yet the boundaries of the zone are not only more rigid under distress but may be more "brittle"; that is, likely to "shatter under attack" (170),

3. Worthington's (1988, 1989) model uses a three-dimensional value system to predict possible client-therapist conflicts. However, Arizmendi, Beutler, Shanfield, Crago, and Hagaman (1985) suggest that specific value similarities and differences, not global value systems, are differentially related to therapeutic improvement, a view partly supported by Richards and Davison (1989).

potentially leading to substantial value change, most likely converging on the therapist's own values.

An unhappy example of clients retreating to rigidly defend their central values under a perceived attack is illustrated by another of our clinical cases. During marital therapy that included teaching the partners more assertive communication patterns, the wife began to value herself and reject her husband's conservative Christian view of marriage. Her insistence on taking part in marital decisions threatened one of his core values and, by extension, his sense of himself. His response was to demand unquestioning "submission," precipitating a crisis, which they resolved by leaving therapy and projecting the threat onto the therapist (whom they labeled as "outside the will of God"). Thus they buttressed the marital alliance by reasserting their old beliefs about the nature of marriage even more strongly—although those old beliefs had not worked.

Hannah's interview case illustrates the shattering of a core value.

> As a child, God was very important to me, but as I grew up he felt so distant. My life was so bad. I went to church to solve my problems, but they didn't go away; in an unhealthy way I was asking God to fix me, but nothing changed. I gave up believing in God. I figured I had to solve my own problems. I couldn't depend on anyone else—so I became the "Invincible Woman." I frantically tried to make things different, but that just kept things stirred up and kept me from thinking rationally and acting effectively. Finally I collapsed physically and emotionally and admitted defeat. In counseling and through Al-Anon, I started looking at myself in a more positive, loving way. I realized I was my own best friend; God gave me that gift and the strength to see things needing change. God has taken away most of my worry and fear. I can't say enough about God in my life now!

Hannah described the collapse of a core value of her childhood, her belief in God, in response to unremitting personal distress. When her belief in herself also collapsed, she came to the heuristic point of reorganizing her core values again. This time, however, with guidance from her therapist and the Al-Anon group, she began re-forming her values on a foundation of more realistic perceptions of God, herself, and others.

Changes in a person's most central values are likely to be accompanied by radical shifts in behavior, relationships, and self-percepts. Hannah was fortunate to be able to recover her faith; many never do. But radical value changes are rare. Just as in the church we see fewer sudden conversions than gradual awakenings at the altar (e.g., Spilka, Hood, and Gorsuch 1985), so in the clinic, our clients are less likely to experience a radical shift in core values, as Hannah did, than changes in less central values.

Some research on the values of highly religious people has been concerned with personality and religious-orientation issues rather than the clinical issues previously reviewed. The most prominent of those issues has been the relation of values to Allport's "intrinsic" and "extrinsic" religious orientations. Allport conceived of intrinsic religion as the central and supreme value of a believer's life, while extrinsic religion was seen as peripheral and subordinate to nonreligious values. He felt that the intrinsic orientation represented a more mature, differentiated faith than the extrinsic orientation, and these different styles of faith have been related to ethnic prejudice (Allport and Ross 1967) and other social and personality variables. Later, Batson and his colleagues added a third conceptual way to be religious, a "quest" orientation where religion is a central value but always open to changes in belief rather than stable or dogmatically closed (Batson and Ventis 1982). The massive literature is not central to this chapter, but for a recent review of both content and methodology see Van Wicklin (1990).

In two multivariate studies of values held by intrinsic-, extrinsic-, and quest-oriented Christian students, Goldsmith and his colleagues (Goldsmith, Goldsmith and Foster 1986; Park and Goldsmith 1985) found that the majority of their highly religious Christian subjects could best be classified as combining the traits of both intrinsics and quest-oriented believers, a religious-orientation type they called "questing intrinsics." These highly religious subjects were characterized as having a core of centrally held, largely coherent religious beliefs that were not open to change. But they also claimed that many of their less central beliefs were open to changes; indeed, these students frequently told the researchers that they were active and felt positive about exploring belief and value alternatives and about modifying their positions. Goldsmith et al.'s highly religious Christian college sample stressed core values from Rokeach's (1973) Value Survey that indicated a primary concern with inner virtues such as "inner harmony," "salvation," "wisdom," "courage" and "forgiveness," while the less orthodoxly religious public college sample chose situational values, such as "a comfortable life," "a world at peace."

Goldsmith et al. (1986) suggested that a "questing intrinsic" orientation might be closer to Allport's notion of mature religion than either the pure "intrinsic" or pure "quest" orientations. The key point here is that their beliefs are fixed at the core but flexible and permeable at the periphery, a pattern that many have considered to represent emotionally healthy religiosity. Watson, Hood, and Morris (1988) found, contrary to Batson's theory, that orthodox, intrinsic believers did not seem to "ignore or hide from existential questions of life" but showed a "commitment to traditional religious resolutions of those problems" (52). These authors further state that adherence to fixed articles of faith does not mean that those beliefs were arrived at by rigid, uncomplicated thought processes and that, in general, there is no consistent evidence that highly religious people are more closed-minded or less cognitively complex than less religious and orthodox people.[4]

Worthington's (1988, 1989) model of a value region of central beliefs surrounded by a zone of toleration appears similar to Goldsmith et al.'s (1986) description of their "questing intrinsics" and to Watson et al.'s (1988) finding of intrinsic believers open to existential questions about life but likely to look for traditional religious solutions. However, in Worthington's model, the zone of toleration applied only to toleration for the perceived beliefs and values of others, notably therapists. On the other hand, Goldsmith et al. and Watson et al. considered only toleration for ambivalence in one's own values.

While recognizing differences in focus of the studies, we believe the similarities in the two models are striking and important. As noted, Worthington (1988, 1989) suggests that people with weakly held or conflicted values often act in ways abhorrent to their central values and that the zone of toleration of painfully distressed clients may become restricted, rigid, and brittle. We propose that, as a highly religious, questing intrinsic believer comes under emotional distress from situational or internal sources, there are related changes to expect in the stability of that person's central core of values and doctrines, the perception and tolerance of internal value ambiguities, and the perception and tolerance of the values of significant others; that is, Worthington's zone of toleration.

We noted Worthington's (1989) criticism of Beutler's notion of "medium centrality" as too global to describe the values of highly religious clients. We agree. However, the concept of zones of toleration in Worthington's model may be too restricted, since it deals only with the perceived values of others. Indeed, while Worthington et al. (1988) found support for some of Worthington's (1988) hypotheses, their attempt to measure and map the zones of toleration met with very little success. As Worthington (1989) notes, there may be several reasons, including methodological ones, for that lack of success, but part of the explanation may lie in the need for a more detailed, more inclusive model of what he means by "toleration" and what Beutler (1981) means by "medium centrality."

We would like to discuss these related cognitive and social-perception changes in highly religious clients in an extended metaphor of a castle, surrounded and protected by a swamp, with hostile land on the other side of the swamp. The castle and its island represent a region of central values, as in Worthington's model. The swamp represents less centrally held, less coherent values, such as Beutler's "medium centrality" values, but also conflicted values, arising from internal ambivalence or perceived

---

4. However, some studies have reported "fundamentalism" to be positively correlated with dogmatism and negatively correlated with cognitive complexity (e.g., Edgington and Hutchinson 1990).

differences from others. The values falling in the swampy areas of the believer's cognitive-value domain are unstable and may frequently shift or even reverse as situational stimuli impinge upon them. In the hostile territory on the other side of the swamp lie the areas of values that are as firmly rejected as those on the castle's island are affirmed.

In an otherwise healthy, highly religious person without unusual emotional distress, the castle, one hopes, is built on a rock and surrounded by firm and pleasant fields that extend to the edge of the swamp. The swamp itself is not wide or frightening. Indeed, the healthy, questing believer may well be regularly draining swampland at the edges of the island to incorporate into productive gardens. That is, the believer, growing in healthy ways, incorporates more value-loaded aspects of life into his or her understanding of self, God, and others. Cognitive complexity and variety increase and toleration for the views of others does, too, even as the issues of value disagreement become better defined. In short, rather than being a source of terror, the swamp is a resource to be used and enjoyed, a source of a richer life while serving to keep the enemies on the hostile shore at a distance.

But the cognitive-value landscape of a distressed client is much different. Frequently old "truths" and virtues no longer seem to be working. Such a person might well wonder whether such traditional values as marital fidelity at home, honestly in business, or humility in church really do work. Moral virtue seems to go unnoticed and unrewarded. Significant others who previously seemed so supportive now are seen as alienated or distant. The Scriptures that once glowed with grace, love, and forgiveness now seem cold and judgmental, as does God himself. The once firm land around the castle is being undermined and pieces are sliding into the swamp of uncertain values. In Koltko's (1990) terms, the metabelief of "importance" remains intact but the metabelief of "potency" is under serious erosion.

At the same time, the believer wonders if values previously rejected are really wrong after all. When God seems distant from us in our distress, we may wonder if maybe the atheists are right that God is just a figment of our imaginations and a projection of our needs. Psalm 73 tells of a believer who felt his feet slipping on the grounds of his faith when he saw how the wicked prospered, and that he "envied the arrogant" (v. 2). In our metaphor, this means that the land on the far shore is crumbling into the swamp, too; that values that had been flatly rejected are now considered as possibilities.

The swamp thus grows wider and wider, while the distressed person watches with anxiety, depression, or confusion. The frightened islander may throw up sandbags and dikes to stop the erosion or may act out in desperation. We believe this is what Worthington meant when he suggested that a client's zone of toleration becomes defensive, restricted, rigid, and brittle and that a client may act in ways sharply dissonant to his or her values. In the extreme case, the island might be swept away and faith and all its related values lost.

At the same time, as Koltko points out, the metabelief that one's religion is (or should be) a potent resource tends to prevent a distressed believer from seeking outside therapeutic help. Prayer, faith, and the support of the religious community should be all one needs. As Koltko notes: "Mormons tend to feel that if they live their religion, they should never need therapy . . . (and) turning to treatment is a denial of faith" (134). Virkler (1979) and others have also noted the reluctance of highly religious people to seek professional counseling. Some have found highly religious clients may prefer religiously compatible, nonprofessional counselors (Sell and Goldsmith 1988). Worthington (1986) concludes that, although religious clients claim they want counselors with similar values, they seem unable to discriminate between counselors with similar and dissimilar values. Koltko insists that therapists need not agree with a highly religious client's faith but need to know the specifics of its main doctrines and workings and, more particularly, what those specifics mean to the client. He adds that a general knowledge of religion is not adequate.

Clearly any therapist will be a key feature on the metaphorical landscape we have been describing. What kinds of religious beliefs and values can the client expect to find in the professional world? In general, most professional therapists have some religious interests and values, but they tend to be nontraditional ones— "spiritual humanism," in Bergin and Jensen's (1990) terms. They are not very open to the religious values of orthodox believers (Bergin and Jensen 1990; Shafranske and Malony 1990). There are powerful negative values in many highly religious clients attached even to seeing a therapist and, short of anecdotes, no one seems to know quite how a client's values actually function in therapy. It seems clear, however, that value change is a major feature of almost any therapy, whether such value change is intended or not. For example, most therapies deal with values about self-evaluation, about perfectionism, and about targets of anger and fear, such as parents.

The interview below indicates some of the value conflicts that can occur between a therapist of the kind Bergin and Jensen (1990) consider typical and a highly religious, orthodox Christian client. Ellen, a Bible-college graduate, complained about the difficulty of working with a therapist who was a relatively new Christian. Although he said he was respectful of her values, he often seemed to disagree with them. At this stage in his spiritual development his therapeutic instincts were probably most guided by the humanistic values of his training and previous experience.

He would question the amount of time I volunteered at church, or suggest that I was expecting too much obedience from my children, and I'd have to analyze—am I being neurotic about this? Am I unrealistic—you know, distorted thinking? Or does he think I'm wrong just because what I'm saying or doing doesn't fit his values? Then I'd have to say, well, are these things important to me because I'm messed up, or because they are God's will for me? Can I trust this baby Christian to know God's will for me? Can I trust myself to know it? I went through a long time in therapy of being really confused about the differences between me and my therapist. I wished he shared my knowledge of the Bible. He seemed to think that because we were both believers we were on the same wavelength. He didn't even seem to be aware of what felt to me like huge conflicts in our values and assumptions about life.

Like many therapists of this sort, he felt sympathetic with the client's religiosity in general but failed to learn or appreciate the specifics of her faith and her religious group norms.

According to Worthington's (1988, 1989) model, the perceived values of significant others—especially those to whom authority is ascribed by the client—will be key to the client's acceptance of psychotherapy; that is, those authorities whose values lie outside the "zone of toleration" will tend to be resisted or rejected. We propose that highly religious clients will see pastors, church leaders, therapists, and other authorities as having firmer, more coherent, better defined values than the clients themselves do. In terms of our metaphor, the distressed islander, faced with eroding lands and an ever-widening value swamp, will tend to see others with solid islands and narrow swamps; that is, as knowing well what they believe and what they reject and as living consistently in accordance with those firm, coherent value systems. While the islander finds that his or her own value boundaries are weak, permeable, and shifting, authorities will be seen as having the well-defined, impermeable value boundaries that allow a consistent and moral lifestyle. The same may well be true of other significant members of the religious reference group, especially if there is little intimacy in the group which would allow glimpses of the other members' human frailties. Sell and Goldsmith (1988) found that social stigma was a major reason their highly religious subjects would be reluctant to seek professional counseling, and Fischer and Turner (1970) found that the ability to tolerate stigma was a major factor in determining a person's orientation toward counseling. As Koltko (1990) describes this kind of self-perception, the islanders may well feel inadequate in comparison to their reference group and perceive themselves as intimidated, stigmatized, spiritual failures.

The problem may be made much more acute if there is perceived disagreement among authorities over religious and life values; for example, if a professional therapist and a pastor are seen to disagree. Such dis-agreement is fairly likely if the client and the pastor represent a conven-tional, orthodox religion. We noted that therapists tend to take a dim view of conventional religion. Clergy are notably wary of professional therapy, too. Meylink and Gorsuch (1988) estimated that less than 4% of clergy refer clientele to psychologists and psychiatrists, and less than 10% to professional therapists of all kinds. Worthington (1986) found that most conservative Christian clergy view their counseling chiefly as imparting "truth" and giving advice; liberal clergy are more Rogerian in approach. Long and Heggen (1988) found that a broad-based sample of clergy described the spiritually ideal adult as "self-reliant," "a leader," "holding strong beliefs," "independent," "aggressive," "obedient," "provid-ing an identity to spouse," "making home a priority." While there is some overlap, their list of ideal spiritual traits differs substantially with the list of ideal mental health traits held by professional therapists (Jensen and Bergin 1988). Further, Long and Heggen found that clergy described the spiritually ideal "adult" and the spiritually ideal "man" in almost identical terms; the spiritually ideal "woman" was described in much different terms, including "follower," "gentle," "submissive." What could the dis-tressed islander, especially a woman, expect from the conflict of author-ities with competing values but more and faster erosion of his or her own values? Confusion and discouragement would seem to follow naturally, along with the risk of radical, undesirable value shifts and accompanying dissonant behaviors.

But where a working alliance is effective, the authority's firmer, coher-ent values will be seen as a potential source of strength by the client. We assume that is one reason that so many clients seek value advice from counselors. However, most therapists, one hopes, seek to help the islanders rebuild their own ravaged lands rather than try to move to the therapists' islands. The result is a dilemma for therapists trying to plan treatment strategies.

We propose that the value swampland, not the castle's rock, is the place for therapists to target effective interventions intended to change values. Strongly affirmed central values—the rock on which our metaphorical castle stands—cannot be changed without great risk, if they can be changed at all. Similarly, flatly rejected values are equally central and are the source of believers' fear that therapists may try to persuade them to do "immoral" acts. Rather, values held ambivalently or with medium centrality are the easiest to change and the place where thera-peutic interventions should have their greatest influence.

The irony is that the therapist sees the greatest potential in the middle of the swamp, but the client wants help at the crumbling shoreline. As Worthington (1989) put it, the client just wants relief. It seems clear that the effective therapist must do both. Indeed, supportive therapy to bolster and repair the castle should probably be done concurrently with interventions intended to change maladaptive and confused values in midswamp. He or she must understand the values that are central to the client and that the client desperately wants saved. The therapist must also target interventions in the areas of greatest value conflict and ambivalence, even though those areas are deep in the swamp where clients feel the least safe.

Obviously, the interactions of values affect the course and outcome of therapy, though not necessarily in ways that we can yet predict. We can, however, suggest ways for the therapist to make use of the values the client brings to therapy. We begin by conceptualizing a map of the client's values, assuming that more accurate knowledge of his or her values will allow greater *precision* of therapeutic focus. Such mapping would first assess the content and salience of values and beliefs. Standard instruments for assessing values, such as Rokeach's (1973) Values Survey and Rotter's (1950) Incomplete Sentences Blank, are helpful. In addition, accurate value mapping requires learning in detail both the official teaching of the client's religion as well as its meaning to the client, as Koltko (1990) suggests. Even clients who profess no religious affiliation at present may give therapeutically significant information if one includes in one's history-taking questions about religious upbringing. Religious upbringing significantly forms the personalities, belief structures, and decision making, even of those who consciously disaffiliate from their religion. A therapist may spot these factors by looking for incongruities that lead to anxiety, guilt, or depression, as Koltko (1990) notes. Further, Tamney, Powell, and Johnson (1989) point out that "nones" who claim no religious affiliation and who have disaffiliated from their religious upbringings may reject religious beliefs and values ("cultural nones"), religious institutions ("structural nones"), or religious people ("marginal nones"). They see these "nones" as innovative and open to changes in values and morals. A clinician should consider these rather different motivations for disaffiliation and recognize that similar feelings may well motivate clients who have not formally disaffiliated but are seriously discouraged in their faith.

The second feature to map is the client's ambivalence or conflict with highly significant others. Our interview with Donna is an example of how conflict with others' values and beliefs causes deep distress in a person with low ego strength.

> As a young believer I was taught and nurtured by some very sincere but very rigid people. I was taught, both by my grandmother and by the church people, that God is an awesome judge; you can work your tail off, but you're never good enough for him. But when I accepted Christ, he accepted me.

Of all the people that knew me, I knew no one who loved me. But God did. My teachers seemed to believe that God always condemned people in the Bible, but I saw in the Bible stories that when people made mistakes and sinned, God kept working in them. Yet, for years my self-esteem was so low that I couldn't really accept emotionally what my mind and even my experience of God told me. I see now that I was repeating to myself all the negative things I had learned at church.

Counseling helped me to straighten out my own thinking to fit with reality. It helped me start to respect my own perceptions and ideas. And it helped me understand what hurt does to people—that the people who taught me their distorted ideas about God and sin were responding to pain in their lives that I may not be able to see.

As a young Christian, Donna had internalized guilt-inducing negative beliefs from her teachers that reinforced shame from her traumatic childhood. Her therapist did not directly challenge her pathological beliefs but chose to strengthen the values with which they were in conflict; that is, her perceptions of God's love and her worth to him.

There is a positive side to the value conflicts with significant others, however, if the significant other is the therapist. Again, the major location is in the swamp of medium centrality. Beutler, Crago, and Arizmendi (1986) report some studies which show that therapeutic success is most associated with initial *dissimilarity* of client and therapist values; other studies show an association of success with initial value *similarity*. These mixed results suggest that whether initial client-therapist value dissimilarity aids or hinders therapy may be situation and person specific. Beutler et al. (1986) add that the degree of dissimilarity on specific attitudes may be more important to success than on general attitudes. Further, Worthington (1989) warns that therapists who share too much about their own specific values risk creating unnecessary value conflicts with their clients; he suggests letting the client project some specific values.[5] Richards and Davison (1989) report that certain of therapists' particular religious values were clearly associated with subjects' willingness to trust those counselors, while other potential therapist values were not related to trust. These authors also report substantial individual differences. These studies all imply that a mix of similar and dissimilar specific beliefs of medium centrality may be optimal for therapeutic improvement. If this supposition is true, the center of Worthington's (1989) "zone of toleration" for client-therapist value differences may be ideal for the therapeutic relationship.

The third feature to map is the degree of emotional distress associated with the client's values. A list of values, such as Rokeach's, or an adjective

---

5. Wyatt and Johnson's (1990) analogue study also suggests that counselors with non-specific positive religious values may be preferred by strongly religious persons.

check list could be useful here if the connotations and associations of the value terms are explored with the client. Such a list should include values specific to the client's faith, however; so lists of general values, such as Rokeach's, may need to be expanded. Clergy or other knowledgeable believers can be useful consultants about such specifics. Projective methods and analysis of resistances are common methods for uncovering ambivalences that create distress. Mapping of values would join other assessment methods and global clinical observations as the basis for planning the course and speed of therapy. This kind of mapping implies a need for constant monitoring of client values as therapy continues, so the therapist can know when to shift to new ground, or help the client retreat temporarily to a more familiar place.

Recall the case of the couple who terminated therapy in order to protect their hierarchical marriage values, a case that might have profited from greater sensitivity to the pain of value conflicts and better mapping of the swamp. As the therapist, I (B. H.) wish I had anticipated their panic and prepared the couple for the increased discomfort and conflict that might arise as they experimented with new ways of relating to each other. I would have explored in more depth with them their beliefs about marriage and would have introduced change more slowly in order to accommodate the anxiety such changes elicited. With better therapeutic methods for dealing with value issues, we hope for happier endings with future clients.

In this chapter we have explored how therapists may conceive of, map, and use highly religious clients' cognitive value-domains. We have pictured the value domain in a metaphor of an island in a swamp, where the swamp is composed of unstable, weakly-held, conflicted, or ambivalent moral and religious values. We have tried to show that these medium-centrality values, especially specific religious values, are important to therapeutic success in a number of ways and that knowledge of and sensitivity to the religious client's value domain offer therapists a fruitful approach to increasing their effectiveness. We have extended Worthington's (1986, 1989) zone of tolerance model to include other sources of conflicted values than those arising from client-therapist value differences. With the theoretical analysis, we have included some real case material to show how clients perceive their value domains. Worthington et al.'s (1988) attempt to measure the zone of toleration was not very successful; our attempt to explore former clients' value-domains with interviews often left us wishing we had asked better, more focused questions. On some occasions the interviewer (B. H.) went back to the interviewee with more questions after we had discussed the first interview. Although we offer some suggestions for techniques to map value-domains, we recognize from our own attempts that it is no short or easy task to map a client's swampland and then reclaim the lost lands.

References

Allport, G. W., and J. M. Ross. 1967. Personal religious orientation and prejudice. *Journal of Personality and Social Psychology* 5: 432–43.

Arizmendi, T. G., L. E. Beutler, S. Shanfield, M. Crago, and R. Hagaman. 1985. Client-therapist value similarity and psychotherapy outcome: A microscopic approach. *Psychotherapy: Theory, Research and Practice* 22: 16–21.

Batson, C. D., and W. L. Ventis. 1982. *The religious experience: A social-psychological perspective.* New York: Oxford Univ. Press.

Bergin, A. E. 1980. Psychotherapy and religious values. *Journal of Consulting and Clinical Psychology* 48: 95–105.

Bergin, A. E., and J. P. Jensen. 1990. Religiosity of psychotherapists: A national survey. *Psychotherapy* 27: 3–7.

Beutler, L. E. 1981. Convergence in counseling and psychotherapy: A current look. *Clinical Psychology Review* 1: 79–101.

Beutler, L. E., M. Crago, and T. G. Arizmendi. 1986. Therapist variables in psychotherapy process and outcome. In *Handbook of psychotherapy and behavior change,* ed. S. L. Garfield and A. E. Bergin, 3d ed., 257–310. New York: Wiley.

Beutler, L. E., S. Pollack, and A. M. Jobe. 1978. "Acceptance," values and therapeutic change. *Journal of Consulting and Clinical Psychology* 46: 198–99.

Edgington, T. J., and R. L. Hutchinson. 1990. Fundamentalism as a predictor of cognitive complexity. *Journal of Psychology and Christianity* 9(1): 47–55.

Fischer, E. H., and J. L. Turner. 1970. Orientations to seeking professional help: Development and research utility of an attitude scale. *Journal of Consulting and Clinical Psychology* 35: 79–90.

Goldsmith, W. M., G. E. Goldsmith, and R. M. Foster. 1986. *Comparative values and religious orientations of students from Christian and public colleges.* Paper presented to the Christian Association for Psychological Studies, Western Region, Oakland, Calif., June.

Jensen, J. P., and A. E. Bergin. 1988. Mental health values of professional therapists: A national interdisciplinary survey. *Professional Psychology* 19: 290–97.

Koltko, M. E. 1990. How religious beliefs affect psychotherapy: The example of Mormonism. *Psychotherapy* 27: 132–41.

London, P. 1964. *The modes and morals of psychotherapy.* New York: Holt, Rinehart and Winston.

Long, V. O., and C. H. Heggen. 1988. Clergy perceptions of spiritual health for adults, men and women. *Counseling and Values* 32: 213–20.

Meylink, W. D., and R. L. Gorsuch. 1988. Relationship between clergy and psychologists: The empirical data. *Journal of Psychology and Christianity* 7(1): 56–72.

Park, J. E., and W. M. Goldsmith. 1985. Values in persons with intrinsic, extrinsic and quest orientations. Paper presented at the Christian Association for Psychological Studies, Western Region, San Diego, June.

Richards, P. S., and M. L. Davison. 1989. The effects of theistic and atheistic counselor values on client trust: A multidimensional scaling analysis. *Counseling and Values* 33: 109–20.

Rokeach, M. 1973. *The nature of human values*. New York: Free Press.

Rotter, J. B. 1950. *Incomplete sentences blank—adult form*. San Antonio, Tex.: The Psychological Corporation, a division of Harcourt, Brace, and Jovanovich.

Sell, K. L., and W. M. Goldsmith. 1988. Concerns about professional counseling: An exploration of five factors and the role of Christian orthodoxy. *Journal of Psychology and Christianity* 7(3): 5–21.

Shafranske, E. P., and H. N. Malony. 1990. Clinical psychologists' religious and spiritual orientations and their practice of psychotherapy. *Psychotherapy* 27: 72–78.

Spilka, B., R. W. Hood, Jr., and R. L. Gorsuch. 1985. *The psychology of religion: An empirical approach*. Englewood Cliffs, N.J.: Prentice-Hall.

Tamney, J. B., S. Powell, and S. Johnson. 1989. Innovation theory and religious nones. *Journal for the Scientific Study of Religion* 28: 216–29.

Van Wicklin, J. F. 1990. Conceiving and measuring ways of being religious. *Journal of Psychology and Christianity* 9(2): 27–40.

Virkler, H. A. 1979. Counseling demands, procedures and preparation of parish ministers: A descriptive study. *Journal of Psychology and Theology* 7: 271–80.

Watson, P. J., R. W. Hood, Jr., and R. J. Morris. 1988. Existential confrontation and religiosity. *Counseling and Values* 33: 47–54.

Worthington, E. L., Jr. 1986. Religious counseling: A review of published empirical research. *Journal of Counseling and Development* 64: 421–31.

_____. 1988. Understanding the values of religious clients: A model and its application to counseling. *Journal of Counseling Psychology* 35: 166–74.

_____. 1989. *Psychotherapy and religious values: An update.* Paper presented to Division 36 of the American Psychological Association, New Orleans, August.

_____. 1991. Psychotherapy and religious values: An update. *Journal of Psychology and Christianity* 10(3): 211–23.

Worthington, E. L., Jr., K. Hsu, K. K. Gowda, and E. Bleach. 1988. *Preliminary tests of Worthington's (1988) theory of important values in religious counseling.* Paper presented at the International Congress on Christian Counseling, Atlanta, November.

Wyatt, S. C., and R. W. Johnson. 1990. The influence of counselors' religious values on clients' perceptions of the counselor. *Journal of Psychology and Theology* 18: 158–65.

Appendix:
Surveys of Therapists'
Religious Values

Bergin and Jensen (1990) surveyed a wide range of American family therapists, clinical social workers, psychiatrists, and clinical psychologists on their religious beliefs and practices. The same authors (Jensen and Bergin 1988) had reported that this sample held a high consensus on "mental health values," which included senses of being a free agent, of identity, worth, purpose, growth, honesty, self-control, and commitment to marriage and physical health. These values are certainly consonant with the prevailing Judeo-Christian religious values. Furthermore, 80% of these psychotherapists claimed a religious preference, a figure that contrasts with the stereotype of the nonreligious or antireligious counselor, as well as with previous research findings. Most (77%) of these therapists said they tried to live up to their religious beliefs, a figure close to that of the lay public (84%). But the religion of therapists tends to be less conventional and more personal than the lay public, "a blend of humanistic philosophy and spirituality" (7). Of these therapists, family therapists reported the highest rates of religious involvement and clinical psychologists the lowest. But although the great majority of these therapists claimed some religious involvement for themselves and most tried to live out their faiths, only 29% said they thought religion was important to the treatment of many clients.

Shafranske and Malony (1990) report a similar survey of members of the American Psychological Association. Self-selection probably resulted in a more religious sample than would be representative, but many of the results are similar to Bergin and Jensen's. Again, there was a high reported rate of religious interest (71% currently affiliated with an organized religion) but most reported they followed an "alternate spiritual path not a part of an organized religion" (74). Many (25%) felt negative about past experiences with organized religion. Nevertheless, 74% felt that religious and spiritual issues can be included appropriately in the scope of psychology and said 66% of their clients expressed themselves in religious language. And, although 52% said spirituality was relevant in their professional lives, most (67%) felt that psychologists, in general, are not trained or skilled in assisting people in their religious development. While most thought the use of religious language was appropriate in psychotherapy, thought a knowledge of the client's religious background was important, and even approved of praying with a client, 55% felt it was not appropriate for a therapist to use religious scriptures or texts in therapy and 73% felt it would be appropriate to recommend a client leave a religion that was seen as hindering psychological growth.

Part 4

Use of and Training in Christian Therapy Techniques

Introduction to Part 4

Techniques of psychotherapy grow intimately from some theory of psychotherapy. The theory articulates a theoretical cause of psychological problems that is derived from an explicit or implicit model of personality. Once the cause is conceptualized, a solution follows logically. For example, in psychoanalytic views, the cause of problems is unconscious conflicts and impulses that dynamically influence a person's behavior in distressing ways. The logical solution to the problem (as conceptualized by psychoanalysis) is to uncover the unconscious conflicts and impulses and exert conscious ego control over them. As another example, the main premise in cognitive therapy is that people have distressing behaviors and emotions because of their maladaptive thoughts. The logical solution is obvious: change maladaptive thoughts to adaptive thoughts, which should produce less distressing behaviors and emotions.

Techniques are ways that therapists act consistently with their theory to bring about the solution to the client's problems. For example, in psychoanalysis, the therapist stimulates resistance (e.g., a symptom, an ego defense, or a transference interaction), usually by being minimally interactive with the client and by probing into the origin or history of behaviors and why they are important. Once resistance is manifested, the counselor—with proper tact and timing and at the proper level of confrontation—interprets the resistance, thus helping the client to become more aware of unconscious dynamic forces. For the cognitive therapist, dysfunctional thoughts are assessed by having clients reflect on their thinking during a narrated memory, by having the client think aloud, or by pointing out directly the logical train of thinking underlying a client's

167

statement. Clients may then be directed to think about the problem differently so that they will experience different emotional and behavioral reactions.

In both cases, techniques were developed to fit a particular theoretical understanding of cause and solution. They are used comfortably within that framework with little concern about internal consistency.

From another perspective, though, therapeutic techniques are remarkably *a*theoretical. Once a technique is developed, it often finds its way into theoretically hostile systems of psychotherapy—yet it may still be used effectively by the therapist. How can this be? How can the behavior therapist provoke a transference interaction yet still use it within the behavior therapy of the client? How can the Gestalt therapist ask a client to think about a past experience and use those thoughts as the basis for a distinctly Gestalt therapy intervention?

Techniques are behavioral procedures that the therapist performs. Yet the procedures are surrounded and given context by the ongoing flow of therapy, which is from an established theoretical perspective. The client sees the procedures within the context of his or her ongoing therapy. The client would thus understand the same procedures differently in behavior therapy as in psychoanalysis. Further, the therapist guides the client's experience and interpretation of the procedures, directing the client's attention to different aspects of the experience.

For example, suppose a behavior therapist provokes her client to confront the therapist in an angry manner, much as the client confronted his mother during his middle school years. This would be understood by a psychoanalytically informed therapist as a transference interaction, perhaps harkening back to late latency/early genital developmental phase. The behavior therapist, however, might interpret the transference interaction as evidence of an incomplete coping repertoire. The client would be understood to have limited ways to handle anger, mostly learned during early adolescence and thus inappropriate for adult-adult interactions. The behavior therapist might then ask her client to examine the therapist-client interaction to analyze which coping behaviors he exhibited. The client might then be prompted to employ a different coping response with the therapist, and they might spend the remainder of the session role playing different ways to cope with confrontation. The same technique—stimulating, interpreting, and exerting ego control over inappropriate confrontation—was used in both psychoanalytically informed therapy and behavior therapy, but it occurred within a different theoretical context and was modified to be consistent with that context.

Christian Techniques

Christian techniques are understood differently by different practitioners. On one extreme, some people believe that Christian counseling has more to do with the therapist's personality and relationship with the client than with any "technique." Such practitioners will attempt to create a relationship that reflects Christ's love, acceptance, mercy, and justice and thus help the client grow into a more mature Christian person.

At another extreme, some therapists believe that only scripturally derived behaviors or behaviors that have originated within the church in pastoral care contexts are appropriate for Christian counseling. Such people would recommend use of Bible exposition, presenting the gospel, confession, seeking and granting forgiveness, praying with and for clients, or anointing with oil, as basic Christian interventions.

A third extreme involves therapists who use fundamentally secular theories of psychotherapy but discuss topics from a Christian point of view. They may deal with explicitly religious beliefs and values from an explicitly Christian point of view. They may or may not employ scripturally or ecclesiastically based interventions.

How can all three approaches claim to use Christian techniques? The answer seems to reside in an understanding of how secular techniques can be *a*theoretical. A technique is Christian not necessarily because it employs one of the scripturally or ecclesiastically derived spiritual disciplines—as Moon et al. label them. Rather, a technique is Christian to the extent that it is interpreted by the clients within a Christian context. This is greatly facilitated by a therapist's acceptance and encouragement of examining difficulties and their solutions from a Christian point of view.

Most Christian therapists know of cases when non-Christian therapists have quoted Scripture in therapy with a Christian to promote humanistic, but not Christian, values. For example, I can recall an instance of a counselor quoting, "Love your neighbor as yourself," to justify advice to a woman to "take care of yourself by divorcing your husband, who obviously is not compatible with you." The thrust of counseling was aimed at reducing distress by terminating a vexing marriage. It was not aimed at nor did it even consider Christian growth. It did not interpret the Golden Rule as Jesus meant it, that is, respecting others' needs as much as we (as fundamentally fallen, flawed people) naturally take care of our own wants and desires. The counselor's intervention centered around Bible exposition, but it was certainly not Christian counseling. Use of explicit Christian techniques doesn't define counseling as being Christian.

Having said that, though, Christian therapists who create a Christian environment for counseling may (or may not) use scripturally or ecclesiastically derived techniques. Papers in the following section explore the frequency of such use. Ball and Goodyear surveyed members of the Christian Association for Psychological Studies (CAPS) to determine their use of such techniques. Some techniques were used more frequently than were others. None could be labeled the sine qua non of Christian counseling.

DiBlasio and Benda surveyed marriage and family therapists in Maryland. They found that self-identification as a Christian was not related to marriage and family therapists' use of forgiveness as a therapeutic technique.

In the final chapter in the section, Moon and his colleagues investigated whether explicitly Christian training programs provided explicit training in the use of Christian techniques as part of therapy. The implication of the chapter is that perhaps more attention should be given to training Christian therapists in the use of techniques that originated in Scripture or pastoral care tradition. Such a conclusion, however, is not necessarily warranted.

Certainly, programs should train their graduate students to establish a vibrant Christian atmosphere for counseling—one that opens the door to deal with Christian beliefs and values explicitly and to consider problems in living from a Christian viewpoint, if that would be helpful to the client.

However, whether explicitly Christian counseling techniques should be used in Christian therapy is an empirical question and a question of spiritual discernment. We should investigate whether use of explicit techniques enhances, detracts from, or does not affect therapeutic progress, with what kinds of clients, under what circumstances. We should investigate the match of such techniques with different theories of psychotherapy and with different therapeutic styles.

As scientists of human behavior who are Christians, our final arbiter of the use of techniques is not empirical investigation. We also need to train students in spiritual discernment, which is enhanced by increasing their spiritual maturity. Spiritual discernment, however, is not merely reliance on internal feelings (which is simply another form of empirical data that is usually less systematic and reliable than scientific research). Spiritual discernment includes maturity in Christian living, wisdom, gifts of the Holy Spirit, understanding of scriptural principles, knowledge of Scripture, prayer, and the ability to hear God's voice.

Graduate training programs for Christian therapists should strive for effective training in both arenas—establishing an empirical basis for therapeutic techniques and spiritual discernment for their use. The three chapters in the present section give an excellent beginning for the first of these.

Self-Reported Professional Practices of Christian Psychotherapists

**ROBERT A. BALL AND
RODNEY K. GOODYEAR**

Mental health professionals' collective response to matters of religion probably is best characterized as one of ambivalence. Both approach and avoidant behavior abounds. Examples of avoidant behavior are to be seen in the theorists from Freud (1964) to Ellis (1980) who have disparaged religious beliefs and in findings that, compared to the general population, disproportional numbers of psychologists embrace atheism or agnosticism (Henry, Sims, and Spray 1971). Perhaps relatedly, the typical training program not only gives scant attention to religious issues, but actually may respond prejudicially to the prospective student who states fundamental religious beliefs (Gartner 1986). Significantly, too, many mental health professionals apparently view client religiosity as an indicator of dysfunction (Bergin 1983).

Yet there also is ample evidence of mental health professionals' fascination for and involvement with things religious. For example, London (1964) has referred to psychotherapists as "secular priests" and Kopp (1971) has considered various metaphors from religious traditions that therapists seem to have adopted to define themselves and

This study was based on a dissertation completed by Robert A. Ball under the supervision of Rodney K. Goodyear.

their roles. And though it is true that psychologists as a group are more frequently agnostic or atheist than the general population, it also is true that they are more likely to have pursued a religious vocation. Goodyear, O'Byrne, Stevens, and Lichtenberg (1989) found this to characterize 9.9% of a national sample of counseling psychology students. But even more to the point of this chapter, there are counselors and psychologists who regularly incorporate religion into their practice. Of these, those who identify as Christian psychotherapists make up a substantial subset.

Christian psychotherapists are important counterparts to the sizable portion of the American lay public who have conservative Christian religious beliefs. King (1978) found that 89% of a sample of evangelical Christians expressed concern that their faith would be unappreciated, misunderstood, or perhaps even ridiculed by counselors who themselves were not Christian. In this context, it also makes sense that clients who have strong religious convictions will have more trust in counselors who disclose their own belief in God (Richards and Davison 1989).

Strong (1980) maintained that Christian counseling can be understood according to both its process and content. Although the *content* might well be Christian-specific, the *process* is indistinguishable from that of counseling in general. Worthingon (1986) offered a more differentiated model when he suggested that Christian counselors might be clustered into those who employ the widely accepted secular counseling models; employ techniques and procedures that originate in the practice of formal religion (e.g., prayer, confession of sins); or employ techniques and procedures drawn from widely accepted secular models, but adapted with a religious content (e.g., systematic desensitization using religious imagery).

Very few studies inform us of the actual practices employed by Christian psychotherapists. The first (and perhaps only previous) real study of this type was conducted just recently by Worthington, Dupont, Berry, and Duncan (1988). But though it was based on work with 27 clients in 92 different sessions, it addressed the work of only 7 therapists, all in one city. For that reason, investigations that replicate and extend this work are essential next steps in investigating the work of Christian psychotherapists.

This article reports two exploratory studies that were undertaken to extend our knowledge of what Christian psychotherapists actually do. The first study employed mailed questionnaires to attempt to identify interventions Christian therapists had used and considered distinct to Christian psychotherapy. The second study used structured interviews to learn more about interventions used by Christian psychotherapists in critical situations they had encountered with their clients.

Study One Method

Participants

Participants in this study were 174 (144 male; 30 female) clinical members of the Christian Association for Psychological Studies (CAPS), from 34 states. This represented a 57.4% return rate for the 303 questionnaires mailed.

Participants' ages ranged from 28 to 72 years ($M = 44.6$; SD = 11.5) and their reported experience ranged from 2 to 51 years ($M = 15$; SD = 8.69). They reported having one of five different degrees, with 134 (77%) Ph.D.s, 16 (9.2%) Ed.D.s, 12 (6.9%) Psy.D.s, 11 (6.3%) D.Min.s, and one (.6%) Th.D. They represented 31 religious denominations, with the 3 most frequent ones listed as Presbyterian (27; 15.5%), nondenominational (21; 12.1%), and Baptist (18; 10.3%).

Participants reported working in ten clinical settings. The majority (94; 54%) were in private practice. The next most frequent settings were group outpatient (18; 10.3%) and hospital (15; 8.6%).

More than 90% of the respondents were represented by the following five of the nine theoretical orientations they reported: cognitive-behavioral (54; 31%), eclectic (37; 21.3%), psychodynamic (35; 20.1%), systems (17; 9.8%), and cognitive (15; 8.6%). Of the seven licensure categories represented by this group, 125 (71.8%) held psychology licenses, 20 (11.5%) held no license, 11 (6.3%) held the California Marriage, Family, and Child Counselor license, and four other licenses were represented among the remaining 18 respondents.

Raters

The raters were four male, fourth-year counseling psychology students at the University of Southern California.

Measure

Respondents completed the "Religious Interventions Questionnaire," which was constructed for this study. The first page requested essential demographic information. Respondents also stated whether they perceived differences in techniques and strategies between Christian and secular counseling. Those responding *no* did not complete the remainder of the questionnaire.

Respondents listed any interventions that they had used one or more times in counseling Christian clients and that they considered *distinct* to Christian counseling. They also described briefly the context in which each intervention had been used. By this method, 436 interventions were generated.

Procedure

The 1988 *International Directory of the Christian Association for Psychological Studies* was used to identify those (N = 454) who were listed as clinical members. Every third one was eliminated; 303 individuals were mailed questionnaires.

Each of the 436 reported interventions was typed on a separate index card. One pair of raters clustered interventions into piles of like-interventions and assigned headings to each cluster. This resulted in 15 clusters. These same raters assigned each intervention, through consensus ratings, to the one of the 15 clusters; and assigned, through consensus ratings, each intervention to one of Worthington's (1986) three categories. A second pair of raters then categorized the interventions into the 15 clusters and Worthington's three categories.

Study One Results

In response to the question of whether they perceived a difference between Christian and secular counseling, only 21 (13%) of the 173 respondents answered *no*. The differences between those answering *no* versus those answering *yes* were statistically significant, X^2 (1, n = 173) = 99.2, $p < .01$.

For the assignment of interventions to the 15 clusters, the two pairs agreed on 386 (87.5%) of the categorizations (a kappa [Cohen 1960] of .80). For assignment to the three Worthington categories, the two pairs agreed on the assignment of 352 (77.5% of the 454) interventions. Those 68 (15%) interventions in the first rating task and 102 (22.5%) for the second on which the pairs of raters did not have agreement were dropped from further consideration and not reported in data summaries.

The 15 categories into which the interventions were clustered and the total proportion of interventions that fit in each cluster are summarized in table 7.1. It depicts each of the categories, examples of the types of interventions that were assigned to that category, and the definition of that category that was supplied by the first pair of raters. The number of interventions assigned to each category is provided, along with the proportion of the 386 that they represented.

Interventions in table 7.1 are depicted in descending order of frequency. Prayer, the most frequently reported intervention, comprised slightly more than one-fourth (26.9%) of the total. The two next most frequently employed intervention types both involved directly teaching the client (the two categories differed in that one involved the direct use of Scripture to establish the intended point; the other did not). When these two categories are collapsed into a single one, they represent 30% of the total interventions, a proportion that exceeded even the use of prayer.

The remaining categories each accounted for less than 10% of the interventions. They range from those interventions that would be closely associated with Christian psychotherapy (e.g., forgiveness, 6.5%; anointing with oil, 1.3%) to those that blend secular interventions with Christian imagery or content (e.g., relaxation techniques, 8%; integration techniques, 2.1%) to those that were strictly secular (2.6%).

The second rating task was to assign the interventions to the three Worthington (1986) categories. The 352 interventions that were rated the same by the two pairs of raters were clustered as follows: *Formal Religious,* 251 (71.3%); *Integration,* 74 (20.9%); and *Secular,* 27 (7.6%).

Study Two Method

Participants

Participants in the second study were 30 (19 male; 11 female) members of CAPS who resided in Southern California. They ranged in age from 34 to 72 ($M = 46.8$; $SD = 10.6$). Their reported range of experience was 3 to 45 years ($M = 14.2$; $SD = 8.6$). In these and other salient characteristics, the composition of this participant group seemed closely to resemble that of Study 1.

Raters

Raters in this study were three first-year counseling psychology graduate students at the University of Southern California, all female.

Procedures

Of those CAPS members mailed the questionnaire in Study 1, those who lived in the Southern California area ($N = 58$) also were sent a brief description of the interview portion of the study and invited to participate. Twenty-one (36%) agreed to participate.

The remaining 31 California CAPS members who were not contacted in Study 1 were invited by letter to participate. The first 9 who responded affirmatively were included as participants.

The typical interview lasted approximately 55 minutes. All were audiotaped and later transcribed. All interviewees were asked to recount five critical incidents, each in the context of treating a Christian client. At the beginning of each interview, the interviewer (the senior author) defined a critical incident as:

> A moment in therapy with a [Christian] client that in some way affected your subsequent skills or approaches to therapy. The importance of recalling these events is that you see the events as crucial moments in your counseling of Christian clients. The only criteria for recounting these events is that they were specific moments in therapy with a Christian client, and that

Table 7.1

Categorization of the Self-Reported Religious Interventions of Participants in Studies 1 and 2

Category	Category Definition	Examples of Interventions	Interventions/Category	
			Study 1	Study 2
Prayer	Use of prayer to help the client. This may occur in many forms, including therapist's silent, in-session prayer.	"The use of prayer for strength in dealing with strong feelings." "Prayer to help clients develop a bigger picture of their suffering and look beyond their current circumstances."	104 (26.9%)	24 (19.8%)
Teaching of concepts	Designed to teach or instruct clients about theological issues, concepts, and values clarification.	"Teaching an awareness of biblical promises of peace, love, and faith." "Help clients view self-worth based on what God says about them."	65 (16.8%)	2 (1.6%)
Reference to Scripture	Differs from the above category in its direct use of Scripture to establish the point.	"Instruction by Scripture to counter such inappropriate feelings as perfectionistic striving." "I cite references to Christ's emotions to help my clients feel at ease about their problems."	51 (13.2%)	2 (3.3%)
Relaxation techniques	The use of guided imagery, meditation, or relaxation—with direct reference to spiritual concepts; often with visualization of God, or Christ.	"The use of imagery and metaphor in biblical stories for relaxation." "Meditation or meditative imagery focusing on Christ and his love."	31 (8.0%)	0 (0.0%)
Forgiveness	Deals with the concept of forgiveness, including any form of confession.	"We discuss how to have forgiveness when a client reports guilt about a behavior or feeling." "I use forgiveness in restoring broken relationships."	25 (6.5%)	7 (5.8%)
Use of self as technique	Therapist self-discloses or models in an attempt to influence the client.	"I have shared aspects of my own spiritual experience." "I attempt to model grace and affirmation."	23 (6.0%)	9 (7.4%)
Homework assignment	Some form of work assigned to be done outside the therapy hour.	"Behavioral and attitudinal homework focusing on a client going to a brother or sister who has offended him or her." "I assign journal keeping of answered prayer."	20 (5.2%)	2 (1.6%)

Table 7.1 (continued)

Category	Category Definition	Examples of Interventions	Interventions/Category Study 1	Study 2
Use of outside resources	Employing the Christian community as extra-therapy resources.	"Referral to a pastor for specific spiritual/theological questions." "Sending a person to a Christian attorney for information."	17 (4.4%)	13 (10.7%)
Inner healing	Interventions that resemble prayer and guided imagery, but distinguished by emphasis on restoration of painful memories	"Healing of memories to deal with hurts from the past." "Helping clients to reform perceptions of painful past experiences and recall repressed memories."	11 (2.9%)	0 (0.0%)
Secular techniques	Standard psychological interventions that did not seem to have religious pertinence.		10 (2.6%)	45 (37.2%)
Integration techniques	Specific therapeutic techniques adapted to include religious content.	"Biblical dream interpretation." "Psychodrama where God is role(played."	8 (2.1%)	5 (4.1%)
Scripture memorization	Interventions specifically using memorization of Scripture to affect change.	"Scripture memorization for thought stopping of obsessive clients and as a means of coping during panic attacks."	8 (2.1%)	0 (0.0%)
Anointing with oil	All responses in this category only briefly mentioned "anointing with oil."		5 (1.3%)	0 (0.0%)
Confrontation /challenge	Interventions that confront a client.	"What does God say about it?" "Asking a client in a bad relationship what they think the Bible says about the relationship."	5 (1.3%)	9 (7.4%)
Screening /intake	Employing the initial therapy session as a way to assess the client's religious status.	"Taking a history of the client's spiritual development when I first see him or her."	3 (0.8%)	1 (0.8%)

Note: Data reported represent the 386 interventions from Study 1 and 121 interventions from Study 2 for which there was rating consensus.

they were critical events or incidents for you as opposed to the client (although both may be present).

For each reported critical incident, the participant was also asked for information about the presenting problem; and their response to the question, Describe the intervention(s) which were used at the time of the critical incident (either before or after). In this study, participants described 144 critical incidents.

Study Two Results

For each of the critical incidents, the respondent described the problem for which the client had sought treatment. The senior author clustered these into 21 intuitively derived categories.

The five most frequently reported client problems together accounted for 54.8% of the cases. Each of these 5 was represented by 10 or more clients; each of the other 16 categories was represented by less than 10. Depression was the most frequent client problem (14.5%), followed in order by marital problems (13.9%), family problems (11.8%), issues of victimization (7.6%), and problems of spirit influence (6.9%). Marital and family issues were differentiated according to whether the focus of treatment was on the marital relationship versus on parenting or discipline problems or problems that affected the entire family. The victim category was employed for molestation victims, crime victims, and adult children of alcoholics. Spirit influence concerned demon possession or influence: six of the participating psychologists reported these instances, with one reporting three such incidents.

The three raters worked independently to assign interventions into each of the two rating systems used in Study 1; Rater A rated for both systems; Raters B and C each rated for only one system. For the 144 responses, the Raters A and B converged in their categorization of 121 (85%) in the first task; Raters A and C converged in their categorization of 125 (86.8%) in the second task. As in the first study, interventions for which there was not convergence were dropped from further consideration.

Table 1 depicts the proportions of the interventions that corresponded to each of the categories. In contrast to Study 1, the most frequently used category of interventions were secular techniques (37.2%). The next two most frequently used intervention types were use of outside resources (10.7%) and prayer (19.8%). There was no use at all of relaxation techniques, inner healing, Scripture memorization, or anointing with oil. Also, whereas teaching of concepts and reference to Scripture together accounted for 30% of the interventions in Study 1, they accounted for 4.9% in Study 2.

Worthington's three categories also reflected a different profile than in Study 1. The assignment of interventions to categories was as follows: *Formal religious,* 39 (31.2%); *Integration,* 13 (10.4%); *Secular,* 73 (58.4%). In Study 1, these percentages were 71.3, 20.9, and 7.6 respectively.

General Discussion

That most respondents in Study 1 believed there to be a difference between the techniques and strategies of secular and Christian counseling was expected because of the respondents' CAPS membership. Nevertheless, this finding was important in validating the rationale for conducting these two studies.

The first of these studies used the larger sample (174 versus 30) and mailed questionnaires as a means of obtaining a picture of the range and frequencies of interventions that these Christian psychotherapists actually have used. The large majority of their reported interventions (71.3%) were coded in Worthington's *formal religious* category. The finer-grained analysis permitted by the other coding system (table 7.1) showed that prayer was the single most frequently used category and that other frequently used religious interventions included teaching clients about theological issues and concepts and direct citations of Scripture. Others, such as the use of forgiveness, were used less frequently, but were interventions clearly anchored in the therapists' religious perspectives.

The different coding systems used in these studies shared two similarly-named categories: *integration techniques* and *secular techniques.* There were some between-system discrepancies in the proportions of interventions assigned to these categories, likely because the first system's greater array of alternative categories allowed more dispersal of intervention assignments than did Worthington's tripartite model. Thus, for example, only 2.6% of interventions were categorized as integration in the first system versus 20.9% in the Worthington system. In fact, though, an examination of table 7.1 suggests how many of the various interventions in multiple categories constitute a blending of established treatment procedures with religious material (e.g., using Scripture memorization for thought stopping; relaxation in which clients were to use images of Christ and his love for meditation).

That both coding systems revealed infrequent use of secular interventions suggests that respondents generally complied with the request to provide examples of interventions distinct to Christian counseling. For the purposes of this study, differences between Christian and secular counseling were forced. Therefore, the relatively low proportion of secular techniques reported in this study likely underrepresents their actual utilization rates by respondents. The profile of Christian counseling techniques depicted in table 7.1 is probably not a profile of the day-to-day practices of these respondents.

In the second study, interviews were employed to obtain more extensive data from a smaller number of therapists. Because these respondents were asked to discuss in some detail their work with specific clients, the information they supplied probably is a more accurate portrayal of their actual behaviors than is true of Study 1. Note, especially, the much larger proportion of secular techniques reported in this study. Yet because the focus was on cases that stood out as especially provocative or challenging to the respondents, it would be inappropriate to conclude that these data represent the *typical* practices of Christian psychotherapists. Thus, although demon possession seemed a notable concern for a small subset of the sample in Study 2, there is no reason to believe it is a typical client concern.

It is especially significant that obtained results of these studies reproduce the findings of Worthington et al. (1988) with such fidelity, despite the variability of research strategies, samples, and coding systems across the three studies. For example, the client problems reported by Worthington et al. were similar to those reported in Study 2. Despite some relatively unique client problems such as spirit influence and the need for spiritual guidance (whose very reporting may be in response to the demand for "critical" situations), the most frequently cited client problems were those that might be seen by any counselor or psychotherapist (e.g., depression; marriage or family problems). This is consistent with the findings in the Worthington et al. study that "the five most prevalent presenting problems were marriage/family, personal/emotional, religious, alcohol/drugs, and parent/child" (p. 286), though most clients present multiple concerns.

Whereas data in Studies 1 and 2 were retrospective accounts of therapists' behavior, those in the Worthington et al. (1988) study were obtained immediately post-session as rating by clients and therapists. Also, data in these two studies were reported as proportions of the total number of interventions, while the Worthington et al. data were reported as proportions of the total number of *sessions* in which particular interventions were employed. Such differences likely account for some of the apparent discrepancies in what are otherwise very congruent findings. For example, Worthington et al. found religious homework assignments and quoting from Scripture to be the two most frequently used interventions. Similar categories of interventions were found in Study 1 to be frequently used.

Although prayer was the most frequently used intervention in Studies 1 and 2, Worthington et al. (1988) found that, of 21 categories, clients reported it third and counselors reported it fifth in frequency (in 43% [client report] versus 32.5% [counselor report] of the sessions). In none of the studies were instances of the laying on of hands reported; anointing with oil was an infrequently reported (1.3%) intervention in Study 1, but not found to occur at all in Study 2 or in that by Worthington et al.

The general convergence of findings across these three studies suggests reliability. It is important, though, to acknowledge some possible cautions in interpreting the findings of Studies 1 and 2. First, there is some slight threat to cross-study comparisons that stems from the fact that raters inadvertently were more advanced male students in Study 1 and less advanced female students in Study 2. A more serious caution results from interventions having been discarded when raters disagreed on their category assignment. Although this increased the degree of certainty that might be accorded the category assignment of the retained interventions, it also resulted in a loss of information that might have changed the results in unknown ways.

The usual caveats about return rates on survey data pertain here. As well, it is important to acknowledge that all respondents were members of one particular association, CAPS. Conclusions about their practices should be extended to Christian counselors or psychologists in general only with caution.

Despite their limitations, the two studies reported in this article add to the small empirical literature on the practices of Christian psychotherapists. Although many mental health professions remain ambivalent about religious matters, attention to these issues is important both to a large constituency of clients and to their therapists. With growth in our knowledge about Christian therapists' interventions, a next step in research will be to examine how they conceptualize their work and their decision rules for using particular strategies and techniques. Increased knowledge of this type has the potential to enrich teaching, supervision, and treatment.

References

Bergin, A. E. 1983. Religiosity and mental health: A critical reevaluation and meta-analysis. *Professional Psychology: Research and Practice* 14: 170–84.

Cohen, J. H. 1960. A coefficient of agreement for nominal scales. *Educational and Psychological Measurement* 20: 37–46.

Ellis, A. 1980. Psychotherapy and religious experience: A response to A. E. Bergin's "Psychotherapy and religious values." *Journal of Consulting and Clinical Psychology* 48: 635–39.

Freud, S. 1964. New introductory lectures on psycho-analysis. In *The standard edition of the complete works of Freud,* vol. 22. Toronto: Clarke Irwin and Co.

Gartner, J. D. 1986. Antireligious bias in admissions to doctoral programs in clinical psychology. *Professional Psychology: Research and Practice* 17: 473–75.

Goodyear, R. K., K. R. O'Byrne, D. Stevens, and J. W. Lichtenberg. 1989. *Beliefs of counseling psychology students: Preliminary data.* Unpublished manuscript, Univ. of Southern California.

Henry, W. E., J. H. Sims, and L. S. Spray. 1971. *The fifth profession.* San Francisco: Jossey-Bass.

King, R. R. 1978. Evangelical Christians and professional counseling: Conflict of values? *Journal of Psychology and Theology* 6: 276–81.

Kopp, S. 1971. *Guru: Metaphors from a psychotherapist.* Palo Alto, Calif.: Science and Behavior.

London, P. 1964. *The modes and morals of psychotherapy.* New York: Holt, Rinehart and Winston.

Richards, P. S., and M. L. Davison. 1989. The effects of theistic and atheistic counselor values on client trust: A multidimensional scaling analysis. *Counseling and Values* 33: 109–22.

Strong, S. R. 1980. Christian counseling: A synthesis of psychological and Christian concepts. *Personnel and Guidance Journal* 58: 589–92.

Taggart, M. 1972. AAPC membership information project. *Journal of Pastoral Care* 26: 219–44.

Worthington, E. L., Jr. 1986. Religious counseling: A review of published empirical research. *Journal of Counseling and Development* 64: 421–31.

Worthington, E. L., Jr., P. D. Dupont, J. T. Berry, and L. A. Duncan. 1988. Christian therapists' and clients' perceptions of religious psychotherapy in private and agency settings. *Journal of Psychology and Theology* 16: 282–93.

8

Practitioners, Religion, and the Use of Forgiveness in the Clinical Setting

FREDERICK A. DIBLASIO
AND BRENT B. BENDA

Forgiveness is the profound pivotal point at which the vertical relationship to the Judeo-Christian Creator and the horizontal relationships between humans intersect, symbolized by the cross on Golgotha, and is the central concept upon which Judeo-Christian theology arises (Buswell 1962). The Scriptures inform us that forgiveness is requisite to establishing a vertical relationship to the Creator (Rom. 3:23–31; Rom. 5; Isa. 55:7) and to healthy spiritual and social relationships between humans (Rom. 2; Mark 11:25; Col. 3:13). Biblically, forgiveness is releasing existing negative feelings and attitudes, such as resentment or bitterness, toward the offending person. Thereby, both parties are freed through forgiveness to engage in more mutually satisfying interactions.

Forgiveness has also been described as "a key part of psychological healing" (Hope 1987, 240), and "a powerful therapeutic intervention" (Fitzgibbons 1986, 630). Its use has been rated as beneficial for a wide range of problems that are brought forth for clinical intervention. It has been deemed particularly useful for clients who have suffered neglect or physical and emotional abuse as children, and as a method to resolve old family-of-origin issues (Framo 1976; Hope 1987). Fitzgibbons (1986) directly connects the use of forgiveness with resolution of anger and depression, settling familial conflict, and assisting in the management of personality disorders. Fisher (1985) and Wolberg (1973) have recommended forgiveness as central in the treatment of clients diagnosed as having a borderline personality. Joy (1985) advocates the use of forgiveness in treating women who experience emotional complications from abortion. Flanigan (1987) described a forgiving process that is posited to restore relationships in alcoholic families. In addition, forgiveness can bring healing to otherwise hurtful and broken relationships in marriages (Worthington and DiBlasio 1990). After receiving or granting forgiveness, clients have indicated a feeling of release and peace, and often view forgiveness as a turning point in their lives. Perhaps forgiveness relieves the pervasive sense of worthlessness, negative views of self and of others, and hopelessness evident in depressed people (Beck 1976) by removing guilt and restoring hope and confidence in relationships.

Although the curative factors induced by forgiveness have been noted by clergy for centuries (e.g., see Rokeach 1979), attention to forgiveness in the literature as a therapeutic concern has been incremental and largely found in religious-oriented journals (Brink 1985; Cunningham 1985; Enright and Zell 1989; Gartner 1988; Pingleton 1989; Sacks 1985; Shontz and Rosenak 1988; Smedes 1983; Todd 1985). More recently, a few secular journals (already cited) have published articles that embraced the concept of forgiveness in therapeutic enterprises. After an extensive literature search, only one empirical study on forgiveness was found (on adolescents and forgiveness; Enright, Santos, and Al-Mabuk 1989). Hence, the present study constitutes the first known empirical investigation of practitioners' attitudes, theories, and uses of forgiveness.

Perhaps a bias exists against therapeutic themes that also incorporate religious ideologies (DiBlasio 1988; Pattison 1982). Some have recognized this problem and have offered recommendations for changes (Bergin 1980). Larson, Pattison, Blazer, Omran, and Kaplan (1986) found that of 2,348 articles reviewed in four psychiatric journals between 1978 and 1982, only 59 included a quantified religious variable (mostly a single measure of religion). They concluded that psychiatric research lacks conceptual and methodological sophistication about religious issues in treatment.

As in any uninvestigated area, the present study proceeds in an exploratory fashion, incorporating the known conceptual literature in hypothesis development. A primary assumption in our analyses was that practitioners who were more religious themselves would have more favorable attitudes toward adherence to theories about forgiveness intervention than would less religious counselors. Specifically, we hypothesized that practitioners who hold strong religious beliefs would more fully embrace positive attitudes about forgiveness as a therapeutic issue; report more development of techniques of forgiveness in their practice;

perceive a greater link between forgiveness and depression; perceive a greater link between forgiveness and anger; and demonstrate more openness to client religious issues in treatment than would clinicians with less religious identification.

Method

Subjects (N = 167) were active clinical practitioners selected primarily from a list of 243 certified members of the American Association of Marital and Family Therapists (AAMFT) in Maryland. A few other therapists from the community were added to the sample. Interviewers read from a standard survey instrument and recorded respondents' answers to 57 questions, typically consisting of five categorical responses.

Subjects ranged from about 25 years old to over 66 years of age (mean age was approximately 43 years old), and more women (n = 112) than men (n = 54) responded. The gender distribution in the sample (67% female) compared favorably to the list of all AAMFT members (approximately 60% female). The highest degrees obtained were undergraduate degrees or less (11%), masters degrees (62%), and doctoral degrees (27%). In addition to their education, 70% of the therapists indicated advanced clinical training (two-thirds of this group reported training of over 176 hours).

The following academic degrees were reported: social work, 45%; psychology, 20%; marital and family therapy, 7%; pastoral, 7%; sociology, 5%; psychiatry, 4%; education, 4%; and other, 8%. For the most part, the therapists offered a range of treatment from individual to group. Some specifically treat in one modality more than the others; for instance, 45% of the therapists reported spending one-third or more time with individuals.

A range of responses were noted on religious questions of the survey. Regarding religious preferences, 56% of therapists identified themselves with a Christian religion, 30% with the Jewish faith, 3% with a Far Eastern faith, and 14% reported "other." Of the Christian group, 31% were Roman Catholic; 21%, Episcopalian; 19%, Baptist or Methodist (because of coding problems these two religions could not be separated); 11%, nondenominational (Christian); 8%, Lutheran; 6%, Presbyterian; and 3%, Pentecostal. The personal importance of religious beliefs ranged from "very important" (51%) to "little or no importance" (17%). Interestingly, subjects rated the impact of religious beliefs on their therapeutic intervention as having significant impact (41%), some impact (48%), and no impact (10%). Yet, 58% of therapists believed that their religious ideologies ought to be "completely" separate from their intervention.

Results

Theoretical and Control Variables

Several variables were developed to test the hypotheses of the study. All theoretical factors were indices comprised of component variables that contained five-point Likert scales (e.g., 1 = never to 5 = always). The component variables and their reliability statistics can be found in table 8.1. Briefly stated, the indices were defined as follows: *forgiveness attitude* (attitude about the importance and usefulness of forgiveness in clinical practice); *forgiveness technique* (techniques for assisting clients with forgiveness); *forgiveness and depression* (perception of the role of forgiveness in resolving depression); *forgiveness and anger* (perception of the role of forgiveness in resolving anger); and *religious openness* (openness to client religious issues as part of therapy). The demographic factors controlled were gender, age, and level of education.

Multivariate Analyses

Five hierarchical regression equations were computed. The procedure allows a determination of the amount of variance that can be explained by control variables, and then in a second entry, an examination of the relative and cumulative effect of religiosity.

After accounting for the variance explained by control factors, religiosity explained only sight variance (R^2 change $\leq .05$) in four of the five theoretical factors (see table 8.2 for summary statistics). Religiosity explained the following amounts of variance: *forgiveness attitude* (R^2 *change* = .05), *religious openness* (R^2 *change* = .05), *forgiveness and anger* (R^2 *change* = .03); *forgiveness techniques* (R^2 *change* = .02). No significant variance was explained in *forgiveness and depression*.

Discussion

The findings indicated minimal differences in theoretical factors produced by religiosity of subjects. Data suggest that while practitioners with stronger religious identification were more receptive than less religious clinicians to forgiveness, and to religious principles as part of therapy, they were about equally inclined to develop forgiveness strategies, and to think that forgiveness was essential to relieving anger or depression. In short, it appears that religious beliefs among practitioners were more influential in general practice ideology than in particular strategies or theoretical linkages. Approximately 95% of the total variance in each of the theoretical factors was not explained by religiosity. Hence, the study's hypotheses were not supported.

Several interwoven explanations of these results are feasible. First, the underdeveloped research and theory in this area may leave clinicians without a body of knowledge from which to work, and without

Table 8.1
Reliability Statistics

	Item-to-total (r)[a]	Alpha
I. **Forgiveness Attitude**		.77
(a) comfort with the notion of forgiveness	.79	
(b) viewpoint about working toward forgiveness	.80	
(c) importance of forgiveness	.79	
(d) forgiveness as a readily thought-about concept	.83	
(e) necessity of formal forgiveness	.45	
II. **Forgiveness Techniques**		.82
(a) techniques for seeking forgiveness	.91	
(b) techniques for granting forgiveness	.88	
(c) techniques for clients' self-forgiveness	.82	
(d) forgiveness as a distinct technique	.61	
III. **Forgiveness and Depression**		.82
(a) depression linked with need to forgive another	.88	
(b) depression linked with need to be forgiven	.83	
(c) depression linked with need to forgive self	.85	
IV. **Forgiveness and Anger**		.75
(a) anger linked with need to forgive another	.79	
(b) anger linked with need to be forgiven	.84	
(c) anger linked with need to forgive self	.81	
V. **Religious Openness**		.83
(a) inquiry to clients' religious affiliation	.76	
(b) inquiry to clients' belief system	.66	
(c) assessment of clients' level of religiosity	.87	
(d) use of clients' religiosity in therapy	.76	
(e) validity of clients' religiosity for therapy	.72	
(f) comfort dealing with clients' religious issues	.66	

[a] All correlations $p < .01$

specific training for implementation. Second, perhaps a strong bias against using religious-related or forgiveness concepts in therapy exists in the professional community, which inhibits professionals from practicing in ways congruent with their more general belief systems. This may be the primary reason or the alienation of therapeutic psychology from religious values (Bergin 1980). And finally, practitioners may perceive that many if not most clients would shun efforts to promote forgiveness.

Several salient limitations of the study need to be addressed. First, most of the sample was made up of AAMFT clinicians, a relatively highly trained and experienced group, which may not be representative of younger professional and those with less training. Second, we have no information about the refusal group; however, the variance in the data was evenly distributed, indicating that therapists of various persuasions toward forgiveness responded. Third, the data are not longitudinal, but are cross-sectional; hence, they do not permit causal statements. For example, we cannot be sure whether strengths of religious beliefs preceded the level of development of forgiveness techniques in practice, or whether experience in using forgiveness intervention may have shaped religious thoughts. Finally, no attempt was made to discover the intervening factors between religious beliefs and any use of them in professional

Table 8.2

Hierarchical Regression Results of Religiosity Level, Gender, Education, and Age on Theoretical Factors

Variable	B	Beta	t	p
Regression I: Forgiveness Attitude				
Entry 1:				
Sex	−1.072	−.142	−1.751	.081
Age	.317	.224	2.713	.007
Education	−.076	−.013	−.155	.876
$F = 2.95$ $p = .034$ Multiple $R = .227$ R^2 changed $= .051$				
Entry 2:				
Religiosity level	.641	.232	2.977	.003
$F = 4.54$ $p = .001$ Multiple $R = .317$ R^2 changed $= .050$ $R^2 = .101$				
Regression II: Forgiveness Techniques				
Entry 1:				
Sex	−.864	−.120	−1.492	.137
Age	.333	.247	3.014	.003
Education	−.507	−.093	−1.085	.279
$F = 5.72$ $p = .001$ Multiple $R = .308$ R^2 changed $= .095$				
Entry 2:				
Religiosity level	.387	.147	1.901	.059
$F = 5.26$ $p = .001$ Multiple $R = .339$ R^2 changed $= .020$ $R^2 = .115$				
Regression III: Forgiveness and Depression				
Entry 1:				
Sex	−.276	−.053	−.640	.523
Age	.236	.243	2.859	.004
Education	−.195	−.049	−.561	.575
$F = 2.92$ $p = .035$ Multiple $R = .226$ R^2 changed $= .051$				
Entry 2:				
Religiosity level	.085	.045	.564	.573
$F = 2.26$ $p = .064$ Multiple $R = .230$ R^2 changed $= .002$ $R^2 = .053$				
Regression IV: Forgiveness and Anger				
Entry 1:				
Sex	−.418	−.085	−1.045	.297
Age	.218	.239	2.856	.004
Education	.029	.007	.091	.927
$F = 2.84$ $p = .039$ Multiple $R = .222$ R^2 changed $= .049$				
Entry 2:				
Religiosity level	.324	.181	2.305	.022
$F = 3.51$ $p = .008$ Multiple $R = .282$ R^2 changed $= .030$ $R^2 = .079$				
Regression V: Forgiveness and Religious Openness				
Entry 1:				
Sex	−.200	−.019	−.244	.807
Age	.051	.026	.326	.744
Education	2.019	.261	3.043	.002
$F = 3.72$ $p = .012$ Multiple $R = .253$ R^2 changed $= .064$				
Entry 2:				
Religiosity level	.879	.235	3.043	.002
$F = 5.24$ $p = .001$ Multiple $R = .338$ R^2 changed $= .050$ $R^2 = .114$				

Note: B is the unstandardized coefficient, whereas Beta is the standardized coefficient.

practice. Future research is clearly needed to sort out and verify events, processes, and sequences.

It seems highly feasible that historically there have been two major flaws in conveying the critical importance of certain fundamental religious concepts such as forgiveness to practitioners in clinical settings: too often these concepts are presented in highly abstract ways without practical applications in everyday problems; and relatedly, there has been a deficiency in developing technologies and guidelines for implementing these concepts in practice. Recently, secular and religious therapists have begun to develop stages of, and strategies for, using forgiveness in treating various human problems (Fitzgibbons 1986; Hope 1987; Pettitt 1987). Given the importance of forgiveness in religious thinking and in resolving problems, more attention should be directed to further development and evaluation of forgiveness interventions. More conceptualization of any link between forgiving oneself and others and emotional conflict needs to occur. And, of course, further empirical work to evaluate conceptual links between factors explored in this study is essential.

Implicit in this discussion has been the implication that forgiveness is important to resolving human afflictions; however, no empirical evidence exists to support this notion. Although many clinicians have reported its usefulness, theoreticians and practitioners must work together to develop forgiveness approaches that can be tested through evaluative research. Only through rigorous research designs can the efficacy of forgiveness theory and techniques be properly evaluated.

References

Beck, A. T. 1976. *Cognitive therapy and the emotional disorders.* New York: International Univ. Press.

Bergin, A. E. 1980. Psychotherapy and religious issues. *Journal of Consulting and Clinical Psychology* 48: 95–105.

Brink, T. L. 1985. The role of religion in later life: A case of consolation and forgiveness. *Journal of Psychology and Christianity* 4(2): 22–25.

Buswell, J. O. 1962. *A systemic theology of the Christian religion.* Grand Rapids: Zondervan.

Cunningham, B. B. 1985. The will to forgive: A pastoral theological view of forgiving. *The Journal of Pastoral Care* 39: 141–49.

DiBlasio, F. 1988. Integrative strategies for family therapy with evangelical Christians. *Journal of Psychology and Theology* 16: 127–34.

Enright, R., and R. Zell. 1989. Problems encountered when we forgive one another. *Journal of Psychology and Christianity* 8(1): 52–60.

Enright, R., M. Santos, and R. Al-Mabuk. 1989. The adolescent as forgiver. *Journal of Adolescence* 12: 95–110.

Fisher, S. F. 1985. Identity of two: The phenomenology of shame in borderline development and treatment. *Psychotherapy* 22: 101–9.

Fitzgibbons, R. P. 1986. The cognitive and emotive uses of forgiveness in the treatment of anger. *Psychotherapy* 23: 629–33.

Flanigan, B. J. 1987. Shame and forgiveness in alcoholism. *Alcoholism Treatment Quarterly* 4: 181–95.

Framo, J. L. 1976. Family-of-origin, a therapeutic resource for adults in marital and family therapy: You should and can go back home again. *Family Process* 15: 193–210.

Gartner, J. 1988. The capacity to forgive: An object relations perspective. *Journal of Religion and Health* 27: 313–20.

Hope, D. 1987. The healing paradox of forgiveness. *Psychotherapy* 24: 240–44.

Joy, S. S. 1985. Abortion: An issue to grieve? *Journal of Counseling and Development* 63: 375–76.

Larson, D., E. M. Pattison, D. G. Blazer, A. R. Omran, and B. Kaplan. 1986. Systematic analysis of research on religious variables in four major psychiatric journals. *American Journal of Psychiatry* 143: 329–34.

Pattison, E. M. 1982. Management of religious issues in family therapy. *International Journal of Family Therapy* 4: 140–63.

Petitt, G. A. 1987. Forgiveness: A teachable skill for creating and maintaining health. *New Zealand Medical Journal* 100: 180–82.

Pingleton, J. D. 1989. The role and function of forgiveness in the psychotherapeutic process. *Journal of Psychology and Theology* 17: 27–35.

Rokeach, M. 1979. *Understanding human values: Individual and societal.* New York: Free Press.

Sacks, J. M. 1985. Religious issues in psychotherapy. *Journal of Religion and Health* 24: 26–30.

Smedes, L. B. 1983. Forgiving people who do not care. *Reformed Journal* 33: 13–18.

Shontz, F., and C. Rosenak. 1988. Psychological theories and the need for forgiveness: Assessment and critique. *Journal of Psychology and Christianity* 7(1): 22–31.

Todd, E. 1985. The value of confession and forgiveness according to Jung. *Journal of Religion and Health* 24: 39–48.

Wolberg, A. R. 1973. *The borderline patient.* New York: Intercontinental Medical Book Co.

Worthington, E. L., Jr., and F. A. DiBlasio. 1990. Promoting mutual forgiveness within the fractured relationship. *Psychotherapy* 27: 219–23.

9

Training in the Use of Christian Disciplines as Counseling Techniques within Christian Graduate Training Programs

GARY W. MOON, JUDY W. BAILEY,
JOHN C. KWASNY, AND
DALE E. WILLIS

Griffith (1983), citing decreases in the financial resources of health and mental health institutions, has called for a collaborative effort that would offer patients "a form of care based on the fusion of Westernized medico-psychological approaches and Christian concepts of healing" (292). More recently, a research group consisting of the American Psychiatric Association's task force on cost-effectiveness in consultation-liaison psychiatry also referenced shrinking federal resources as a motivation factor to their appeal for "innovative approaches . . . needed to stimulate research in new or undeveloped clinical areas" (Larson et al. 1987, 1106). Certainly, the clinical application of the classic Christian disciplines represents a relatively undeveloped clinical area, and perhaps, one that offers a unique possibility of fusing medico-psychological approaches and Christian concepts.

For two decades Clinebell's (1970) reference to the clergy and the churches they pastor as "collectively representing a sleeping giant of huge potential of barely tapped resources for fostering mental health"

(46) has been quoted to underscore the enormous potential of the church in the arena of mental health service delivery. It is possible, however, that a second giant slumbers. This giant is not the physical and human resources of the Christian church, but rather the wealth of unique Christian counseling techniques—Christian disciplines—which have been developed, practiced, and honed over the centuries by the church's physicians of the soul.

A growing swell of support for the use of overtly Christian counseling techniques is already present in the literature. There is evidence that Christian clients prefer Christian counselors because of perceived similarities (Worthington and Gascoyne 1985); are reluctant to seek help from secular counselors (Fisher and Cohen 1972; Gilbert 1981); perceive needs to practice certain Christian disciplines such as confession, forgiveness (Worthington, Dupont, Berry, and Duncan 1988), and prayer (Morgan 1982; Larson, Pattison, Blazer, Omran, and Kaplan 1986) as a means of help for emotional problems. More specifically, Spilka, Hood, and Gorsuch (1985) summarize empirical investigations that share the theme of "Religion as Therapy" (301–5). The positive mental health benefits of prayer (Appel 1959), conversion (Strauss 1979), glossolalia (Hutch 1980; Kelsey 1964; Kildahl 1972), confession (Boisen 1958; Mowrer 1961), religious imagery (Propst 1980), and mystical experience (Spilka 1980; Trew 1971) are documented. Additionally, Finney and Malony (1985) and Carlson, Bacaseta, and Simanton (1988) cite evidence for the mental health benefits of Christian meditation. Wilson (1974) references the general psychological benefits of Christian maneuvers in therapy. And, Fitzgibbons (1986), Wolberg (1973), and Worthington and DiBlasio (1990) promote forgiveness as an appropriate psychotherapeutic technique.

While the existing literature contains promise, there is still little experimental research in the area of practical integration. Larson et al. (1986) conclude from their review that, "the data suggest that the academic knowledge and skills needed to evaluate religion have not been absorbed into the psychiatric domain" (329). This lack of "absorption" may be partially because mental health professionals do not view and value religion as a major factor in their lives (Larson et al. 1986). The Christian disciplines face an added barrier. They are kept outside the boundaries of psychotherapy by many because of being seen as belonging within a separate discipline, that is, spiritual direction. Some, such as Edwards (1980), imply that psychotherapy and spiritual direction are different, almost orthogonal, processes involving distinct subjects, goals, attitudes, and methods. The disciplines are seen as methods for spiritual direction, but not as techniques for psychotherapy.

Another barrier to the clinical application of Christian disciplines is the lack of their specific and precise definitions. A limited number of articles exist that refer to religious or spiritual counseling intervention (Nelson and Wilson 1984; Winger and Hunsberger 1988; Worthington 1986; Worthington et al. 1988), but these articles do not give the specific criteria for the selection of the techniques. Worthington et al. (1988) offer the only extensive list of spiritual guidance techniques that are proposed for use in clinical practice. And, indeed, many of these techniques are specific Christian disciplines. However, only limited information is provided concerning definition and selection factors.

There is an additional practical barrier to the clinical application of Christian disciplines—that is, the lack of training for counselors who wish to employ them in treatment. In spite of the growing number of graduate training programs that teach the integration of psychology and theology, there is little empirical evidence that Christian counselors are receiving training in uniquely Christian interventions, however these interventions are defined. This appears true in spite of many calls for specialized training for mental health professionals in the area of religious or Christian intervention (Collins and Tornquist 1981; Nelson and Wilson 1984; Worthington et al. 1988). Indeed, Nelson and Wilson (1984) have made the following observation concerning this need:

> Since most medical and psychological education does not include instruction as to the use of spiritual intervention, training is necessary for anyone who wishes to do Christian psychotherapy. As in other aspects of psychotherapy the application of spiritual interventions requires proper supervision by a trained Christian therapist. (21)

However, there is little evidence that these calls are being answered, and the question remains, who will provide the training?

The present study is an exploratory examination of four hypotheses about graduate training practices and procedures regarding the use of Christian disciplines as counseling techniques: Will content validation, through expert agreement, be found for the proposed list of Christian disciplines? Which Christian disciplines (if any) are taught in these graduate training programs? Does accreditation affect training practices and procedures? Will disciplines associated with certain religious traditions (i.e., holiness, charismatic) be taught more or less than those associated with other traditions?

Method

Participants

Representatives of 27 of the 87 programs surveyed responded. Only 20 of the returned surveys contained usable data. Respondents included 4 deans, 2 coordinators, 4 directors, 5 chairpersons, 3 professors, and 2 assistants to chairpersons. The respondents were 15 men, 3 women, and 2 respondents whose gender was unspecified. Nine of the graduate training programs were Catholic and 11 were non-Catholic. All major geographic areas of the United States were represented.

Additional demographic data reveal the following. Seventeen of the 20 graduate programs were accredited. Five of these 17 were accredited by the American Psychological Association. Sixteen of the programs reported a theological orientation. Of these, 44% reported a conservative identification, 25% reported a moderate identification, and 31% listed themselves as liberal. All of the programs offered some form of master's degree, while 40% offered either a Ph.D. or a Psy.D. degree. Seventy-five percent of the programs listed professional counseling or psychology as their primary training emphasis.

Instrument

One survey form and a list of Christian disciplines with operational definitions were developed. Because this is an initiatory study, neither instrument is supported by reliability or validity data. Worthington's (1986) description of "a religious counseling technique as any practice used in counseling that originated within the practice of formal religion" (427) provided the general qualification for the Christian counseling techniques included on the list. Three sources were used to generate the specific list of Christian disciplines and their definitions: the hermeneutical examination of biblical text relating to religious practices; Christian writers and spiritual directors from the time of Christ to the present, found in Kepler (1948), Crabb (1977), Leech (1977), Edwards (1980), May (1982), Neufelder and Coehlo (1982), Sanford and Sanford (1982), Tyrrell (1982), Peck (1983), Benner (1988), Collins (1988), Foster (1988); and journal articles generated through a database search, particularly that of Worthington et al. (1988).

All of the disciplines included on the list were found in at least two of the above mentioned sources. A figure of twenty was arbitrarily set as the maximum number of disciplines to be examined. The twenty Christian disciplines judged to receive the greatest amount of support across the three sources were selected. Greatest weight was given to the category of scriptural support. Initial content validity was to be further assessed by the responses of the program directors to the survey questions regarding scriptural support. Brief definitions of each technique were written and pertinent Scripture references for each technique selected. The disciplines are summarized in table 9.1.

A survey form was designed to elicit the respondents' ratings of each Christian counseling technique in four areas: emphasis in the curriculum, scriptural support, therapeutic utility, and subjective value. Four 5-point Likert-type scales were developed: for emphasis in the curriculum, 1 = not taught, 2 = not in a syllabus but receptive atmosphere to discussion, 3 = discussion encouraged but left to professor's discretion, 4 = writ-

Table 9.1

Working Definitions and Scriptural References
for the Twenty Christian Disciplines

Meditation: ". . . to engage in contemplation or reflection . . . to focus one's thoughts on: reflect on or ponder over" (Webster 1986, 738).

1. Concrete meditation–A focus of thoughts on Scripture (individual words and/or phrases). This may also include concrete objects of God's creation. Ps. 119:15, 99, 148.
2. Abstract meditation–An activity closely related to (1), which encourages more active use of the imagination, such as a passive focus on one or more of the attributes of God. Ps. 63:6; 143:5.

Prayer: Communion and/or conversation with God.

3. Intercessory prayer–A form of prayer that involves making our requests known to God, either as they relate to ourselves or others. Eph. 6:18; Phil. 4:6.
4. Contemplative prayer–A particular type of interpersonal response to God which seeks to create a passive openness to the experience of God through nonanalytical focus of attention (Finney 1984). Often contemplative prayer transcends words and images due to the inadequacy of these vehicles to capture God. Ps. 46:10; 27:4.
5. Listening prayer–A process similar to contemplative prayer, but with the exception that the primary focus is upon receptivity to communication (words/images) from God. Ps. 130:5–6; 1 Sam. 3:9, 10.
6. Praying in the Spirit–As a type of verbal prayer, a specific experience which often involves the presence of verbal utterances—usually not recognizable speech (Finney 1984); as "prayer of interior surrender" (Finney 1984), an ongoing process of awareness of God's presence. Rom. 8:26; 1 Thess. 5:17; 1 Cor. 12:10.

Scripture: God's written revelation as contained in the scriptural canon.

7. Counselor: Pro-active–Didactic use of Scripture involving teaching, discussion, exhortation, and encouragement. 2 Tim. 3:14–17; Col. 3:16.
8. Client: Pro-active–Encouragement of Scripture study, memorization, and application as a structured homework technique. Ps. 119:9–16; 2 Tim. 2:15.
9. Confession–"Taking personal responsibility for" transgressions of thought or deed and entering into a process of metanoia (turning away, repentance) that involves admitting to God and/or others our sin (Foster 1988, 148). Ps. 51:1–3; James 5:16.
10. Worship–Giving to God our praise, thanksgiving, allegiance, honor, and adoration, both individually and in fellowship with other believers. Rom. 12:1; Ps. 9:1–2; Heb. 10:25.
11. Forgiveness–The complete canceling of a debt or penalty for an offense, which generally involves cleansing and freedom from sin and its effects. 1 John 1:9; Matt. 6:14–15.
12. Fasting–Abstaining from normal pleasures for a period of time for the purpose of spiritual growth/insight. Matt. 6:16–18; Ps. 35:13.
13. Deliverance–Releasing a person from oppression or possession by evil spirits or demons. Matt. 10:8; Mic. 6:31.
14. Solitude/silence–Drawing away from the crowds or distractions in order to meet with God alone (Foster 1988). It further involves the attitude of inner stillness as one brings the heart and mind into focus on the Lord. Ps. 131:2; Mic. 6:31.
15. Discernment–A gift of divine insight for the purpose of rightly distinguishing between good and evil, truth and error. 1 John 4:1, 6; 1 Cor. 12:10; Heb. 5:14.
16. Journal keeping–A written expression of emotions, thoughts, experiences, and/or dreams which serves as an outpouring of the soul as well as an encouragement for self or others. Psalms.
17. Obedience–The giving up of personal autonomy, entering into a life of freely accepted servanthood to God (Foster 1988). Phil. 2:5–8; 1 John 5:3; 1 Cor. 12:1–31.
18. Simplicity–A life lived with singleness of desire as expressed in Matthew 6:33, which involves the freedom of being detached from worldly concern. Matt. 6:22–34; Col. 3:1–5.
19. Spiritual history–A type of case history which involves the structured discussion of one's religious background, spiritual journey, and other specific events that relate to relationship with God. 1 Thess. 3:5–6; 2 Tim. 1:5–6.
20. Healing–A dynamic, miraculous process of being made whole (physically and/or emotionally) which often involves laying on of hands or anointing with oil. Mic. 6:13; James 5:14–15.

ten into syllabus of at least one class and receives up to three hours lecture time, and 5 = written into syllabus of at least one class and receives more than three hours lecture time; for scriptural support, 1 = no support for this practice in Scripture, 3 = some indirect support as a valuable Christian practice, and 5 = clearly supported as a valuable Christian practice; for therapeutic utility, 1 = I believe this practice has no place in our training program, no therapeutic utility, 5 = I believe this should be an integral part of our training program, clear therapeutic utility; for subjective value, 1 = I consider this technique to have no value, 3 = I consider this technique to have moderate value, 5 = I consider this technique to have very high value.

Procedure

Respondent schools were identified in *Peterson's Education Directory* (Miers and Goldstein 1986) as religious, and as offering graduate degree programs in counseling and/or psychology. Additional schools known to have these qualifications were also included. Eighty-seven schools were sent a survey, along with the list of the techniques and their definitions, a return envelope, and a cover letter explaining the purpose of the survey. In the cover letter, the directors were made aware that the purpose of the investigation was to obtain information regarding the training practices and perspectives of their programs specifically concerning the use of Christian disciplines as counseling techniques. Surveys not returned within eight weeks were followed by a second mailing. Twenty-seven surveys (31%) were returned. Seven of these were not usable, leaving 20 (23%) with data suitable for analysis.

Results

Mean scores and standard deviations for each cell and overall column means (practices or perspectives across all twenty disciplines) are summarized in table 9.2. The overall mean scores (reported on 5-point Likert-type scales) were emphasis in curriculum (2.25); scriptural support (4.53); therapeutic utility (3.32); and subjective value (4.29). The scriptural support rating is encouraging and is seen as offering at least minimal backing for the content validity of the list of disciplines. Seventeen of the twenty disciplines were rated as either a 4 or a 5 on the scriptural support rating scale by at least 80% of the respondents. The exceptions were simplicity (75%), spiritual history (64%), and journal keeping (33%).

Also reported in table 9.2 are the percentages of the respondent graduate programs that devote significant lecture time to the teaching of specific disciplines. Of all the disciplines, only one, forgiveness, was both written into a course syllabus and given at least three hours of lecture time in a specific course by at least 25% of the programs. Contemplative

Table 9.2
Mean Ratings and Standard Deviations of Techniques Concerning Training Practices and Perspectives

Techniques[a]	Emphasis in Curriculum[b]		Scriptural Support[c]		Therapeutic Utility[d]		Subjective Value[e]	
	Mean	SD	Mean	SD	Mean	SD	Mean	SD
Concrete meditation (10)	2.15	1.39	4.83	0.28	3.50	1.17	4.67	0.69
Abstract meditation (10)	2.10	1.37	4.50	0.50	3.36	1.12	4.36	0.57
Intercessory prayer (10)	2.26	1.40	4.92	0.21	3.14	1.17	4.64	0.47
Contemplative prayer (20)	2.45	1.56	4.83	0.28	3.29	1.24	4.45	0.58
Listening prayer (5)	2.15	1.28	4.85	0.29	3.36	1.28	4.75	0.33
Praying in the Spirit (0)	1.84	0.91	4.36	0.85	2.86	1.21	3.73	1.05
Scripture: counselor pro-active (15)	2.37	1.49	4.67	0.66	3.27	1.35	4.00	1.04
Scripture: client pro-active (5)	2.32	1.38	4.75	0.64	3.73	1.24	4.55	0.57
Confession (15)	2.28	1.48	4.92	0.21	3.80	1.27	4.73	0.48
Worship (15)	2.21	1.43	4.92	0.21	3.20	1.27	4.09	0.92
Forgiveness (25)	2.60	1.66	4.93	0.22	3.67	1.33	4.64	0.47
Fasting (0)	1.90	1.09	4.62	0.59	2.87	1.26	3.73	0.95
Deliverance (0)	2.11	1.26	4.50	0.67	3.07	1.32	3.82	0.99
Solitude/ silence (0)	2.25	1.18	4.50	0.61	3.53	1.18	4.45	0.48
Discernment (0)	2.50	1.39	4.38	0.74	3.13	1.22	4.45	0.58
Journal keeping (0)	2.89	1.51	3.00	1.04	3.40	1.13	4.17	0.61
Obedience (0)	1.95	1.12	4.62	0.67	3.23	1.23	4.18	0.88
Simplicity (0)	2.00	1.00	4.42	0.68	3.47	1.17	4.36	0.47
Spiritual history (10)	2.16	1.35	3.18	1.13	3.07	1.24	3.82	0.93
Healing (10)	2.53	1.50	4.86	0.29	3.43	1.29	4.17	0.99
Overall Mean	2.25	1.15	4.53	0.35	3.32	1.04	4.29	0.70

[a] Teaching is defined as written into syllabus of at least one class—receives more than three hours lecture time. Percent of responding programs that teach each discipline is recorded in parenthesis after the name of the discipline.

[b] n range = 18–20. Each item was rated either: 1 = not taught; 2 = not in a syllabus; receptive atmosphere to discussion; 3 = discussion encouraged but left to professor's discretion; 4 = written into syllabus of at least 1 class—receives up to 3 hours lecture time; 5 = written into syllabus of at least 1 class—receives more than 3 hours lecture time.

[c] n range = 11–14. Each item was rated on a 5-point scale with: 1 = no support for this practice in Scripture; 3 = some indirect support as valuable Christian practice; 5 = clearly supported as valuable Christian practice.

[d] n range = 13–15. Each item was rated on a 5-point scale with: 1 = I believe this practice has no place in training program, no therapeutic utility; 5 = I believe this should be an integral part of training program, clear therapeutic utility.

[e] n range = 11–12. Each item was rated on a 5-point scale with: 1 = I consider this technique to have no value; 3 = I consider this technique to have moderate value; 5 = I consider this technique to have very high value.

prayer, teaching with Scripture, confession, and worship were the next most frequently taught disciplines. Six of the disciplines were not given at least three hours of lecture time by any of the programs. These disciplines are praying in the Spirit, fasting, deliverance, solitude/silence, obedience, and simplicity.

The effects of program accreditation on each of the dependent variables (emphasis in curriculum, scriptural support, therapeutic utility, and subjective value) were examined. The 17 accredited programs were compared with the 3 nonaccredited programs on the mean ratings for each of these variables, using a one-way analysis of variance (ANOVA). A significant relationship between accreditation and emphasis in curriculum or subjective value was not found. The respective F (1, 18) values = 1.02, and 2.27. It was observed, however, that the nonaccredited programs were more likely to perceive the disciplines as having scriptural support, F (1, 18) = 8.60, but less likely to view the disciplines as having therapeutic utility, F (1, 18) = 5.72.

The 5 APA approved programs were compared with the 15 non-APA approved programs on mean ratings for each of the 4 dependent variables, using a one-way analysis of variance (ANOVA). APA approved programs differed from their non-APA approved counterparts in that APA-approved programs were less likely to subjectively value the disciplines than were non-APA approved programs, $F(1, 18) = 9.88$, $p < .05$. The respective $F(1, 18)$ values for the other dependent variables (emphasis in curriculum, scriptural support, and therapeutic utility) = 1.11, 2.51. and 1.37, p = ns.

The 9 programs which identified themselves as Catholic were compared with the 11 non-Catholic programs on mean ratings for each of the dependent variables, again using a one-way analysis of variance (ANOVA). Catholic programs were more likely than non-Catholic programs to view the disciplines as having scriptural support, F (1, 18) = 7.40, $p < .05$. The respective F (1, 18) values for the other dependent variables (emphasis in curriculum, therapeutic utility, and subjective value) = 1.76, 2.82, and 1.97, p = ns.

It was thought that the association of certain disciplines with particular religious traditions might cause a selective valuing of some disciplines relative to others. Using the booklet RENOVARE published by Renovare, Inc., 5 traditions were identified: contemplative, holiness, charismatic, social justice, and evangelical. Four raters independently categorized each technique according to which tradition the technique was most associated with. Not all disciplines were assigned because consensus among raters was not found. Assignments to religious traditions were as follows: contemplative—contemplative prayer, listening prayer, solitude/silence; holiness—confession, fasting, simplicity; charismatic—praying in the Spirit, deliverance, discernment; social justice—intercessory prayer, healing; evangelical—Scripture teaching by the counselor ("counselor pro-active"), and Scripture study as homework ("client pro-active").

Four one-way analyses of variance (ANOVA) were used to investigate whether disciplines in each of the 5 traditions were rated differently on each of the dependent variables (e.g., emphasis in the curriculum, scrip-

Table 9.3

Means for Training Practice and Perspectives by Religious Tradition of the Disciplines

Training Practices/ Perspectives	Contemplative (n=20)	Holiness (n=20)	Charismatic (n=20)	Social Justice (n=20)	Evangelical (n=20)	$F(4, 15)$
	Religious Tradition					
Emphasis in Ccurriculum	2.28^{a}	2.06^{a}	2.15^{a}	2.39^{a}	2.34^{a}	0.27
Spiritual support	4.73^{a}	4.65^{ab}	4.42^{b}	4.89^{a}	4.71^{ab}	2.89*
Therapeutic utility	3.39^{a}	3.38^{a}	3.02^{a}	3.29^{a}	3.50^{a}	0.50
Subjective value	4.55^{a}	4.27^{ab}	4.00^{a}	4.40^{b}	4.27^{ab}	2.43*

Note: Techniques included under each grouping include: Contemplative (contemplative prayer, listening prayer,solitude/silence), Holiness (confession, fasting, simplicity), Charismatic (praying in the Spirit, deliverance, discernment), Social Justice (intercessory prayer, healing), Evangelical (Scripture: counselor pro-active, Scripture: client pro-active).

[a,b] means with different superscripts are different at $p < .05$, using Duncan's Multiple Range Test.

$^{*}p < .05$

tural support, therapeutic utility, and subjective value—see table 9.3). The effect of tradition of origin on perceived scriptural support, and subjective value was significant, $F(4, 15) = 2.89$, $p < .05$, and $F(4, 15) = 2.43$, $p < .05$, respectively. Duncan's test revealed that the training directors were significantly more likely to view the "charismatic" disciplines as having less scriptural support and as being less valued than the disciplines from the other four traditions (e.g., contemplative, holiness, social justice, and evangelical).

Discussion

Several areas of weakness are apparent in this study. Despite the use of two mailings there was a low return rate for the surveys. Only 23% of surveys were returned and proved to be usable. This low response may not speak well for interest in this area of practical integration, even among religiously oriented programs. The selection process for graduate training programs may have been overly inclusive and yielded some programs with only nominal interest in Christian practices. It would also have proven enlightening to have provided the program directors with the opportunity to provide comment concerning their attitudes toward teaching the Christian disciplines as therapeutic techniques in counseling and to have asked specific questions concerning their views of boundary issues between Christian counseling and spiritual direction.

Concerning the teaching of the disciplines in Christian graduate training programs, it is noteworthy that, in spite of increasing calls for specialized training for mental health professionals involving religion/Christian interventions (Collins and Tornquist 1981; Quackenbos, Privette and Klentz 1986; Worthington et al. 1988), the results of this study generally support the hypothesis that instruction in the Christian disciplines is a rarity. Indeed, it would seem that the pervasive training attitude toward these disciplines as counseling techniques is: ". . . they are not specifically listed in a course syllabus, but a receptive atmosphere for discussion is present and sometimes encouraged." While it is encouraging to note that some training is occurring, one is left to ponder the possible validity of Propst's (1980) assertion that Christian mental health professionals often have a tendency to "ignore, or at the very least, feel embarrassed about, so called 'spiritual approaches to mental health'" (107).

It was hypothesized that program accreditation would suppress the amount of instruction time allotted. Results indicate that program accreditation does not have a significant effect on instruction time. There were no significant relationships observed between any of the demographic variables assigned and amount of instruction apportioned (APA-approved programs were less likely to assign subjective value to the disciplines than non-APA approved programs). However, it must be observed that the overall mean "emphasis in curriculum" ratings were low—leaving little room for differentiation.

Somewhat surprisingly, nonaccredited programs viewed the disciplines as having less therapeutic utility than did the accredited programs. This was true in spite of the fact that these nonaccredited programs perceived the disciplines to possess greater scriptural support than did the accredited programs. It is possible that the nonaccredited programs are more closely aligned to a pastoral counseling model than a scientist-practitioner model and subsequently are more inclined to view such maneuvers in terms of underlying scriptural support, but less likely to conceptualize in terms such as "therapeutic potential."

When the disciplines were grouped according to major Christian traditions (i.e., contemplative, holiness, charismatic, social justice, and evangelical), it was observed that the "charismatic" disciplines were rated significantly lower than the other grouping in the areas of perceived scriptural support and subjective value. This may reflect a bias against certain disciplines which, interestingly enough, may possess the highest potential to bring about dramatic change (i.e., deliverance).

It seems promising that the Christian disciplines were viewed as possessing therapeutic potential and subjective value. Indeed, one is left to wonder if some established therapeutic techniques such as "script analysis," hypnosis, or dream interpretation would receive such high utility ratings from these same directors collectively representing such a spectrum of orientations. Given this hint of receptivity, and the present zeitgeist which reflects diminishing financial resources for mental health services, the general public's positive value of religion, and conceptual advances in the discipline of integration, the charge of Quackenbos et al. (1986) rings with poignancy. They state: "It is timely for those in the counseling professions to consider seriously specialized education and certification in religious counseling" (82). It is our primary contention that Christian counseling can legitimately make more use of explicitly Christian techniques that arise from within the Christian traditions.

References

Appel, K. E. 1959. Religion. In *American handbook of psychiatry*, vol. 2, ed. S. Arieti. New York: Basic.

Benner, D. G. 1988. *Psychotherapy and the spiritual quest*. Grand Rapids: Baker.

Boisen, A. T. 1958. Religious experience and psychological conflict. *American Psychologist* 13: 568–70.

Carlson, C. R., P. E. Bacaseta, and D. A. Simanton. 1988. A controlled evaluation of devotional meditation and progressive relaxation. *Journal of Psychology and Theology* 16: 362–68.

Clinebell, H. J., Jr. 1970. The local church's contribution to positive mental health. In *Community mental health: The role of church and temple*, ed. H. J. Clinebell, Jr., 46–56. Nashville: Abingdon.

Collins, G. R. 1988. *Christian counseling: A comprehensive guide*. Rev. ed. Dallas: Word.

Collins, G. R., and L. M. Tornquist. 1981. Training Christian people helpers: Observations on counselor education. *Journal of Psychology and Theology* 9: 69–80.

Crabb, L. J. 1977. *Effective biblical counseling*. Grand Rapids: Zondervan.

Edwards, T. H. 1980. *Spiritual friend*. New York: Paulist.

Finney, J. R. 1984. *Contemplative prayer and its use in psychotherapy*. Unpublished doctoral dissertation, Fuller Theological Seminary.

Finney, J. R., and H. N. Malony, Jr. 1985. Empirical studies of Christian prayer: A review of the literature. *Journal of Psychology and Theology* 13(2): 104–15.

Fisher, E. W., and S. L. Cohen. 1972. Demographic correlates of attitudes toward seeking professional psychological help. *Journal of Consulting and Clinical Psychology* 39: 70–74.

Fitzgibbons, R. P. 1986. The cognitive and emotive uses of forgiveness in the treatment of anger. *Psychotherapy* 23: 629–33.

Foster, R. J. 1988. *Celebration of discipline*. Rev. ed. San Francisco: Harper and Row.

Gilbert, M. G. 1981. Characteristics of pastors related to pastoral counseling and referral. *Journal of Pastoral and Counseling* 16: 30–38.

Griffith, E. E. 1983. The impact of sociocultural factors on a church-based healing model. *American Journal of Orthopsychiatry* 53: 291–302.

Hutch, R. A. 1980. The personal ritual of glossolalia. *Journal for the Scientific Study of Religion* 19: 255–66.

Kelsey, M. T. 1964. *Tongue speaking: An experiment in spiritual experience.* Garden City, N.Y.: Doubleday.

Kepler, T. S., ed. 1948. *The fellowship of the saints* (an anthology of Christian devotional literature). New York: Abingdon-Cokesbury.

Kildahl, J. P. 1972. *The psychology of speaking in tongues.* New York: Harper and Row.

Larson, D. B., L. C. Kessler, B. J. Burns, H. A. Pincus, J. C. Houpt, S. Fiester, and L. Chaitken. 1987. A research development workshop to stimulate outcome research in consultation—liaison psychiatry. *Hospital and Community Psychiatry* 38: 1106–9.

Larson, D. B., E. M. Pattison, D. G. Blaser, A. R. Omram, and B. H. Kaplan. 1986. Systematic analysis of research on religious variables in four major psychiatric journals, 1978–1982. *American Journal of Psychiatry* 143: 329–34.

Leech, K. 1977. *Soul friend: The practice of Christian spirituality.* San Francisco: Harper and Row.

May, G. G. 1982. *Care of mind/care of spirit: Psychiatric dimensions of spiritual direction.* San Francisco: Harper and Row.

Miers, P., and A. J. Goldstein, eds.1986. *Peterson's graduate education directory.* Princeton, N.J.: Peterson's Guides.

Morgan, D. D. 1982. Needs assessment in churches: A Christian community's need for professional counseling services. *Journal of Psychology and Theology* 10: 242–50.

Mowrer, O. H. 1961. *The crisis in psychiatry and religion.* Princeton, N.J.: D. Van Nostrand.

Nelson, A. A., and W. P. Wilson. 1984. The ethics of sharing religious faith in psychotherapy. *Journal of Psychology and Theology* 12: 15–23.

Neufelder, J. N., and M. C. Coelho, eds. 1982. *Writings on spiritual direction.* New York: Seabury.

Peck, M. S. 1983. *People of the lie: The hope for healing human evil.* New York: Simon and Schuster.

Propst, R. L. 1980. A comparison of the cognitive restructuring psychotherapy paradigm and several spiritual approaches to mental health. *Journal of Psychology and Theology* 8: 107–14.

Quackenbos, S., G. Privette, and B. Klenz. 1986. Psychotherapy and religion: Rapprochement or antithesis? *Journal of Counseling and Development* 65: 82–85.

Sanford, J., and P. Sanford 1982. *The transformation of the inner man.* Tulsa: Victory House.

Spilka, B. 1980. *Toward a psychosocial theory of religious mysticism with empirical reference.* Paper presented at the convention of the Rocky Mountain Psychological Association, Tucson, Arizona, April.

Spilka, B., R. W. Hood, and R. L. Gorsuch. 1985. *The psychology of religion: An empirical approach.* Englewood Cliffs, N.J.: Prentice-Hall.

Strauss, R. A. 1979. Religious conversion as a personal and collective accomplishment. *Sociological Analysis* 40: 158–65.

Trew, A. 1971. The religious factor in mental illness. *Pastoral Psychology* 22: 21–28.

Tyrrell, B. J. 1982. *Christotherapy II.* Ramsey, N.J.: Paulist.

Webster's ninth new collegiate dictionary. 1986. Springfield, Mass.: Merriam-Webster.

Wilson, W. P. 1974. Utilization of Christian beliefs in psychotherapy. *Journal of Psychology and Theology* 2: 125–31.

Winger, D., and B. Hunsberger. 1988. Clergy counseling practices, Christian orthodoxy and problem solving styles. *Journal of Psychology and Theology* 16: 41–48.

Wolberg, A. R. 1973. *The borderline patient.* New York: Intercontinental Medical Book Co.

Worthington, E. L., Jr. 1986. Religious counseling: A review of published empirical research. *Journal of Counseling and Development* 64: 421–31.

Worthington, E. L., Jr., and F. A. DiBlasio. 1990. Promoting mutual forgiveness within the fractured relationship. *Psychotherapy* 27: 219–23.

Worthington, E. L., Jr., P. D. Dupont, J. T. Berry, and L. A. Duncan. 1988. Christian therapists' and clients' perceptions of religious psychotherapy in private and agency settings. *Journal of Psychology and Theology* 16: 282–93.

Worthington, E. L., Jr., and S. R. Gascoyne. 1985. Preferences of Christians and non-Christians for five Christian counselors' treatment plans: A partial replication and extension. *Journal of Psychology and Theology* 13: 29–41.

Part 5

An Eye to the Future

Introduction to Part 5

Thus far, the book has examined the current status of religious values in psychotherapy. A variety of suggestions have been advanced about needed research and theory. In the final section of the book, four chapters take a more focused look at the future.

Tjeltveit challenges a purely empirical examination of the field of religious values in psychotherapy, arguing that Christian ethics and scientific psychology must be linked for a meaningful understanding of the field. Tan reviews the status of Christian lay counseling, which will undoubtedly gain in popularity during the next decade. Bergin and Payne argue that investigators of religious psychology currently use approaches that do not reflect the spiritual reality of existence. They call for approaches to personality and psychotherapy that are truly spiritual rather than merely reflecting a naturalistic worldview. In the final essay, I speculate about the future, the role of Christian therapy within the future, and how to be proactive in helping shape a future in which Christian therapy can thrive.

10

Christian Ethics and Psychological Explanations of "Religious Values" in Therapy: Critical Connections

ALAN C. TJELTVEIT

Absent theological explanation, vital dimensions of "religious values" in psychotherapy will be overlooked. Explanations based solely on empirical studies will be fatally flawed. Put more positively, theology, including Christian ethics, can lead to a decidedly deepened grasp of the spiritual, ethical, *and psychological* aspects of human beings, values, religion, and therapy.

But ought *psychologists* address such a broad range of issues when ample empirical questions remain unexamined? Yes, for two major reasons: first, three types of problematic attempts to resolve the tension between science and faith may be seen. Some have sought to eliminate Christianity's "discordant" notes by harmonizing it with the intellectual fancy of the day. What is a common result? Key doctrines have been diluted and essential teachings compromised.

But some Christians reject all new ideas, including those in scientific theories. Most notorious was their once doggedly insisting that the sun revolved around the earth. Should Christians stick their heads in the sand in this way? By no means! We ought to be, not ostriches, but ospreys, ris-

The author gratefully acknowledges the comments of William Jennings and Franklin Sherman on an earlier draft of this chapter.

ing above tradition with psychology's disciplinary tools to see what we otherwise could not.

Christians unwilling to learn from psychology are not the only ostriches. There is another type: the psychologist so busy investigating the sand—often with impeccable experimental design—that the broader context and essential aspects of that being investigated, including its meaning, are lost. Here, theology can help. Indeed, it is when we give *both* science and theology careful critical attention that we avoid problematic resolutions of the science-faith tension.

Second, for those who want to connect or integrate psychology and theology, few issues are of more theoretical and pragmatic import than religion and values in therapy. Why? Psychology here enters into the very heart of faith. The promise is great, as is the peril. Psychology and theology now unabashedly address the same subjects. And both provide explanations—psychological, ethical, and religious—that influence individuals receiving therapy.

Defining "values" clarifies the difficulty. Does "value" mean what is *regarded* as valuable, for instance, a *belief, attitude, or feeling* that it is good to worship God? Or does value mean what *is* valuable, for instance, that it is *actually valuable or good* to worship God, intrinsically good even if having no measurable consequences? About the latter, psychology as science has little to say, but theology much.

A further difficulty results from the term *religious values*, a phrase so ambiguous I refrain from using it here. Does it refer to values about distinctively religious matters? If yes, values in which sense of the word, and what are those "distinctively religious matters"? Are "religious values" rooted in religious faith or convictions (so *all* values are religious for the Christian)? How are these "religious values" related to moral values, to theological assertions, and to faith? Ought scholars use McMinn's (1984) assumption, which he saw implicit in Bergin (1980), that "religious values are similar to other values operating in a client-therapist relationship" (26)? Or, though both may be rational, are *theological* explanations different in kind from explanations that natural science methods provide (Clayton 1989)?

In this chapter I will examine the respective competencies of science and Christian ethics to explain what is good, right, and virtuous in psychological, ethical, and religious realms connected to therapy. After reviewing basic approaches to Christian ethics, I consider explanations from traditional scientific methods and from Christian ethics. Though both are vitally important, the focus is on how Christian ethics appropriately adds to and challenges psychological explanations of religion, values, and therapy.

Christian Ethics

Theology, systematic reflection on beliefs about God (as understood in Christian texts and tradition) and the relationship of God with people and the world, includes ethics. Long (1967, 1982), in a classic taxonomy, discusses how Christian ethicists set ethical standards. He discusses three motifs, which may, of course, be combined. The connection to therapy is that therapists set goals (which include values or ethical standards) and work to implement those goals.

The first, the deliberative motif, emphasizes reason, which is either a major (e.g., Aquinas) or the sole (e.g., Kant) source of ethical standards. For other ethicists, reason provides philosophical categories in which distinctively Christian values are expressed.

The prescriptive motif stresses ethical injunctions (prescriptions) whose content and authority stem from the will of God revealed in Scripture (e.g., Calvin, Carl Henry, and claims that the Bible is an infallible guide of conduct), from a particular community, or both.

In the relational motif, "the direction of action is shaped by the sense of excitement or gratitude which arises from a live, dynamic, and compelling encounter with the source of moral guidance" (Long 1967, 117). For Augustine, Luther, and Jonathan Edwards the source of moral guidance is God, whose redemptive deed "brings into existence" (Sittler 1958, 25) action and character only later thought of as moral. The *relationship* produces moral behavior, not values or prescriptions of philosophical or biblical origin.

Long (1967) concludes irenically by calling for a "comprehensive complementarity" (310), in which each motif corrects the others' weaknesses. Indeed, all find some support in Scripture and Christian tradition.

Christian ethicists have recently focused on the importance of character (or virtue) and community (e.g., Hauerwas 1975, 1981; Meilaender 1984). (The terms are far richer in connotation than the similar psychological terms, "traits" and "situations," though character and community are also seen as interacting.) Character, according to Birch and Rasmussen (1989), refers "to moral elements we often consider 'internal' to the person or group—motives, dispositions, attitudes, intentions, and perceptions" (40). Christian ethicists are thus using *psychological* explanations.

Two other aspects of most Christian ethics are germane: Most Christian ethicists (save some Calvinists—though Muller and Vande Kemp [1985] assert that Calvin was not a philosophical determinist) assume some measure of genuine human freedom or agency; and Christian ethicists discuss values both in terms of what *has* value and also in connection with God (and often the church). Thus their explanations of values are broader in scope than (and often different in kind from) those of the scientific psychologist.

Explanations in Science and Christian Ethics

Scientific Explanations

Psychologists qua scientists make crucial contributions to an understanding of how religion, values, and therapy are related. Researchers can measure values (defined as what is *felt* or *believed* to be valuable), measure value changes, investigate some (but, to the extent relationalists are right, not all) change processes, and investigate some of the relationships between religion, values, and other variables. In this way, regularities may be discovered. Of particular importance is science's role in testing plausible hypotheses empirically (e.g., Bergin 1980; Beutler 1989; Kelly 1990; Worthington 1988, 1989). Ideas that seem true may thereby be shown to be false.

Psychologists also provide facts ethicists need in order to make optimal ethical decisions. (And therapists addressing ethical issues function as ethicists). For instance, Rosenthal's (1955) study spawned an empirical research program indicating that therapists often influence client values (Beutler 1981). This research provides knowledge that helps resolve the associated professional ethical issues (Tjeltveit 1986, 1989a).

Nevertheless, recent developments in the philosophy of science (e.g., Hill 1989; O'Donohue 1989; Ratzsch 1987) may require some qualification of the traditional claims made by psychologists for science (but need not lead to relativism, cf. Van Leeuwen 1988, or a total rejection of those claims). Scientific knowledge is not value free; it involves both scientific values (e.g., objectivity) and extra-scientific values. In this regard, the science-religion difference is one of degree, not kind (Barbour 1974).

Further, Clayton (1989), Evans (1989), Van Leeuwen (1985), and others argue that natural science methods alone are inadequate to address certain *psychological* questions. Other approaches (discussed subsequently) are needed to explain some human phenomena.

Scientific methods also cannot, by themselves, produce *ethical or theological* knowledge. If scientific research establishes that therapy changes values or that therapy involving religion-related values produces changes in some measure of mental health, that does not establish that those changes are *good* or *should* occur, but only that they occur. Establishing that such changes are good or right requires arguments that are *ethical* in nature, not scientific. This point has been missed by theorists who, influenced by the idea of evolution, imply that survival is a value derived from science. But survival and the related ideals of growth and development are not necessarily good, as the phrases *survival of racism, growth of cancer*, and *development of explosive violence* suggest.

Finally, Schwartz (1990) provides evidence that suggests "values are often contextually determined, sociohistorical phenomenon" that are mistakenly confused with "eternal, natural" truths (7) discoverable by traditional scientific methods. Thus, attempts to discover a "universal structure of values" by strictly empirical means (e.g., Schwartz and Bilsky 1987) are flawed, because value, by its nature as contingent and historical, cannot be fully apprehended by traditional scientific methods. Schwartz therefore argues that, in the study of values, we need "a perspective that is both metaphysically and epistemologically more inclusive than science" (8). Theology, of course, provides one type of "more inclusive" perspective.

Theological Explanations

Theological explanations address the context within which psychotherapy occurs, its ultimate (and often aspects of its penultimate) meaning, values in the sense of what is valuable or most valuable, certain change processes, the nature and destiny of the human beings involved, and the role of God in therapy and in the lives of therapy participants. The richness, wisdom, and truth of theological explanations emerges, in part, from centuries of religious experience, including experience related to problems therapy now addresses. Finally, clients often use theological explanations to which therapists must be attuned.

Theological explanations can contribute to, be complementary to, or conflict with scientific explanations. Theology *contributes* to psychological explanations through alternative psychological methods and through proposing hypotheses to be tested by traditional scientific methods. Bergin's (1980) hypotheses illustrate the latter. The importance of theology was documented by Donahue (1989), who illustrated how the failure to consider theological issues has led to misleading research conclusions.

More controversial are theological *challenges* to psychological explanations. Ought Christian ethicists here remove themselves from a realm best addressed by the scientific methods of the psychologist? Birch and Rasmussen (1989) offer an emphatic no. Critical analysis, they assert, is "an indispensable requirement of an adequate Christian ethic" (78).

The degree to which theological challenges are controversial depends on their nature. For instance, some scientists deny epistemic status to theological assertions. In Christian circles, criticism of such "scientific" assertions is relatively uncontroversial. But when theology challenges the idea that *only* traditional scientific methods should be used to obtain psychological knowledge, Christians are divided.

To clarify theology's contributions and challenges to psychological explanations of religion and values in therapy, I will discuss three issues raised by Evans (1989): values (meaning what *is* valuable for human beings), freedom, and meaning.

Values. When explaining religion, values, and therapy, Christians ethicists address what is good, right, and virtuous. Explanations can include not simply pertinent facts, but evaluations about the goodness and rightness of what occurs in therapy and accounts of therapy's ultimate dimension or context.

This means that Christians—whether scientists, practitioners, or theologians—face both constructive and critical tasks as they explain values in therapy. The constructive task is to clarify what is good, right, and virtuous in therapy, using the deliberative, prescriptive, and relational motifs of Christian ethics. The goal? To set forth the evaluative aspects of the model of human beings used, to explicate ideal visions about human beings, to clarify life's context (including what is ultimately important) (Tjeltveit 1989c), and to balance or order the good outcomes of therapy and life—outcomes like mental, moral, and spiritual health. Values (including those most therapists endorse) and their underlying theories need to be clarified, evaluated, and justified. These tasks, Browning (1987) suggests, are best carried out in critical dialogue with persons not sharing Christian assumptions.

A critical task is also necessary. Christian ethics properly challenges certain psychological explanations of values in therapy—whether made by scientist or practitioner. This includes explanations that claim to be value-free, those in which ethical or religious judgments are made implicitly, or those that contain judgments about ethical and religious issues that vary from those of the Christian faith. Post-positivist philosophers of science have ravaged the claim that explanations can be value-free. So, *any* explanation of values in therapy will include ideas about goodness and rightness. This does not mean the values are wrong or wrongly present, but simply that they are present. As such, they may and should be evaluated in terms of Christian ethics.

Values in theories of therapy have recently received much scholarly attention. Browning (1987) discussed at length the implicit ethical and religious convictions of Freud, Skinner, Rogers, and others, doing so critically from the perspective of theological ethics. Evans (1989) argued it is both legitimate and desirable to use an explicitly value-critical perspective in developing psychological explanations.

The idea that psychologists should evaluate the rightness or correctness of values in therapy as part of a comprehensive explanation of values will seem wrong to many. Psychologists are generally socialized to value *not* making value judgments. Indeed, there *are* dangers in making value judgments, as there are in not doing so. But suppose post-positivist philosophers of science are correct about science's value-ladenness, and suppose there is some truth to Christian claims about values. Then the only questions about using a value-critical perspective in our explanations are how explicitly we do so and how well.

Freedom. Explanations hinge, in part, upon whether or not people are believed to be free, or capable of "agency," defined by Rychlak (1988) as "the capacity for an organism to behave in compliance with, in addition to, in opposition to, or without regard for biological or sociocultural stimulations" (84). Many psychologists deny we are free in that sense; others believe we are (e.g., Rychlak 1979, 1988).

Almost all Christian ethicists (e.g., Birch and Rasmussen 1989; Smedes 1983; Thielicke 1958/1979) believe we are in some measure free, in part because the Christian conviction that persons are morally responsible requires freedom (Evans 1977, 1989). Indeed, Birch and Rasmussen (1989) assert that the Bible "promotes moral agency" (189).

The relevance of this debate for understanding religion, values, and therapy is this: Explanations including agency are profoundly and significantly different from those that do not. In this connection, Bergin's (1985) assertion that "obedience to moral law is, in principle, no different from obedience to physical laws" (111), which appears inconsistent with a belief in moral agency, is illustrative. A belief in moral agency suggests that there *is* a relevant difference between a person, who can choose whether or not to tell a lie, and a rock, which, if unsupported in the air, cannot choose whether or not to fall. A person can disobey; a rock cannot. To be sure, consequences follow from the actions of either a person or a rock, and these consequences may show discoverable regularities. But intrinsic to *morality* is the human capacity to choose. A person who chooses dishonesty is blameworthy in a way a rock that falls is not, and cannot be. Explanations, *especially* about morality, that omit this human capacity to choose are thus different in kind from those that include it.

Freedom, or agency, also makes a difference in explanations of faith and religious behavior. For instance, in making sense of Joshua saying to the tribes of Israel, "Choose this day whom you will serve" (Josh. 24:15 RSV), explanations that deny human agency are different from those that argue those individuals could have chosen to serve *or* not to serve. Indeed, the very idea of a *relationship* with God may *require* that human beings, as persons, be agents.

Meaning. Some psychologists, theologians, and philosophers hold that important knowledge is gained when the *meaning* of human action is considered (Evans 1977, 1989; Gerkin 1984; Hauerwas and Jones 1989; Lindbeck 1984; MacIntyre 1984; McAdams and Ochberg 1988; Messer, Sass, and Woolfolk 1988; Thiemann 1985; Van Leeuwen 1985; Vitz 1990). But "meaning" is defined in particular ways here. Although definitional consensus has not developed, general features can be outlined.

Meaning in this technical sense has to do with persons actively and often tacitly striving to make sense of life as they act. For instance, to grasp the meaning of the actions of researchers or clinicians, it is necessary to consider their attempts to *make sense* of persons, *interpret* their behavior, *give significance to* some aspects of situations but not to others, and *construct* some more (or less) coherent account of persons' actions. The intentions and motivations of the researchers or therapists, especially their "actively striving to," are critical in this use of "meaning." To leave them out is to be blind to essential aspects of human action.

Meaning usually includes a number of key elements: narrative, interpretation, agency, intention, and context. Grasping the meaning of a person's action often requires understanding how the action fits within the overall narrative or story of his or her life. Determining meaning in a particular instance requires tailored or idiographic interpretation. This is partly because agency and intention—the choices persons make, the goals they intend to reach—preclude explanations that *exhaustively* account for a given action in terms of universal *laws* of behavior. Choices, goals, and intentions are historical and contingent in nature. So a person's *own* interpretation of an action is often needed to explain it adequately. Finally, context also matters: The same behavior or cognition may have different meanings in different settings.

But the well-trained scientific psychologist is by now surely asking why traditional scientific approaches cannot address these issues. They can, and should. The central issue is whether these newer methods lead to explanations scientific methods do not, and so should be used *in addition to* them. The extensive discussions about appropriate methodology in psychology cannot be reviewed here, but a brief discussion is warranted.

Take, for instance, the idea of loving one's neighbor as a response of faith. Scientific research provides explanations of prosocial behavior. Does the *story* of the Good Samaritan *add* to our understanding of the idea of love? Does it provide a type of explanation that existing scientific laws do not? That any conceivable set of scientific laws could not? Could Jesus have done better? In the sense that if Jesus were to return when scientific psychology is complete and wanted to explain that idea, would the story convey the meaning of love in a way those laws would not?

Likewise, when we try to understand client actions, does it help to consider not only scientific results but also the meaning of particular actions in the context of the client's life *story*? to consider clients' *intentions*? how clients *interpret* their actions?

Several claim that explanations focusing on meaning are distinctive. Packer (1985) argued they are of a different type than those based on rationalism and empiricism. For example, rather than explaining the good Samaritan's actions in terms of "formal structures, where logical rules operate on abstract elements whose only 'context' is the formal system they define" (1088) or as a particular expression of causal and empirical contingencies expressed in universal human laws, an explanation focused on meaning would stress the *particular* meaning of his action, his *purposes,* his *making sense of* the situation *in that particular historical context,* and his *choices.* Similarly, Vitz (1990) reviews evidence that suggests narrative thinking is qualitatively different from scientific (or propositional) thinking. Birch and Rasmussen (1989) suggest that narrative thinking produces coherence and a type of insight. Perhaps this is because the Gestalt dictum, the whole is greater than the sum of its parts, is true.

Are there problems with this narrative approach? Certainly. In addition to language that is often difficult to understand and the inescapable problem of multiple interpretations of an action, there is another problem. Some advocates focus so exclusively on individuals' freedom to construct meaning that they believe there are no valid grounds to challenge claims about meaning. For example, Shweder and Fiske (1986; cf. Van Leeuwen 1988) appear to have properly applied the term *relativist* (10) to Gergen's (1986) approach. His radical social constructionism is ironically at odds with the qualities of his personal and ethical convictions, convictions for which his theory denies any (save perhaps subjectivistic) truth claims. The end result of such positions? Any particular interpretation is as meaningful as the next, or, better, as meaningless.

Is relativism inevitable? Need one *choose* between methods focusing on meaning and psychology's traditional methods? Decidedly not. Tests of the adequacy of explanations of meaning have been proposed, and Evans (1989) argues persuasively that the search for empirical regularities and the interpretation of meaning not only can but inevitably do occur concomitantly. Empiricists, in fact, take meaning into account in some aspects of what they do. Likewise, social constructionists rely on beliefs about empirical regularities whose legitimacy their theory denies. Empirical regularities and an account of meaning are thus interdependent and inescapably intertwined. What must be addressed, then, is the balance of the two we employ, and how intentionally and well we do both.

But why does it matter whether we consider meaning when we look at values and religion in therapy? Apart from its importance for explanation, two reasons emerge: ethics and Christian faith. Some claim that both, by their nature, have to do with agents making sense of life. So meaning simply cannot be left out.

Hauerwas (1977) claims that "story teaches us to know and do what is right" (16). Taylor (1989) argues that narrative and ideas about goodness are intertwined, inescapable, and integral to our concepts of self and identity (understood in a strong sense). Finally, Niebuhr (1963) argued that all responsible or moral action is *interpreted* action. To the extent this is true, an explanation of values in therapy that fails to take into account the meanings, interpretations, and intentions of the actors involved, that is, a meaning-less concept of morality, is, if not meaningless, at least inadequate and impoverished.

Do issues of meaning and narrative take on any added significance when we turn from ethics to *Christian* ethics? Yes, because Christian ethics both points beyond itself to Christ and is a part of Christian faith. And, as Birch and Rasmussen (1989) point out, "Christianity as a faith has a narrative character about it" (105). We need to understand life (including ethics and psychotherapy) in terms of biblical accounts, the biblical *story* of God's past, present, and future involvement with us. When we see *anything* as part of that narrative, we gain a new element of explanation.

Indeed, some (e.g., Clayton 1989; Jodock 1989) argue that religious explanations, though they can be rational, are different in scope and content from other kinds including those of the natural and social sciences. Lindbeck (1984) points out that religions employ "comprehensive interpretive schemes . . . told with a particular purpose or interest" (32), that of pointing to what is most important. If this is the case, *"religious* values" ought *not* be understood as other types of values are (McMinn 1984), but in accordance with their particular character. Clayton asserts that theological explanations are distinctive, involving a commitment both to rational discourse and to a particular religious tradition, Scripture, and community. Therefore, "direct epistemological connections between the natural sciences and theology commit a type of category mistake" (vii), a conclusion I have drawn on different grounds (Tjeltveit 1989b). So, when the distinctive character of religious life is considered, explanations need to account for the distinctive meaning of religion.

A crucial point remains. Christian faith, expressed in Christian narratives, includes a particular understanding of human beings. Evans (1990) recently documented how the Christian philosopher Kierkegaard set forth that understanding. In doing so, Kierkegaard functioned as a psychologist (and however much it may not be their primary role, philosophers and theologians are as much inescapably psychologists—of some sort—as psychologists are inescapably philosophers and theologians—of some sort). His goal was "to understand meanings as human life possibilities" (37), in part because he was convinced people failed to understand Christianity "because they did not understand human existence profoundly enough" (21). So Kierkegaard developed a psychology of human beings as spiritual, a psychology rooted in the ultimate context of life's meaning as viewed from a Christian perspective.

To summarize, some argue that Christian faith has an inextricably narrative character, involving a particular understanding about the ultimate context of human experience. So human existence needs to be understood in a particular way, as spiritual. This means a psychology profound enough to account for our spiritual nature and our place in that narrative is needed. If we do not have a sufficiently rich psychology, we prevent people from seeing the true nature of Christian faith. To try to account for "religious values in therapy" without a psychology of adequate depth is thus to blind us to what is needed to become fully Christian. A psychology of adequate depth must take meaning with utmost seriousness. Therefore, when the psychological approach to be used in understanding religion and values in psychotherapy is discussed, those wishing to be faithful to the Christian faith need to recognize that the stakes are very high.

Conclusion

Providing explanations of religion and values in therapy is vitally important. Christian ethics connects with that task on three levels: it contributes to scientific psychology by suggesting hypotheses; it addresses what is valuable and life's ultimate context, elements of explanation beyond the scope of science; and it may challenge traditional approaches in psychology by calling for richer psychological explanations of religion and values in therapy, explanations including moral agency and meaning.

Beutler (1989) described two lines of empirical investigation for those attempting to specify the values of most importance to therapy: "(1) assessing the values that distinguish and characterize patients and therapists, and (2) assessing the differential influence that specific patient and therapist values have on treatment process and outcome" (8).

Explanations that draw upon both psychology and theology (whether from a strictly scholarly motivation or as a foundation for clinical practice) need two, and possibly three, additional approaches:

Assessing therapy in terms of *goodness, rightness, and virtue*. This is the ethical task: Which therapy outcomes are good outcomes? With which values ought therapy be laden? What kind of value influence should occur in therapy? What can the deliberative, prescriptive, and relational motifs of Christian ethics, and community and character, contribute to the needed dialogue with "secular" psychotherapeutic theorists and practitioners about these issues?

Assessing the *ultimate context* of life. This is the theological task: What is that ultimate context? Which perspective or perspectives point to it most clearly and deeply? What does Scripture say? What theological traditions need to be considered? What is God's nature and how is God involved in history? in therapy? What is the role of the Holy Spirit in therapy? How should human behavior, including that in therapy, involve spiritual maturity? guilt? repentance? forgiveness? reconciliation? grace? freedom?

Assessing the *meaning* of moral and religious aspects of therapy—using the concepts of agency, intentionality, and narrative. This is the interpretive task: What is the meaning of therapy? for a particular person? of a particular moment in therapy? the ethical meaning? the religious meaning? How is moral agency exercised in therapy? by therapist? by client? What are the limits of that freedom? What does the client intend? the therapist? intend regarding mental health? regarding moral health? regarding spiritual health? In addressing those questions, how can therapy narratives, for example, case histories, help? ethical narratives, for example, stories of ethically praiseworthy or morally tragic persons? religious narratives, for example, stories from Scripture or about spiritually praiseworthy persons alive today?

The last is, of course, most controversial. Some deny it can be helpful and argue that only standard empirical psychology and traditional theology should be used. Others see it as helpful, but answer, "Yes, but is it psychology?" with a hearty no.

Suppose we assume the last task contributes to explanation in some way. On one level it perhaps matters little whether it is given the honorific title *psychological*. Those who want a comprehensive understanding of religion and values in therapy (or seek integrated personal growth joining mental, moral, and spiritual health) will address meaning whatever its disciplinary home. But on another level, this approach uses terms, like perception, intention, motivation, attitudes, and values, that certainly appear to be psychological. And if bringing moral agency and meaning within psychology enables us and clients to better see what is good, right, virtuous, and spiritually mature, to better see the grace of God in Christ, there may be reason for such an inclusion. There is historical precedent: The psychology of William James, Rambo (1980) notes, "delineated the human capacities which enable a person to engage in vigorous moral agency for the improvement of the community" (50); and Kierkegaard argued that a more profound psychology is vitally important—so persons can become truly Christian, that is, truly human. Perhaps, then, the choice of whether to include questions of freedom and meaning within psychology is not simply a scientific or disciplinary decision, but also one inescapably ethical and spiritual.

In summary, Christian ethics needs to be connected to explanations of religion and values in therapy. Because such explanations are important in both research and practice, the Christian psychologist ought to pay close attention to what both the psychotherapeutic disciplines and Christian ethics have to say. Rigorous reflection on both—and on their connections—is absolutely essential. Often the two approaches can be reconciled; sometimes a conflict requires us to choose what, or whom, we will serve.

References

Barbour, I. G. 1974. *Myths, models, and paradigms*. New York: Harper and Row.

Bergin, A. E. 1980. Psychotherapy and religious values. *Journal of Consulting and Clinical Psychology* 48: 170–84.

———. 1985. Proposed values for guiding and evaluating counseling and psychotherapy. *Counseling and Values* 29: 99–116.

Beutler, L. E. 1981. Convergence in counseling and psychotherapy: A current look. *Clinical Psychology Review* 1: 79–101.

_____. 1989. *Psychotherapy and religious values: An update.* Paper presented at the annual meeting of the American Psychological Association, New Orleans, August.

Birch, B. C., and L. L. Rasmussen. 1989. *Bible and ethics in the Christian life.* Rev. ed. Minneapolis: Augsburg.

Browning, D. 1987. *Religious thought and the modern psychologies: A critical conversation in the theology of culture.* Philadelphia: Fortress.

Clayton, P. 1989. *Explanation from physics to theology: An essay in rationality and religion.* New Haven: Yale Univ. Press.

Donahue, M. J. 1989. Disregarding theology in the psychology of religion: Some examples. *Journal of Psychology and Theology* 17: 329–35.

Evans, C. S. 1977. *Preserving the person: A look at the human sciences.* Downers Grove, Ill.: InterVarsity.

_____. 1989. *Wisdom and humanness in psychology: Prospects for a Christian approach.* Grand Rapids: Baker.

_____. 1990. *Søren Kierkegaard's Christian psychology: Insight for counseling and pastoral care.* Grand Rapids: Zondervan.

Gergen, K. J. 1986. Correspondence versus autonomy in the language of understanding human action. In *Metatheory in social science: Pluralisms and subjectivities*, ed. D. W. Fiske and R. A. Shweder, 136–62. Chicago: Univ. of Chicago Press.

Gerkin, C. 1984. *The living human document: Revisioning pastoral counseling in a hermeneutical mode.* Nashville: Abingdon.

Hauerwas, S. 1975. *Character and the Christian life: A study in theological ethics.* San Antonio: Trinity Univ. Press.

_____. 1977. *Truthfulness and tragedy.* Notre Dame: Univ. of Notre Dame Press.

_____. 1981. *A community of character: Toward a constructive Christian social ethic.* Notre Dame: Univ. of Notre Dame Press.

Hauerwas, S., and L. G. Jones, eds. 1989. *Why narrative? Readings in narrative theology.* Grand Rapids: Eerdmans.

Hill, P. C. 1989. Implications for integration from a new philosophy of psychology as science. *Journal of Psychology and Christianity* 8(1): 61–74.

Jodock, D. 1989. *The church's Bible: Its contemporary authority.* Minneapolis: Fortress.

Kelly, T. A. 1990. The role of values in psychotherapy: A critical review of process and outcome effects. *Clinical Psychology Review* 10: 171–86.

Lindbeck, G. A. 1984. *The nature of doctrine: Religion and theology in a postliberal age.* Philadelphia: Westminster.

Long, E. L., Jr. 1967. *A survey of Christian ethics.* New York: Oxford Univ. Press.

_____. 1982. *A recent survey of Christian ethics.* New York: Oxford Univ. Press.

MacIntyre, A. 1984. *After virtue: A study in moral theory.* 2d ed. Notre Dame: Univ. of Notre Dame Press.

McAdams, D. P., and R. L. Ochberg, eds. 1988. *Psychobiography and life narratives.* Durham, N.C.: Duke Univ. Press.

McMinn, M. R. 1984. Religious values and client-therapist matching in psychotherapy. *Journal of Psychology and Theology* 12: 24–33.

Meilaender, G. C. 1984. *The theory and practice of virtue.* Notre Dame: Univ. of Notre Dame Press.

Messer, S. B., L. A. Sass, and R. L. Woolfolk, eds. 1988. *Hermeneutics and psychological theory: Interpretive perspectives on personality, psychotherapy, and psychopathology.* New Brunswick, N. J.: Rutgers Univ. Press.

Muller, R., and H. Vande Kemp. 1985. On psychologists' uses of "Calvinism." *American Psychologist* 40: 466–68.

Niebuhr, H. R. 1963. *The responsible self: An essay in Christian moral philosophy.* New York: Harper and Row.

O'Donohue, W. 1989. The (even) Bolder model: The clinical psychologist as metaphysician-scientist-practitioner. *American Psychologist* 44: 1460–68.

Packer, M. J. 1985. Hermeneutic inquiry in the study of human conduct. *American Psychologist* 40: 1081–93.

Rambo, L. R. 1980. Ethics, evolution, and the psychology of William James. *Journal of the History of the Behavioral Sciences* 16: 50–57.

Ratzsch, D. 1987. *Philosophy of science: The natural sciences in Christian perspective.* Downers Grove, Ill.: InterVarsity.

Rosenthal, D. 1955. Changes in some moral values following psychotherapy. *Journal of Consulting Psychology* 19: 431–36.

Rychlak, J. F. 1979. *Discovering free will and personal responsibility.* New York: Oxford Univ. Press.

_____. 1988. Explaining helping relationships through learning theories and the question of human agency. *Counseling and Values* 32: 83–92.

Schwartz, B. 1990. The creation and destruction of value. *American Psychologist* 45: 7–15.

Schwartz, S. H., and W. Bilsky. 1987. Toward a universal psychological structure of human values. *Journal of Personality and Social Psychology* 53: 550–62.

Shweder, R. A., and D. W. Fiske. 1986. Introduction: Uneasy social science. In *Metatheory in social science: Pluralisms and subjectivities*, ed. D. W. Fiske and R. A. Shweder, 1–18. Chicago: Univ. of Chicago Press.

Sittler, J. 1958. *The structure of Christian ethics*. Baton Rouge: Louisiana State Univ. Press.

Smedes, L. B. 1983. *Mere morality: What God expects from ordinary people*. Grand Rapids: Eerdmans.

Taylor, C. 1989. *Sources of the self: The making of the modern identity*. Cambridge, Mass.: Harvard Univ. Press.

Thielicke, H. 1979. *Theological ethics*, vol. 1, *Foundations*. Grand Rapids: Eerdmans. (Original work published 1958.)

Thiemann, R. F. 1985. *Revelation and theology: The gospel as narrated promise*. Notre Dame: Univ. of Notre Dame Press.

Tjeltveit, A. C. 1986. The ethics of value conversion in psychotherapy: Appropriate and inappropriate therapist influence on client values. *Clinical Psychology Review* 6: 515–37.

_____. 1989a. Dealing with value dilemmas in therapy. In *Innovations in clinical practice: A source book*, ed. P. A. Keller and S. R. Heyman, vol. 8, 405–15. Sarasota, Fla.: Professional Resource Exchange.

_____. 1989b. The impossibility of a psychology of the Christian religion: A theological perspective. *Journal of Psychology and Theology* 17: 205–12.

_____. 1989c. The ubiquity of models of human beings in psychotherapy: The need for rigorous reflection. *Psychotherapy* 26: 1–10.

Van Leeuwen, M. S. 1985. *The person in psychology: A contemporary Christian appraisal*. Grand Rapids: Eerdmans.

_____. 1988. Psychology's "two cultures": A Christian analysis. *Christian Scholar's Review* 28: 406–24.

Vitz, P. C. 1990. The use of stories in moral development: New psychological reasons for an old education method. *American Psychologist* 45: 709–20.

Worthington, E. L., Jr. 1988. Understanding the values of religious clients: A model and its application to counseling. *Journal of Counseling Psychology* 35: 166–74.

_____. 1989. *Religious values in psychotherapy: An update*. Paper presented at the annual meeting of the American Psychological Association, New Orleans, August.

11

Religious Values and Interventions in Lay Christian Counseling

SIANG-YANG TAN

Religious values in psychotherapy or counseling is an area that has received substantial attention in recent years in the general psychological literature (e.g., see Beit-Hallahmi 1975; Bergin 1980a, 1980b, 1983, 1988a, 1988b; Bergin and Jensen 1990; Bergin, Masters, and Richards 1987; Bergin, Stinchfield, Gaskin, Masters, and Sullivan 1988; Ellis 1980; Lovinger 1984; Miller and Martin 1988; Quackenbos, Privette, and Klentz 1986; Spero 1985; Spilka 1986; Stern 1985; Walls 1980; Worthington 1986, 1988), which included a recent special issue of *Psychotherapy* (vol. 27, no. 1, Spring 1990) on "Psychotherapy and Religion." The Christian literature on integrating psychotherapy or counseling and spirituality or Christian faith has also recently grown considerably (e.g., see Anderson 1990; Backus 1985; Benner 1987a, 1987b, 1988; Benner and Palmer 1986; Collins 1980, 1988; Crabb 1977, 1987, 1988; Finch 1989; Gilbert and Brock 1985, 1989; Jones 1989; Jones and Butman 1991; McLemore and Brokaw 1986; McMinn and Lebold 1989; Propst 1988; Seamands 1985; Southard 1989; Tan 1987a, 1987b, 1988a, 1990a; Tyrrell 1982; Ward 1977; Wright 1986), including an ongoing series of books entitled *Resources for Christian Counseling,* under the general editorship of Dr. Gary Collins and published by Word.

More specifically, Bergin and Jensen (1990) have pointed out that one-third of the American population still avow that religious commitment is the most important dimension of their lives, and another third consider religion as very important, according to recent Gallup surveys (*Religion in America*, 1985). Bergin and Jensen (1990) concluded:

> A majority of the population probably prefer an orientation to counseling and psychotherapy that is sympathetic, or at least sensitive, to a spiritual perspective. We need to better perceive and respond to this public need (Bergin 1988a; 1988b). Indeed, it is still evident that most people prefer counsel from clergy rather than mental health professionals (Veroff et al. 1981). Thus, while professional opposition to a spiritual framework is still evident (Ellis 1980; Seligman 1988), it is hard to justify (Bergin 1983).
>
> The importance of religiosity for many clients requires a careful re-education of therapists whose conceptual/clinical frameworks have room only for secular and naturalistic constructs. (6–7)

It should be noted that a Continuing Education Workshop led by Edward Shafranske, Siang-Yang Tan, and Robert J. Lovinger on "Psychotherapy with Religiously Committed Clients" (#108) was conducted for the first time recently at the 98th Annual Convention of the American Psychological Association, held in Boston, Massachusetts, August 1990. The registration for the workshop was full, reflecting the growing interest in further training and education in this crucial area.

Religious clients have often expressed concern about being misunderstood by a secular counselor or psychotherapist who might pathologize or ignore spiritual issues, fail to understand religious ideas and terminology, and negate revelation as valid epistemology (Worthington and Scott 1983). Orthodox Christians in particular have been found to prefer the use of prayer and the Scriptures in counseling or psychotherapy (Gass 1984), as well as counselors who are seen to have similar religious beliefs (Dougherty and Worthington 1982; Worthington and Gascoyne 1985).

While there appears to be a preference for religiously oriented counseling or psychotherapy by religious clients, it should be pointed out that such "religious therapy" is difficult to define precisely because it is not a unitary approach to therapy. For example, Worthington, Dupont, Berry, and Duncan (1988) found that Christian therapists used three spiritual guidance strategies (encouraging forgiving others, encouraging forgiving God, and assigning spiritual homework) with a wide range of frequencies, and gave quite divergent ratings of their effectiveness, although these strategies were perceived to be very helpful by clients.

More recent studies have found mental health professionals, including clinical psychologists, to have a significant degree of religious preference or affiliation (e.g., see Bergin and Jensen 1990; Shafranske and Malony 1990). In one study, 80% of mental health professionals stated that they have some type of religious preference [with the most common group (38%) being Protestants], and 41% claimed they attend religious services regularly, but only 29% felt that religious matters are important in therapeutic work with clients (Bergin and Jensen 1990).

In another survey of clinical psychologists in particular, similar results were found, with 71% of the respondents being affiliated with an organized religion and 41% with regular attendance at religious services (Shafranske and Malony 1990). However, this study also found that clinical psychologists in general appreciated the religious and spiritual aspects of their clients' experiences, although 55% agreed that it was inappropriate to use religious Scripture or texts in therapy, and 68% felt it was inappropriate for a psychologist to pray with a client. About 85% of the respondents indicated they had little or no training in the area of psychology and religion.

Professional counselors and therapists, therefore, appear to be personally more religiously or spiritually oriented today than in the past, but the majority are still not likely to employ explicit religious interventions, like the use of prayer and Scripture, in therapy. Religious clients, on the other hand, especially Christian clients, seem to prefer more explicit forms of religiously-oriented counseling and therapy, although one recent study suggested that the need for religiously-oriented counselors may not be as great as some have claimed (Wyatt and Johnson 1990). While the professional counseling or psychotherapy field may still be somewhat reticent about the use of religious values and interventions in therapy, the field of lay Christian counseling is definitely more open.

Lay Christian counseling is a field that has also grown significantly in recent years, and has become an important part of current Christian ministry and local church contexts (see Tan 1981, 1987, 1988b, 1989a, 1990b, 1991). Collins (1986) has described lay counselors as nonprofessional or paraprofessional counselors who lack the training, education, experience, or credentials to be professional therapists, but who nevertheless are involved in helping people cope with personal problems. Lay Christian counseling or helping is therefore lay counseling done by Christians, usually within an explicitly Christian or biblically-based model or framework of people-helping (e.g., Tan 1981, 1991).

Overview of Lay Christian Counseling

Three basic levels, categories, or models of lay Christian counseling have been described (see Tan 1988b, 1989a, 1991). The first is the "informal, spontaneous" model, which assumes that lay Christian counseling should take place spontaneously and informally in relationships and interactions already present in the existing structures of the church or other religious organization and hence only some basic caring or helping skills training should be made available to as many leaders and interested members in the church or organization as possible. The second is the "informal, organized" model, which assumes that lay Christian counseling should be a well-supervised and organized ministry that should still occur in informal settings (homes, hospitals, restaurants) as far as possible. The third and final one is the "formal, organized" model, which assumes that lay Christian counseling should be an organized and well-supervised ministry to be conducted in a more formal way, by means of a lay counseling center or service established in a local church or parachurch organization.

It is difficult to estimate the number of churches and parachurch organizations involved in each of the models or levels of lay Christian counseling ministry, but it is probably accurate to state that the majority of churches are involved more in the "informal, spontaneous" model where organized, ongoing lay counselor training and regular supervision are absent.

However, a significant number of churches have become involved in the "informal, organized" model of lay Christian counseling ministry, which is also particularly appropriate for ethnic minority churches where the stigma against formal counseling may still be great (see Tan 1989b). A good example of such a model is the Stephen Series on Christian caregiving developed by Kenneth Haugk (see Haugk 1984), which is currently being used in more than 2500 congregations in 58 denominations in all 50 states in the United States, 7 provinces in Canada, and 6 other countries. From 1978–1989, 50 Leader's Training Courses have been held, with a total of 9468 Stephen Leaders trained in Christian caregiving or lay helping skills, including a 50-hour training program [for more information contact Stephen Ministries, 1325 Boland, St. Louis, MO 63117, tel. (314) 645–5511].

Another good example of this second model of lay Christian counseling ministry is the Lay Pastors Ministry developed by Melvin J. Steinbron (see Steinbron 1987), which includes lay pastoral care and counseling. Steinbron started this ministry in 1978 with only five lay people when he was Minister of Pastoral Care at College Hill Presbyterian Church in Cincinnati, Ohio. It has now expanded to at least 36 states in the United States, 5 Canadian provinces, and 2 foreign countries, with a network of churches that have equipped their lay people to provide pastoral care and counseling [for further information, Steinbron can be contacted at Hope Presbyterian Church, 7132 Portland Avenue S., Minneapolis, MN 55423, tel. (612) 866–4055].

A growing number of local churches are also involved with the "formal, organized" model of lay Christian counseling. Sturkie and Bear (1989) have described the following four successful ones: Lay Counseling Ministry of the La Canada Presbyterian Church in La Canada, California; Neighbors Who Care—Lay Counseling Ministry of the Neighborhood Church in Bellevue, Washington; Christian Counseling Ministry of the Elmbrook Church in Waukesha, Wisconsin; and the North Heights

Lutheran Church Counseling Clinic of the North Heights Lutheran Church in Roseville, Minnesota. Other local churches that have (or had) successful lay counseling centers or services using the "formal, organized" model include Peoples Church of Montreal in Canada (which no longer has an active lay counseling service), and North Park Community Chapel in London, Ontario, Canada (see Tan 1991); First Presbyterian Church in Boulder, Colorado; College Hill Presbyterian Church in Cincinnati, Ohio, and a number of other local churches in Southern California, for example, Sierra Madre Congregational Church, Arcadia Presbyterian Church, Glenkirk Presbyterian Church, Bel Air Presbyterian Church, Hollywood Presbyterian Church, Rolling Hills Covenant Church, and First Evangelical Free Church of Fullerton.

Lay counseling ministries have also been extended beyond the local church context to parachurch organizations (e.g., Youth For Christ, Young Life, and the Navigators), prison ministries, retirement and nursing homes, Christian mental health centers or programs (e.g., New Directions Counseling Center in the San Francisco Bay Area), and missions (see Tan 1991).

Lay Christian counseling is therefore a widespread ministry today that continues to mushroom and grow both within and beyond the local church context. In both the "informal, organized" and "formal, organized" models, which will be the primary focus of this chapter, systematic and ongoing training and supervision in effective lay Christian counseling or helping skills are provided. The role of religious values and interventions, and more specifically, Christian or biblical values and spiritual interventions like the use of prayer and the Scriptures, explicit discussion of spiritual issues, and referral to church or parachurch groups (see Tan 1988a, 1990a) in such lay Christian counseling will now be considered under two major headings: the findings of a survey of 15 evangelical church-based lay counseling ministries conducted by the Center for Church Renewal in Plano, Texas; and a brief review of some well-known existing training programs for lay Christian counselors.

Lay Counseling Survey Findings

A survey of 15 evangelical church-based lay counseling ministries (utilizing primarily the "formal, organized" and/or "informal, organized" models) was conducted in 1986 by the Center for Church Renewal in Plano, Texas [for further information, a copy of the "Lay Counseling Survey" is available from Pastor Floyd Elliott, Director of Counseling and Family Renewal, Center for Church Renewal, 200 Chisholm Place, Suite 228, Plano, TX 75075, tel. (214) 423–4262; also see chap. 10 of Tan 1991].

The 15 churches surveyed ranged in size from 450 to 9000 members with 14 of them describing themselves as "large," and none of them as rural (5 described themselves as urban and 10 as suburban). They represented a variety of denominational affiliations (e.g., Assemblies of God [1], Bible [1], Christian Church [1], Conservative Baptist [2], Evangelical Presbyterian [1], Independent [1], Missionary Church [1], Presbyterian Church USA [5], Reformed Churches of America [1], and Southern Baptist Churches [2]—one church belonged to both the Conservative and Southern Baptist denominations), geographical locations, and lay counseling philosophies and models. They provided information in response to the survey in three major areas: lay counselor training, lay counseling, and evaluation. Only information relevant to the use of religious values and interventions in the areas of lay counselor training and lay counseling will now be briefly summarized.

Lay counselor training. The average length of the lay counselor training programs provided was about eight months, with eight churches having training programs that lasted six months or less. The average number of classes conducted was 36, with a range from 6 to 135. Most of the training classes were held on a weekly basis, lasting 1–2 hours each class.

Of the 13 churches that responded to a question on the survey concerning the content of the training program, 4 stated that they were heavily influenced by Larry Crabb's lay counselor training approach (i.e., "biblical counseling"), although they also described their training content or curriculum as eclectic. Two other churches used mainly the Stephen Series or Ministry materials for their training program. One church used only Gerard Egan's *The Skilled Helper,* and another only Gary Collins's *People Helper Pack.*

The most frequently mentioned training topics included the following, with their frequencies provided in parentheses: counseling skills (12), training for specific issues (9), crisis counseling (8), marital counseling (8), use of the Bible in counseling (8), theology of human nature (7), theology of change (7), how or when to refer (5), relationship of psychology and religion (4), and self-understanding in lay counseling (2). Other more specific topics mentioned only once included the following: authority of Scripture, adult personality inventory, assertiveness training, assessment/diagnosis, categories of problems, Christian thinking, communication process, confidentiality, depression, feelings, issues of counseling, legal issues, organization, philosophy of counseling, prayer, psychopathology, relating to others, sin, telephone care, and thinking through your faith.

Lay counseling. The types of counseling situations in which the trained lay counselors minister included the following, with their frequencies mentioned given in parentheses: parenting problems (12), depression (11), marital disputes (11), grief (10), premarital (10), drugs/alcohol abuse (8), self-image (7), anxiety (7), anger (6), child abuse (5), guilt (5), suicide (4), teen pregnancy (4), extramarital affairs (4), vocational (3), relationships (3), adjustment difficulties (3), adolescents (2), shut-ins (2), support counseling (2), family (2), and death (2). The counseling situations, therefore, included a wide range, from relatively light calling activity or visitation to more serious situations like suicide, substance abuse, and marital difficulties.

When the churches surveyed were asked about their philosophy of counseling and more specifically which theorist(s) most directly influenced their counseling model and ministry, most of the churches described themselves as philosophically eclectic. However, 10 of the 15 mentioned Reality Therapy (William Glasser) as influential in shaping their philosophy of counseling. Other theorists mentioned at least twice included the following, with their frequencies of mention provided in parentheses: Larry Crabb (7), Norm Wright (3), Jay Adams (2), Gerard Egan (2), Gary Collins (2), Kenneth Haugk and the Stephen Series (2), Carl Rogers (2), and Virginia Satir (2). Among the theorists mentioned once were Assagioli, the Bobgans, Bowen, Ellis, Carkhuff, Friedman, Meier, Minirth, Walters, Welter, and Worthington. From these survey findings, it appears therefore that evangelical churches with lay counseling ministries tend to use a variety of training materials including both secular as well as Christian authors. However, a strong emphasis on a biblical perspective to people-helping (e.g., by the influence of authors such as Crabb, Wright, Adams, Collins, and Haugk) including the use of Christian values and spiritual interventions (like the use of Scripture) is evident in the answers given on the survey. Such churches are also involved in helping people with a wide range of problems, so that the importance of ongoing training and supervision covering ethical and legal issues and when and how to refer cannot be overemphasized.

While the findings of the lay counseling survey just mentioned are helpful and interesting, the limitations of such a survey should also be pointed out. First, the number of churches surveyed was relatively small (i.e., 15). Second, a significant majority of the churches (i.e., 14) were relatively large ones, and none of the churches was located in a rural area. Hence, while some attempt was made to survey a variety of evangelical churches with different denominational affiliations, geographical locations, and lay counseling models and philosophies, the survey results are limited to a small sample of relatively large evangelical churches in urban or suburban parts of the United States. The findings from the survey should, therefore, not be generalized to other smaller evangelical churches, to other nonevangelical churches, to parachurch organizations and other contexts of lay counseling ministry, or to other countries. Finally, there are also some methodological limitations inherent in the use of the survey method for collecting data or information. Questions of reliability and validity are crucial ones, since the survey method often requires answers that are based on memory or retrospective accounts.

Despite the limitations mentioned, the lay counseling survey conducted by the Center for Church Renewal is still helpful and is a significant step in the right direction. More comprehensive surveys are needed before definitive conclusions can be made about lay Christian counseling in general.

A Brief Review of Some Lay Christian Counselor Training Programs

Several well-known training programs for lay Christian counselors, some of which were mentioned in the survey findings, will now be briefly reviewed. All of them are founded on biblically-based models of lay Christian counseling or people-helping, with an explicit commitment to biblical, Christian values and perspectives, including the use of the Scriptures and prayer with clients, and sharing the gospel or Christian faith with non-Christian clients where appropriate.

Crabb (1977) has developed a well-known biblical counseling approach (which emphasizes the need to change unbiblical, erroneous thinking to biblical thinking based on the Scriptures) for the training of lay Christian counselors (also see Crabb 1982, 1987, 1988; and Crabb and Allender 1984). He has also written a training manual that is available only through the Institute of Biblical Counseling and its workshops or seminars on biblical counseling.

Collins (1976) has described a "people-helping" (or discipleship counseling) approach to lay Christian counseling. He has put together the People Helper Pack containing a text, a growthbook, and audiotapes for training lay Christians in basic helping skills in 12 sessions. More recently he has developed a more extensive and comprehensive training program in Christian counseling that can be used for training lay as well as professional Christian counselors. It is called the Christian Counselor's Library. Produced by Word, the Christian Counselor's Library contains 40 audio cassettes, a counselor's manual, counselee worksheets, and a copy of his revised textbook on Christian counseling (Collins 1988).

Adams (1970, 1973) is well-known for his nouthetic counseling approach (centered in the Scriptures), which he has also developed for use in training lay nouthetic counselors (Adams 1981), including a "Competent to Counsel" Training Kit that is available from the National Association of Evangelicals (450 Gunderson Drive, Wheaton, IL 60187). A similar approach, called the Biblical Counseling Training Program, with two foundational training courses and three levels of advanced courses, has been developed by John C. Broger and made available through the Biblical Counseling Foundation [P. O. Box 925, Rancho Mirage, CA 92270, tel. (619) 773–2667].

Tan (1981, 1986, 1987b; also see chap. 7 of Tan 1991) has described a basic (12-session) as well as a more extensive year-long training program for lay Christian counselors, using a biblically-based, largely cognitive-behavioral model of Christian counseling, which borrows heavily from authors like Crabb, Collins, Adams, and a few others. More recently, he has emphasized the need to focus more on the power and gifts of the Holy Spirit in lay counseling ministries (Tan 1990b).

Sweeten (1987) has an approach to lay Christian counseling, which he calls "discipleship counseling," that attempts to integrate psychology, Christian theology, and the power of the Holy Spirit. He has produced books, audiotapes, and videotapes, and he conducts "Counseling with Power" seminars for training lay Christian counselors and pastors. His training program has four major components: "Apples of Gold I and II," (focusing on interpersonal helping skills), "Rational Christian Thinking," and "Breaking Free from the Past." It is being used in 40 states and 25 countries. [Dr. Gary Sweeten can be reached at Equipping Ministries International, 4015 Executive Park Drive, Suite 309, Cincinnati, OH 45241, tel. (513) 769–5353].

Lukens (1983) has proposed a model for training paraprofessional or lay Christian counselors, with the following six sequential levels of training, each lasting 8–10 weeks in duration: Level 1—"Body Life Skills I"; Level 2—"Theory and Theology"; Level 3—"Personal Awareness"; Level 4—"Body Life Skills II"; Level 5—"Practicum" (a minimum of 40 client hours and 10 supervision hours); and Level 6—"Advanced Training," in areas like marital and family counseling, vocational and financial counseling, and prayer for inner healing and deliverance. [Dr. Horace Lukens can be contacted at 7320 South Yale, Tulsa, OK 74136, tel. (918) 496–9588.]

As mentioned earlier, Haugk (1984) has written a helpful book on lay Christian caregiving as a way of life that serves as a textbook with other training materials for his Stephen Series of lay caring ministry. Lay caregivers, called Stephen Ministers in his training program, are trained for 50 hours in a variety of topics, including the effective use of the traditional resources of Christianity like prayer and the use of Scriptures. While the Stephen Series focuses on lay caregiving (or lay pastoral care), it involves a certain degree of lay Christian counseling or helping.

Similar to Crabb's biblical counseling approach, Backus (1985) has written a textbook for training lay Christian counselors in Misbelief Therapy, which he developed as a Christian, biblical approach to cognitive-behavior therapy, using the Scriptures to overcome misbeliefs or erroneous, unbiblical beliefs. [Dr. William Backus can be contacted at 2701 North Rice Street, Roseville, MN 55113, tel. (612) 484–2049].

A more recent lay Christian counselor training program has been developed by William H. "Skip" Hunt, who is president of Christian Helplines, Inc., a national association of Christian telephone counseling ministries formed over three years ago. Hunt has written a number of training courses, including "How Can I Help?" which is a college level course in personal counseling and evangelism that prepares the ordinary lay person to help friends in crisis. It is also used by Christian crisis centers across the country to train staff and volunteers. [Skip Hunt can be contacted at P. O. Box 10855, Tampa, FL 33679, tel. (813) 874–5509].

Another lay counselor training program that has been recently developed uses mainly videocassettes with accompanying leader's guide and learner's manuals/textbooks. It consists of four courses (Introduction, Relationship, Realization, and Responsibility), featuring people like Dr. Joyce Hulgus, H. Norman Wright, Rev. Rex E. Johnson, and Richard J. Mohline on videotape. Each course involves eight weekly sessions of 2-1/2 to 3 hours' duration, with additional homework assignments. This unique videotape training program is available from Innovations in Learning, 7018 El Paseo St., Long Beach, CA 90815.

Other relatively well-known books relevant to the training of lay Christian counselors include Baldwin (1988), Bobgan and Bobgan (1985), Drakeford and King (1988), Foster (1986), Grunlan and Lambrides (1984), Hughes (1982), Linquist (1976), Miller (1978), Morris (1974), Peterson (1980), Sala (1989), Solomon (1977), Somerville (1978), Steinbron (1987), Sturkie and Bear (1989), Varenhorst with Sparks (1988), Walters (1983), Welter (1978, 1985), Worthington (1982, 1985), and Wright (1977).

The literature available for the training of lay Christian counselors has therefore mushroomed in recent years. It appears that the most widely used and better known training programs and books or materials are those based on biblical models of people-helping that explicitly affirm Christian values and spiritual interventions like prayer and the use of Scripture. There is still a need, however, for more critical evaluation of such programs and models (see Hurding 1988; cf. Browning 1987, and Tan 1991).

Concluding Comments

Religious values and interventions, especially explicitly biblical values and Christian spiritual interventions, therefore occupy a central place in the ministry of lay Christian counseling. They should also be incorporated more frequently and centrally in professional Christian therapy in order to practice what has been called "explicit integration in psychotherapy or Christian counseling" (Tan 1988a, 1990a). Such explicit integration, however, should be conducted in a clinically competent and ethically responsible way since the danger of abusing rather than appropriately using spiritual interventions and resources does exist. Nelson and Wilson (1984), in the context of professional psychotherapy, have provided some helpful ethical guidelines for sharing religious faith in psychotherapy, which can also be applied to the context of lay Christian counseling. They suggested that it is ethical for counselors and psychotherapists to share their religious faith and values if they are addressing problems that would be helped by spiritual intervention, if they are working within the client's belief system (so that counselors or therapists will not force their own beliefs on the client), and if they have carefully defined the therapy or counseling contract to include spiritual intervention. It is, therefore, important to clarify these issues at the beginning of counseling with clients.

It should also be pointed out that the limited research evidence available from two controlled studies comparing religious and nonreligious approaches to cognitive therapy have yielded conflicting findings, so that the superiority of a religious, Christian approach to cognitive therapy still has not been conclusively established (Pecheur and Edwards 1984; Propst 1980). In fact, a more recent dissertation study (Johnson 1990) comparing religious (Christian) and nonreligious rational-emotive therapy with religious (Christian) clients revealed no significant differences between the two forms of therapy, which were both found to be effective. More controlled and refined outcome studies are needed, however, before more definitive conclusions can be made. In particular, well-controlled outcome studies should be conducted on the relative effectiveness of Christian approaches to therapy that explicitly use counselors with appropriate spiritual gifts (e.g., exhortation or encouragement, healing, wisdom, knowledge, discerning of spirits, and mercy) who rely on the presence and power of the Holy Spirit and the use of spiritual resources like prayer and the Scriptures, versus Christian approaches that do not explicitly do so. The importance of other mediating factors like client variables, technique variables, and client-counselor match also warrant further attention.

In conclusion, it is proposed that a biblical approach to counseling (whether conducted by lay or professional Christian counselors) that explicitly utilizes Christian religious values or perspectives and interventions (e.g., prayer and the use of Scripture), and relies on appropriate spiritual gifts and the power and ministry of the Holy Spirit, makes unique contributions to counseling effectiveness, especially with religious, Christian clients. Further research is needed to determine the empirical validity of this proposal. It is encouraging to note that lay Christian counseling in general tends to be characterized by such a biblical approach to people-helping while not ignoring the need for systematic training in basic counseling or helping skills. It is hoped that professional Christian counseling or psychotherapy will also be more and more likewise characterized.

References

Adams, J. E. 1970. *Competent to counsel.* Grand Rapids: Baker.

_____. 1973. *The Christian counselor's manual.* Grand Rapids: Baker.

_____. 1981. *Ready to restore: The layman's guide to Christian counseling.* Grand Rapids: Baker.

Anderson, R. S. 1990. *Christians who counsel: The vocation of wholistic therapy.* Grand Rapids: Zondervan.

Backus, W. 1985. *Telling the truth to troubled people.* Minneapolis: Bethany House.

Baldwin, C. L. 1988. *Friendship counseling: Biblical foundations for helping others.* Grand Rapids: Zondervan.

Beit-Hallahmi, B. 1975. Encountering orthodox religion in psychotherapy. *Psychotherapy: Theory, Research and Practice* 11: 357–59.

Benner, D. G. 1988. *Psychotherapy and the spiritual quest.* Grand Rapids: Baker.

Benner, D. G., ed. 1987a. *Christian counseling and psychotherapy.* Grand Rapids: Baker.

_____, ed. 1987b. *Psychotherapy in Christian perspective.* Grand Rapids: Baker.

Benner, D. G., and S. L. Palmer. 1986. Psychotherapy and Christian faith. In *Psychology and the Christian faith*, ed. S. L. Jones, 156–77. Grand Rapids: Baker.

Bergin, A. E. 1980a. Psychotherapy and religious values. *Journal of Consulting and Clinical Psychology* 48: 95–105.

_____. 1980b. Religious and humanistic values: A reply to Ellis and Walls. *Journal of Consulting and Clinical Psychology* 48: 642–45.

_____. 1983. Religiosity and mental health: A critical reevaluation and meta-analysis. *Professional Psychology* 14: 170–84.

_____. 1988a. Three contributions of a spiritual perspective to counseling, psychotherapy and behavior change. *Counseling and Values* 33: 21–31.

_____. 1988b. The spiritual perspective is ecumenical and eclectic (rejoinder). *Counseling and Values* 33: 57–59.

Bergin, A. E., and J. P. Jensen. 1990. Religiosity of psychotherapists: A national survey. *Psychotherapy* 27: 3–7.

Bergin, A. E., K. S. Masters, and P. S. Richards. 1987. Religiousness and mental health reconsidered: A study of an intrinsically religious sample. *Journal of Counseling Psychology* 34: 197–204.

Bergin, A. E., R. D. Stinchfield, T. A. Gaskin, K. S. Masters, and C. E. Sullivan. 1988. Religious life-styles and mental health: An exploratory study. *Journal of Counseling Psychology* 35: 91–98.

Bobgan, M., and D. Bobgan. 1985. *How to counsel from Scripture.* Chicago: Moody.

Browning, D. S. 1987. *Religious thought and the modern psychologies.* Philadelphia: Fortress.

Collins, G. R. 1976. *How to be a people helper.* Santa Ana, Calif.: Vision House.

_____. 1986. *Innovative approaches to counseling.* Waco: Word.

_____. 1988. *Christian counseling: A comprehensive guide.* Rev. ed. Dallas: Word.

_____, ed. 1980. *Helping people grow: Practical approaches to Christian counseling.* Santa Ana, Calif.: Vision House.

Crabb, L. J. 1977. *Effective biblical counseling.* Grand Rapids: Zondervan.

_____. 1982. *The marriage builder.* Grand Rapids: Zondervan.

_____. 1987. *Understanding people: Deep longings for relationship.* Grand Rapids: Zondervan.

_____. 1988. *Inside out.* Colorado Springs: NavPress.

Crabb, L. J., Jr., and D. Allender. 1984. *Encouragement: The key to caring.* Grand Rapids: Zondervan.

Dougherty, S. G., and E. L. Worthington. 1982. Preferences of conservative and moderate Christians for four Christian counselors' treatment plans. *Journal of Psychology and Theology* 10: 346–54.

Drakeford, J. W., and C. V. King. 1988. *Wise counsel: Skills for lay counseling.* Nashville: The Sunday School Board of the Southern Baptist Convention.

Ellis, A. 1980. Psychotherapy and atheistic values: A response to A. E. Bergin's "Psychotherapy and religious values." *Journal of Consulting and Clinical Psychology* 48: 635–39.

Finch, J. G. 1989. *Intensive therapy and the three ways.* Pasadena, Calif.: Integration.

Foster, T. 1986. *Called to counsel.* Nashville: Oliver Nelson.

Gass, S. C. 1984. Orthodox Christian values related to psychotherapy and mental health. *Journal of Psychology and Theology* 12: 230–37.

Gilbert, M. G., and R. T. Brock, eds. 1985. *The Holy Spirit and counseling: Theology and theory.* Peabody, Mass.: Hendrickson.

_____. 1989. *The Holy Spirit and counseling: Principles and practice.* Peabody, Mass.: Hendrickson.

Grunlan, S., and D. Lambrides. 1984. *Healing relationships: A Christian's manual for lay counseling.* Camp Hill, Penn.: Christian Publications.

Haugk, K. C. 1984. *Christian caregiving: A way of life.* Minneapolis: Augsburg.

Hughes, S. 1982. *A friend in need.* Eastbourne, East Sussex: Kingsway.

Hurding, R. F. 1985. *The tree of healing.* Grand Rapids: Zondervan.

Johnson, W. B. 1990. *The comparative efficacy of religious and nonreligious rational-emotive therapy with religious clients.* Unpublished doctoral dissertation, Graduate School of Psychology, Fuller Theological Seminary, Pasadena, Calif.

Jones, S. L. 1989. Rational-emotive therapy in Christian perspective. *Journal of Psychology and Theology* 17: 110–20.

Jones, S. L., and R. E. Butman. 1991. *Modern psychotherapies: A comprehensive Christian appraisal.* Downers Grove, Ill.: InterVarsity.

Lindquist, S. E. 1976. *Action helping skills.* Fresno, Calif.: Link-Care Foundation.

Lovinger, R. J. 1984. *Working with religious issues in therapy.* New York: Jason Aronson.

Lukens, H. C., Jr. 1983. Training of paraprofessional Christian counselors: A model proposed. *Journal of Psychology and Christianity* 2(2): 61–66.

McLemore, C. W., and D. W. Brokaw. 1986. Psychotherapy as a spiritual enterprise. In *Psychology and the Christian faith*, ed. S. L. Jones, 178–95. Grand Rapids: Baker.

McMinn, M. R., and C. J. Lebold. 1989. Collaborative efforts in cognitive therapy with religious clients. *Journal of Psychology and Theology* 17: 101–9.

Miller, P. M. 1978. *Peer counseling in the church.* Scottsdale, Penn.: Herald.

Miller, W. R., and J. E. Martin, eds. 1988. *Behavior therapy and religion: Integrating spiritual and behavioral approaches to change.* Newbury Park, Calif.: Sage.

Morris, P. D. 1974. *Love therapy.* Wheaton, Ill.: Tyndale House.

Nelson, A. A., and W. P. Wilson. 1984. The ethics of sharing religious faith in psychotherapy. *Journal of Psychology and Theology* 12: 15–23.

Pecheur, D., and K. J. Edwards. 1984. A comparison of secular and religious versions of cognitive therapy with depressed Christian college students. *Journal of Psychology and Theology* 12: 45–54.

Peterson, E. 1980. *Who cares? A handbook of Christian counseling.* Wilton, Conn.: Morehouse-Barlow.

Propst, R. L. 1980. The comparative efficacy of religious and nonreligious imagery for the treatment of mild depression in religious individuals. *Cognitive Therapy and Research* 4: 167–78.

_____. 1988. *Psychotherapy in a religious framework.* New York: Human Sciences.

Quackenbos, S., G. Privette, and B. Klentz. 1986. Psychotherapy and religion: Rapprochement or antithesis? *Journal of Counseling and Development* 65: 82–85.

Religion in America. 1985. Princeton, N.J.: The Gallup Report. Report No. 236.

Sala, H. 1989. *Coffee cup counseling: How to be ready when friends ask for help.* Nashville: Nelson.

Seamands, D. 1985. *Healing of memories.* Wheaton, Ill.: Victor.

Seligman, L. 1988. Invited commentary: Three contributions of a spiritual perspective to counseling, psychotherapy, and behavior change (Allen E. Bergin). *Counseling and Values* 33: 55–56.

Shafranske, E. P., and H. N. Malony. 1990. Clinical psychologists' religious and spiritual orientation and their practice of psychotherapy. *Psychotherapy* 27: 72–78.

Solomon, C. R. 1977. *Counseling with the mind of Christ.* Old Tappan, N.J.: Revell.

Somerville, R. B. 1978. *Help for hotliners: A manual for Christian telephone crisis counselors.* Phillipsburg, N.J.: Presbyterian and Reformed.

Southard, S. 1989. *Theology and therapy.* Dallas: Word.

Spero, M. H., ed. 1985. *Psychotherapy of the religious patient.* Springfield, Ill.: Charles C. Thomas.

Spilka, B. 1986. Spiritual issues: Do they belong in psychological practice? Yes—but! *Psychotherapy in Private Practice* 4: 93–100.

Steinbron, M. J. 1987. *Can the pastor do it alone? A model for preparing lay people for lay pastoring.* Ventura, Calif.: Regal.

Stern, E. M., ed. 1985. *Psychotherapy and the religiously committed patient.* New York: Haworth.

Sturkie, J., and G. Bear. 1989. *Christian peer counseling: Love in action.* Dallas: Word.

Sweeten, G. R. 1987. Lay helpers and the caring community. *Journal of Psychology and Christianity* 6(2): 14–20.

Tan, S.-Y. 1981. Lay counseling: The local church. *CAPS Bulletin* 7(1): 15–20.

_____. 1986. Training paraprofessional Christian counselors. *The Journal of Pastoral Care* 40(4): 296–304.

_____. 1987a. Cognitive-behavior therapy: A biblical approach and critique. *Journal of Psychology and Theology* 15(2): 103–12.

_____. 1987b. Intrapersonal integration: The servant's spirituality. *Journal of Psychology and Christianity* 6(1): 34–39.

_____. 1987d. Training lay Christian counselors: A basic program and some preliminary data. *Journal of Psychology and Christianity* 6(2): 57–61.

_____. 1988a. *Explicit integration in psychotherapy.* Invited paper presented at the International Congress on Christian Counseling, Atlanta, November.

_____. 1988b. Lay Christian counseling: Present status and future directions. Invited paper presented at the International Congress on Christian Counseling, Atlanta, November.

_____. 1989a. Lay counseling (An interview). *The Christian Journal of Psychology and Counseling* 4(2): 1–5.

_____. 1989b. Psychopathology and culture: The Asian-American context. *Journal of Psychology and Christianity* 8(2): 61–75.

_____. 1990a. Explicit integration in Christian counseling (An interview). *The Christian Journal of Psychology and Counseling* 5(2): 7–13.

_____. 1990b. Lay Christian counseling: The next decade. *Journal of Psychology and Christianity* 9(3): 46–52.

_____. 1991. *Lay counseling: Equipping Christians for a helping ministry.* Grand Rapids: Zondervan.

_____, ed. 1987c. Lay Christian counseling. (Special issue) *Journal of Psychology and Christianity* 6(2): 1–84.

Tyrrell, B. J. 1982. *Christotherapy II.* New York: Paulist.

Varenhorst, B. B., with L. Sparks. 1988. *Training teenagers for peer ministry.* Loveland, Colo.: Group.

Veroff, J., R. A. Kulka, and E. Douvan. 1981. *Mental health in America.* New York: Basic.

Walls, G. B. 1980. Values and psychotherapy: A comment on "Psychotherapy and religious values." *Journal of Consulting and Clinical Psychology* 48: 640–41.

Walters, R. P. 1983. *The amity book: Exercises in friendship skills.* Grand Rapids: Christian Helpers, Inc.

Ward, W. O. 1977. *The Bible in counseling.* Chicago: Moody.

Welter, P. 1978. *How to help a friend.* Wheaton: Tyndale House.

Welter, P. 1985. *Connecting with a friend: Eighteen proven counseling skills to help you help others.* Wheaton: Tyndale House.

Worthington, E. L., Jr. 1982. *When someone asks for help: A practical guide for counseling.* Downers Grove, Ill.: InterVarsity.

_____. 1985. *How to help the hurting: When friends face problems with self-esteem, self-control, fear, depression, loneliness.* Downers Grove, Ill.: InterVarsity.

_____. 1986. Religious counseling: A review of published empirical research. *Journal of Counseling and Development* 64: 421–31.

_____. 1988. Understanding the values of religious clients: A model and its application to counseling. *Journal of Counseling* 35: 166–74.

Worthington, E. L., P. D. Dupont, J. T. Berry, and L. A. Duncan. 1988. Christian therapists' and clients' perceptions of religious psychotherapy in private and agency settings. *Journal of Psychology and Theology* 16: 282–93.

Worthington, E. L., and S. R. Gascoyne. 1985. Preferences of Christians and non-Christians for five Christian counselors' treatment plans: A partial replication and extension. *Journal of Psychology and Theology* 13: 29–41.

Worthington, E. L., and G. G. Scott. 1983. Goal selection for counseling with potentially religious clients by professional and student counselors in explicitly Christian or secular settings. *Journal of Psychology and Theology* 11: 318–29.

Wright, H. N. 1977. *Training Christians to counsel: A resource curriculum manual.* Eugene, Ore.: Harvest House.

Wright, H. N. 1986. *Self-talk, imagery, and prayer in counseling.* Waco: Word.

Wyatt, S. D., and R. W. Johnson. 1990. The influence of counselors' religious values on clients' perceptions of the counselor. *Journal of Psychology and Theology* 18: 158–65.

12

Proposed Agenda for a Spiritual Strategy in Personality and Psychotherapy

ALLEN E. BERGIN
AND I. REED PAYNE

The effort to implement spiritual values[1] in psychotherapy is a worthy goal, but we must remember that such an enterprise exists in a context. It is the purpose of this article to outline a broad spectrum of effort that must be pursued if value-oriented therapeutic practices are to attain optimal meaning and efficacy. We propose, therefore, that those who are motivated to develop such an approach join in addressing an agenda of tasks to be accomplished in establishing a spiritual strategy. We use the term *strategy* in keeping with the usage defined by Liebert and Spiegler (1990), who refer to the major approaches to personality and psychotherapy in this manner. Their text on personality is subtitled "Strategies and Issues" and they have avoided using the phrase *personality theories*.

1. By "spiritual values" we mean those deriving from our Judeo-Christian heritage. An eclectic, ecumenical spiritual strategy will likely also include approaches rooted in compatible values from diverse sources, both secular and religious.

The authors of this chapter are grateful to Mark Chamberlain, Patricia Loftus, and David Greaves for substantial assistance with this chapter. The work was supported by an intramural grant from the College of Family, Home and Social Sciences, Brigham Young University.

This important distinction implies that existing major approaches are not technically theories as such, but are strategies or approaches to the main issues of personality and therapeutic change. The modern versions of these strategies are actually collections of "micro-theories" concerning related topics rather than "macro-theories" that explain all behavior in a single overarching conceptualization. Strategies include concepts regarding the origins, development, and dynamics of personality, the organization or structure of personality, assessment or measurement of personality, and personality change. Liebert and Spiegler (1990) outline the details of the traditional theories within this structure, such as the psychoanalytic, dispositional, phenomenological, and behavioral strategies.

We suggest that specific approaches to therapy based upon Christian and other religious traditions are actually embedded in a broad array of assumptions and professional procedures that are part of the beginnings of a new "spiritual strategy" in the psychosocial and mental health fields. Although the specific assumptions on which these works rest are often not explicitly articulated, they exist and need to be specified more overtly as part of a plan for a comprehensive approach.

It is our view that a spiritual approach contributes distinctive factors to a strategy of personality and therapeutic change, but that such an approach also necessarily partakes of some characteristics of other approaches. It is our view that a spiritual approach contributes uniquely to a conception of human nature, a moral frame of reference and specific techniques of change. In addition, a spiritual approach, if it is to be a viable option in the professional domain, needs to be empirical, eclectic, and ecumenical. Finally, specialized aspects of a spiritual strategy can be denominationally specific and contribute meaningfully to the religious diversity and plurality that exists among the public clientele. As we proceed to outline each of these dimensions to a spiritual strategy, we will provide reference to articles that attempt to define each of these particular areas. When we have completed this outline, it will hopefully be much clearer how a value-oriented approach within a spiritual strategy can contribute to a more comprehensive understanding of personality and psychotherapy.

A Conception of Human Nature

To have a spiritual approach to psychology has profound implications for personality theory. The assumptions that this approach brings to theory are rooted in theology and have been outlined by several writers (Bergin 1988a, 1988b; Collins 1977, 1980). One of the essential points is recognizing the existence of a spiritual reality as a fundamental assumption. As we read in the Book of Job (32:8): "There is a spirit in man and the inspiration of the Almighty giveth them understanding." The exact nature of a person's spirit may be disputed in its details across denominations, but there is a clear agreement that the essential identity of a person is eternal, has a spiritual or an invisible aspect, and can respond to the spirit of God through prayer and other means of inspiration that have direct effects upon thought, feelings, and conduct. There are many other fundamentals that derive from a spiritual perception of the world and of man's place in it that could and should help to shape a new perspective on personality. Some of these concern "Identity," "Agency," "Integrity," "Power," "Intimacy," "Family," and "Value Systems." It is essential that the hard work required to develop and integrate such concepts be undertaken. Although hermeneutic, existential, humanistic, cognitive, and social constructionist thought all open the way to a spiritual approach to theory, none of these has bridged the secular-to-sacred gap. Transpersonal psychology attempts this but its all-inclusive style is alien to an approach rooted in biblical concepts and practices. While no truly systematic spiritual strategy has yet appeared, there are worthy beginnings in efforts to tie theology to concepts of personality and psychotherapy.

One example of this is Jones's (1989) attempt to show the relationships between a Christian perspective and rational-emotive theory and therapy. Jones points out a number of apparent similarities between the two perspectives that have been noted by other Christian writers; but his analysis is telling in that while there are some regions of overlap, such as the importance of beliefs in guiding behavior, there are actually many incompatibilities at a fundamental level. He notes that the rational-emotive conception of self is basically atomistic and that it "undermines persons seeing themselves as agents, as substantive selves; as responsible moral agents with continuous identities through life" (117). Another key point of potential conflict is in the definition of "rational." Theology suggests beliefs, such as *dependence* upon God, that may be viewed as irrational by secular theorists. We are thus challenged to show what healthy dependency is and how it is an integral aspect of human nature. Both the difficulties Jones identifies and the possibilities he outlines provide a meaningful attempt toward a Christian strategy of personality.

Spilka and Bridges (1989) provide another interesting effort at comparing and contrasting theological assumptions with psychological theories. They evaluate contemporary "process," "liberation," and "feminist" theologies and show certain parallels between them and social cognitive theory. "The importance of the role of the self and needs for meaning, control, and self-esteem are stressed, indicating that theology can serve as psychological theory that both psychology and theology might benefit from increased interaction between the disciplines" (343). The paper is not specifically denominational in orientation, but deals with modern struggles to interpret our understanding of God in relation to groups who have suffered social oppression and who seem to be alienated from traditional religious identifications. The authors note that one approach to process theology emphasizes the themes of God as "presence," "wisdom," and "power" (347). This apparently does not deny the additional biblical conceptions of God but attempts to show that "a sense of God's *presence* may be tied to feelings of self-worth." God as *wisdom* may be associated with meaningfulness through the faith that "no matter what threats and contingencies we may experience, God is faithful and is leading us to creative modes of dealing with problems" (347). Finally, God as *power* "may reflect personal capability in being able to influence the world" (347).

The notion is that if people can perceive God's influence along these dimensions then therapeutic change in one's life may be more likely. "Meaninglessness, powerlessness, and low self-esteem are correlates of cultural realities that deprive people of opportunities to realize their potential" (347). This type of thinking certainly has implications for a theory of personality and shows how such a theory can be enhanced by theological thought. A further task for a spiritual strategy would be to link traditional concepts of sin, forgiveness, and salvation in a significant way to meaning, a sense of personal capacity and self-esteem.

In sum, these articles demonstrate the fact that thoughtful people are struggling with the problem of developing a conceptual framework for a spiritual strategy. Human nature transcends the empirical with meaning emanating from relationships with God and fellow humans. We endorse such efforts and believe that as they become more systematic, a more powerful conceptual framework may be arrived at which can guide theory, research, and practice in personality and psychotherapy.

A Moral Frame of Reference

An important contribution of a spiritual perspective is that it anchors values in universal terms. Since evidence shows that psychotherapy is a value-laden process, this makes the spiritual strategy immediately and especially relevant to the therapeutic situation. Although therapists are often unaware of their particular moral frames of reference and especially how they impact upon clients, this situation is rapidly changing. It is becoming abundantly clear that values must be dealt with more systematically and effectively if therapeutic change is to be lasting. To be optimal, values must also affect one's life style and one's impact upon others (Bergin 1991).

No more powerful value themes could be invoked in this context than the teachings of Jesus Christ.[2] An eternal and universal morality can inform or impact professionals and their clientele in profound ways.

---

2. We begin with Jesus Christ because we revere him as our Lord and Savior; but we naturally also include the teachings of the biblical prophets and apostles and our own Latter-day Saint tradition. In addition, we respectfully rely upon compatible virtues and values that are emphasized in other traditions.

How to do this with efficacy and with respect for other noble traditions is an essential task for the future. For our purposes here, some illustrative work will suffice.

In contrast to earlier assertions that values are "relative" and that psychotherapy should be "value-free," it seems more likely (implicit though it may be) that there may be certain values which mental health care workers see as "better" or as underlying healthy adjustment. Many values "imply a frame of reference for guiding behavior and regulating life style so as to prevent or ameliorate psychopathologies . . ." (Bergin 1985, 106). Making these implicit values explicit in therapy, particularly in the spiritual realm, may in actuality promote freedom in the therapeutic environment by promoting specific and open deliberation about values (Bergin 1988a, 1988b).

In a national survey of mental health care workers, Jensen and Bergin (1988) found considerable consensus on values assessed to be pertinent to both mental health and psychotherapy. These included: a sense of being a free agent, a sense of identity and feelings of worth, being skilled in interpersonal communication, sensitivity, and nurturance, being genuine and honest, having self-control and personal responsibility, being committed in marriage, family, and other relationships, having orienting values and meaningful purposes, having deepened self-awareness and motivation for growth, having adaptive coping strategies for managing stresses and crises, finding fulfillment in work, and practicing good habits of physical health. These, in essence, are traditional values, which are correspondingly many of the same values that underlie practices and beliefs espoused in religious environments.

Sprinthall and McVay (1987) give examples of progress toward a generalized conception of universalistic values that may bridge the gap between such "clinical" values and spiritual values. They note an increasing consensus between religious and secular value theories in a common ground of universal and humane principles. While religion as an organized system of faith concerns itself with universals, spirituality *is* a universal. Dombeck and Karl (1987) state, "Every person can be understood to have a spiritual life, although some persons do not subscribe to any established religion" (184).

When value-related problems are encountered in therapy, both the client's and the therapist's values may need to be examined or articulated to provide an ethical and open atmosphere. Though a therapist's and client's values may differ at points, this need not discourage value exploration and problem solving. Indeed, some divergence may be preferred to total value agreement (Beutler, Crago and Arizmendi 1986; Propst, Ostrom, Watkins, Dean, and Mashburn 1992). If values become a problem in therapy the therapist should approach them openly, and, if conflict between client and therapist persists, referral elsewhere may be required.

Referrals based on value discrepancy, client need, and/or therapist bias need to be made from a position of value knowledge and professional integrity. Therapy techniques or strategies need to be justified and explained, especially if they are other than what traditional therapy might offer (cf. Bergin 1985, 1991).

Is it ethical to provide services to persons who have diverse backgrounds if those backgrounds are not understood? Certainly this point has been made when dealing with cross-cultural counseling or therapy with minorities and might well be made in terms of values or working with clients who have a distinct religious or value orientation. Psychologists will encounter more religious diversity than any other kind of diversity.

Both Meyer (1988) and Lovinger (1984) suggest that it may be appropriate to become acquainted with major teachings and dilemmas typical of clients of diverse religious orientations. To deny service to a client who wants to deal with spiritually related issues seems to Meyer no more appropriate than "to deny service to a student coping with educational issues or a terminally ill patient struggling with medical concerns" (488). According to Meyer, clarification of values and biases with regard to religion could be better understood through research, role playing, exploratory papers, or additional education aimed at understanding spiritual issues, both process and content, in research and in practice. It is important in understanding religious clients that the therapist both appreciate the value pattern of the individual's particular group and understand the individual's personal value pattern within that group (Worthington 1986).

Implications of a moral frame of reference for therapy are seen in this vignette: If a client is bothered by the habit of viewing or using pornography and remains uncomfortable, how might this dilemma be approached? A traditional therapist might reason that viewing or not viewing pornography is not the issue, but reducing the guilt or conflict (the real culprits) is of concern. Since the therapist may not know of any data indicating pornography is damaging, there would be little motivation to suggest the client's discontinuance of the habit. Yet, if the client's values of human dignity, sensitivity, reverence for life, or respect for persons are brought into awareness, the client has clear justification and motivation to modify this behavior while remaining within his or her value system.

It is paradoxical that traditional psychology and psychotherapy, which foster individualism, free expression, and tolerance of dissent, would be so reluctant to address one of the most fundamental concerns of humankind—morality and spirituality. In fact, therapeutic efforts have studiously avoided controversy, concern, and needs associated with religion. Regarding this conspiracy of silence, one could accusingly reflect that we speak of wholeness but insist on parts; we value openness but stay partly closed; we like to be accepting but only of some things; it is good to be tolerant but not of things we don't understand. In the larger matrix of sociocultural variables, religion cannot be avoided as subject or object, cause or effect, noumena or phenomena.

The danger of a moral philosophy or moral frame of reference not anchored to spirituality or religion is that of relativeness, expediency, and an ever-changing hierarchy of values. With no standard of measure or no reference point, it is easy to manipulate moral issues to meet merely expedient needs. Defense mechanisms and self-justifications can be used to reconcile questionable intentions or "needs" with situational moral imperatives. An entire domain of human experience may be neglected by ignoring the spiritual and moral frame of reference. Ignorance of spiritual constructs and experience predispose a therapist to misjudge, misinterpret, misunderstand, mismanage, or neglect important segments of a client's life which may impact significantly on adjustment or growth. Therapy may clumsily tread on sensitive areas. If the therapist is blind to the spiritual or moral realities of the client, resistance and transference will remain only partially appreciated.

We have suggested several important issues for the therapist and client. Spiritual, religious, and moral diversity are givens that we must acknowledge. It is argued that a moral frame of reference might be appropriately and advantageously anchored to the spiritual and religious. The therapeutic process encounters value dilemmas on every side. As therapists, we must prepare to understand and address these complex issues more effectively. This will require an interaction and combining of traditional techniques adapted to value issues and techniques emanating from moral and spiritual strategies.

Specific Techniques of Change

As with other approaches, a spiritual strategy implies hypotheses and techniques of change. Although these have special applicability to normal and mildly disturbed persons, which is the special province of spiritual approaches, they are also frequently applicable to more severe disorders, usually in conjunction with techniques from secular sources.

Essentially there are two categories of counseling techniques used in dealing with religious or spiritual issues: those grounded in traditional psychological theories or emanating from professional secular sources, which are then adapted to religious content, and those originating specifically from within spiritual or religious frameworks, which are used therapeutically in coping with both standard symptoms and religious issues. This section will explore examples of the use of techniques, traditional and religious, applied to diverse issues.

Illustrative of applying traditional techniques with religious content, Propst (1980) found that cognitive behavioral therapy with religious imagery and a religious placebo (group discussion of religious issues) showed more of a treatment effect in mild depression for religious subjects than did a nonreligious imagery treatment. In a subsequent study, 59 clinically depressed subjects (nonpsychotic, nonbipolar) were treated with two forms of cognitive-behavioral therapy, one with religious content and one without (Propst et al. 1992). Religious and nonreligious therapists were used in each group. There was also a pastoral counseling treatment group. Subjects in the religious content treatment and pastoral counseling treatment reported significantly lower rates of posttreatment depression and better adjustment scores than the waiting list controls or the subjects in the nonreligious cognitive therapy. It is also of interest that the nonreligious therapists, using the religious approach, had the highest level of treatment effect.

In an article addressing religious values and therapy, Aust (1990) reviews techniques mentioned by several authors. Success with imagery is detailed by Propst (1980), Worthington (1978), and Frank (1973). Wilson (1974) notes client improvement with "Christian therapeutic maneuvers" consisting of commitment or rededication, confession or uncovering, forgiveness of self and others, and fellowship or community. Moral Reconation Therapy (Little and Robinson 1988) is a step-by-step treatment program applied to treatments for antisocial or drug abuse clients. The authors report that the approach appears effective in promoting moral growth and behavior improvement. They also indicate that it fosters commitments to goals and development of identity.

One of the unique aspects of Moral Reconation Therapy is the requirement for clients of a payback to society in the form of public service, such as working with Special Olympics, rebuilding park structures, or building food boxes for the poor at Christmas time. Briefly, the treatments appear to involve the following behaviors: the clients are responsible for their own treatment as well as the treatment of others, confrontation is an important aspect, and a formal written assessment of the self is required. Activities that raise the person's awareness of relationships with others are implemented. A connection between freedom and responsibility is taught. The client must provide service to others where there is no overt gain for the client. The strategies include an effort to decrease clients' decisions based on pleasure and pain. Also, they are taught to tolerate delays in gratification. They are exposed to problems and moral dilemmas at the various stages of moral development. Trust and honesty in relationships are points of focus. Ongoing self-assessment, in conjunction with receiving assessment from other clients and staff, are required. Preliminary research suggests that there is an encouraging level of success.

The concept of forgiveness, with its roots in religion, has been espoused as a spiritual therapy technique (Bergin 1980; Brandsma 1985; Hope 1987). Hope (1987) states:

> Choosing to forgive is a paradoxical act that releases a person from the need to seek payment or revenge for past insults or disappointments through an up-leveling or reframing process. Forgiveness is a core value of Christianity and other major religions . . . It is proposed that understanding the dynamics of forgiveness can serve as a powerful therapeutic tool. (240)

Forgiveness, Hope further indicates, is a voluntary act, a decision about how a person deals with the past. In dealing with injustice, disappointment, and humiliation, one needs to learn how to reinterpret, let go, or accept the past in a way that frees one for future growth. Although anger and indignation may be therapeutic and essential in some cases, lasting change requires transcending one's sense of victimization. Hope indicates that by choosing to forgive we increase our options and freedom to grow. Further, it is suggested that "forgiveness can be seen as a metaaction, as a reframing of how one views the world . . ." (242). The opposite of forgiveness is a desire to seek vindication, which delivers a person into a crippling state of ambivalence towards people who are important. Forgiveness of others, then, may be a necessary requisite for forgiving one's self. Hope also explains, "for those who also view life from a spiritual dimension, forgiveness becomes an act of faith, a way of actualizing religious beliefs" (242). Hope quotes Fillipaldi (1982, 75), who states that "forgiveness is a focus on the present that frees from the past and opens up the future." A series of steps in the forgiving process is outlined by Donnelley (1982).

Confession and contrition are two preliminaries seen as preparatory acts to healing (Harrison 1988). Involved in these processes is the radical lowering of one's defenses. Often involved is a reordering of values and the freeing of energies that are bound up in the process of trying to hide. Contrition is equated with desire to change and is the opposite of defensiveness. It implies pliancy. In practicing each virtue, the complementary vice is rendered ineffective or nonexistent. "The individual is made a new creature bit by bit and each aspect of moral goodness is acquired by deliberate choice" (315). Harrison continues,

> . . . Much of what is involved in psychotherapy is similar to the practices intrinsic to religious purgation. The point to be made here is not that psychotherapy is equivalent to the process of sanctification, but that it is often compatible with it and in some cases may contribute to it by exposing attitudes and personal difficulties that the individual does not want to face. . . . But the larger task, the perfecting of the entire person, necessitates a larger process—one which is supernatural as well as human and more intimate and more pervasive than any earthly method could be (317).

Specific therapy techniques mentioned by Lovinger (1984) include religious imagery, for example, comparing Christian charity with being a

Christian doormat, using alternative Bible translations, considering context, special use of words, and other interpretations of Scriptures, using contradictory imperatives, wherein the meaning is modified by other scriptural statements, corrective experiences, literary resources, denominational resources, forgiveness, and service. It is mentioned that the hallmark of effective therapy (Freud) is increased capacity to work and to love.

Some Cautions

Caveats are warranted in this venture of implementing spiritual strategies. Because religious techniques are espoused for a variety of reasons, it need not be assumed that those who are promoting spiritually based methods are always competent, honest, or ethical in their approach. There may be hidden agendas, exploitiveness, and manipulations for implicit reasons, which reflect something less than integrity.

Potentially, the directness, evangelism, and conversion agenda of a pastoral counselor or a religiously oriented therapist may not be compatible with the traditional therapeutic value of autonomy and independent choice. However, there is no inherent reason why a spiritual approach or moral frame of reference need be any more directive than other approaches to psychotherapy. The value of personal choice and growth based on independent judgment can be equally valued by those with a religious orientation and those who do not espouse any religious framework.

Many therapists may not know how to deal with values and spiritual concerns in a constructive, helpful manner because they have not been taught to do so. They have avoided the process of helping others cope with spiritual issues and controversial values in a religious context. When dealing with values, certain principles may need to be observed in preserving human agency or freedom of choice. Though working with a client's spiritual values may promote growth and change in a positive direction, the therapist should remain "within" the client's own value system in this endeavor. To impose the therapist's own religious values onto a nonreligious client may not only be counterproductive, it may also violate professional ethics.

No blanket statement that religious techniques are universally beneficial in therapy is endeavored. The usefulness of such therapeutic techniques is predicated on several criteria such as religiosity of the client, desire by the client to employ such techniques, comfort level of the therapist, skill of the therapist in the use of religious techniques, and, ultimately, empirical proof of efficacy.

Dual or unwarranted roles should be avoided as well. Both the client and the therapist should understand that though the therapist may be sensitive to and discuss the client's religious issues, the therapist does not possess the same role assigned to members of the client's particular ecclesiastical leadership. A proper referral in cases where the client may need to speak with an appropriate member of the faith may be necessary to comply with the expectations of a client's religious affiliation.

Despite such cautions, there is a vast untapped potential for spiritual approaches to therapeutic change. The way is open for creative Christian counselors and others to develop and assemble a repertoire of useful techniques that add to what is already known and can be done. At the same time, we need to remember our obligation to be empirical, eclectic, and ecumenical.

The Empirical Dimension

It is essential that a spiritual strategy have an empirical dimension if it is to have credibility in the profession at large and if we are serious about using all of the sources of truth God has given to us. Certainly, the scientific method in its various forms (experimental, correlational, qualitative, descriptive) is a rich source of truth that we cannot afford to ignore, even though we may be emphasizing processes that are not easy to observe in traditional scientific ways. Nevertheless, we can observe many of the effects or consequences of invisible spiritual processes such as spiritual experience. Just as in biology or physics, many of our phenomena will be inferred from observable events. It has been noted for instance that there seem to be material consequences to spiritual conviction. This is manifested in the fact that physical health of people who have a sense of coherence in their lives or a certain way of believing in God are healthier than others (Antonovsky 1979; McIntosh and Spilka 1990). We also note that there are correlations between the quality of one's lifestyle, the nature of one's belief system and mental health indices (Bergin 1991).

Although the psychology of religion field, as exemplified by the work of the members of The Society for the Scientific Study of Religion, is pertinent to the empirical dimension of a spiritual strategy, much of it is essentially secular social psychology. We need to carefully identify those subsections of research that are particularly pertinent to an approach that openly acknowledges the reality of the invisible spiritual dimension in life. Much of psychology of religion research simply ignores the possibility of a spiritual reality. On the other hand, Hood's work on mystical and religious experiences constitutes a set of studies and measures that give us an observational handle on a very private domain of phenomena (Spilka, Hood, and Gorsuch 1985). Hood's mysticism scale expressly identifies and quantifies self-reports of transcendental spiritual experiences. This work exemplifies the encounter of empiricism with spiritual phenomenology that is not intimidated by behavioristic, mechanical, or other objectivistic strictures that might otherwise inhibit good research in this area.

At the same time, we would not want to ignore objectivist research that is pertinent to the cause of the spiritual agenda. For instance, there is an abundant literature in the area of prevention of mental disorders and social pathology that shows a positive effect of religion (Payne, Bergin, Bielema, and Jenkins 1991). Many other research areas, for example the study of Intrinsic and Extrinsic religious orientations, illustrate the value of standard psychology of religion research (Donahue 1985; Kirkpatrick 1989).

In entering the empirical domain, we do not want to be limited entirely to traditional designs, however. Qualitative, descriptive research may be important in analyzing the relation between a religious lifestyle and personality traits and mental health indices. In addition, we need to be brave enough to consider a spiritual method itself as a form of empiricism. That is, a researcher may use a spiritual perception of the characteristics of a person being studied that is not accessible by ordinary observational techniques. In this sense spirituality overlaps with intuition, inspiration, illumination, and creativity. Such phenomena have been noted by some therapists who have touched on the transpersonal realm and have referred to the possibility that therapists may be able to perceive characteristics of a client and to commune with the spirit of that client in a way that goes beyond ordinary empathic perception (Rogers 1980).

This kind of spiritually enhanced perception can occur in research as well as in therapy and might become the focus of new studies in which spiritual tests become part of the realm of empirical testing. By spiritual tests we mean that the researcher tests the communications from or impressions received from a subject against a sensed perception of the truth as witnessed by the spirit to the observer. This is a type of internal consistency or a reliability on which validity is based. Such perception still needs to be checked against the perceptions of equally qualified observers and against consensually established scriptural criteria of truth. A balance is required between idiographic and nomothetic perceptions in order to avoid self-deception. Although this method may seem radical, it will be essential to consider it in the repertoire of assessment devices available within a spiritual strategy. Although there are many dangers to this, there are also many potentialities. This procedure takes research beyond the ordinary qualitative and descriptive methods of the empirical approach. Reports of its use are rare, but as a prototype it could become an essential ingredient of a spiritual strategy.

Eclectic

Since much of the ground we are currently exploring in developing a spiritual strategy is uncharted, there is considerable opportunity for creativity. We must take care, however, that we do not reinvent the wheel. There are resources within the behavioral sciences that can be tapped for the purpose of our effort. Therefore, as we seek to integrate psychological theory and technique, eclecticism will be a valuable guiding principle as we select what is useful from a variety of sources.

Consider some examples of efforts toward such an integration. Jones (1989), as previously discussed, attempted to integrate some aspects of the theory and practice of the rational-emotive approach into a religious framework while also discarding major aspects of the theory. Smith and Hendelman (1990) have made similar efforts with regard to religion and psychoanalytic thought. The goal of their book, *Psychoanalysis and Religion,* is to help bridge the gap that has so long existed between psychoanalysts and religious thinkers, especially in identifying healthy ego processes in religious experience and expression. Another exemplary effort is a book edited by Miller and Martin, *Behavior Therapy and Religion* (1988), which attempts to establish integration of spiritual and behavioral approaches to change. Of particular note is Martin and Carlson's (1988) chapter on health psychology in which they ". . . emphasize . . . combining modern, well-tested medical and behavioral health interventions with appropriate spiritual ones . . ." (103). They note an interesting series of exploratory studies showing a positive effect of a "Divine Love" film on measures of immune function.

Propst et al. (1992) have also demonstrated the value of integrating religious content into cognitive therapy of depression. When Propst's Religious Cognitive Therapy was conducted according to a prescribed technique manual, Christian religious clients benefited more from the religiously integrated therapy than from standard cognitive techniques. We would do well to follow the lead of these and other pioneers in seeking to broaden the interface between religion and secular psychology.

In addition to learning from secular approaches, a spiritual strategy has much to offer psychology at large, especially regarding the way it deals with religious and spiritual issues. It may be that those who are currently ignoring relevant spiritual and religious content would be less likely to do so if it were translated into the terms of their espoused strategy. By first understanding other strategies and then asking ourselves how religious and spiritual issues fit into their system (by "speaking their language"), we will be better prepared to extend contributions from the spiritual strategy to other strategies. The fact that they are framed in a familiar language will make it more likely that those from other strategies will recognize these potential contributions.

Dombeck and Karl (1987) have created a model as an aid for understanding how spiritual aspects of mental health care fit into four different helping professions: medicine, nursing, humanistic psychology, and pastoral counseling. They explore the distinctions between the professions, seeking to understand how spiritual needs might fit uniquely into the framework of each. Case illustrations are given, including one of a man who had become elated after an inspirational religious experience during a retreat. He was diagnosed as hypomanic but the psychiatrist recognized the religious experience as valid and separate from the man's pathology. Diagnosis and treatment allowed for retention of the religious dimension following mental improvement. Neither the psychiatric nor the religious perspective dominated, but each did its respective part in a balanced, eclectic approach to the helping process.

In addition to educating therapists and sensitizing them to religious issues, Miller and Martin (1988) offer the following possibilities for spiritual contributions to psychology: enlarging the scope of inquiry, stretching the science, unlocking training, raising clinical issues, improving effectiveness and accessibility of therapy, and broadening perspectives.

In sum, a spiritual strategy can be eclectic in two ways. First, by integrating useful technique and theory *from* a variety of sources within psychology, and second, by seeking to introduce a spiritual perspective or frame of reference *to* traditionally secular techniques and theories.

Ecumenical and Denominational

One avenue we must pursue in seeking to increase the utility of our work is that of breaking down the barriers that can prevent productive communication of thought between denominations. In order to be of maximum benefit, our work must be ecumenical in the following ways: areas of agreement should be sought and specified, rather than focusing upon narrow areas of disagreement, and even in areas where disagreement on specific doctrinal issues or beliefs exist, we can seek ways to apply things learned within the context of one denomination to other denominations.

The interface between psychology and religion is only part of a larger ecumenical movement noted by Sprinthall and McVay (1987). The spirit of their essay suggests that those interested in the interface between religion and psychotherapy may learn from each other and learn together in spite of divergence in belief systems or denominations. In order to be truly ecumenical, this exchange must include not only traditional Christian religion but other religions as well, and, in our culture, this should include particular attention to our Judaic heritage. Hutch (1983) points out that some bridges can be built between Christian and eastern philosophies in their approaches to anxiety, human suffering, and insight into the human condition.

Perhaps there are bridges that should not be built, but generally a free interchange between denominations and even across cultures opens the door for research and theorizing to be done in a broad manner. We may then comprehend human nature and human need in a worldwide way that will better fulfill the purposes of the Lord and those who wish to serve the Lord.

Beit-Hallahmi (1975) provides an example of how issues on therapy—even those that are denominationally specific on content—can be reported in an ecumenical manner. He uses specific examples from case studies to illustrate more general or universal issues in working with religious clients.

For example, he presents a therapy case of an individual from an orthodox Jewish background. He discusses the importance of understanding that Israeli society is divided into a religious subculture and a secular subculture. Understanding this division and the coinciding differences in terms of beliefs, appearance (dress), and behavior allowed the therapist to work more effectively with the client in his struggles within the context of that society. This example is used to illustrate the universal problem of understanding the client's specific religious group and the client's way of defining himself or herself within it.

In addition, Beit-Hallahmi (1975) uses this case to illustrate the general issue of dealing with the gap in religiosity between the client and the therapist. Since Beit-Hallahmi did not wear a skullcap, it was obvious to the client that he did not practice orthodox Judaism. He describes how the tension that resulted from the client-therapist religious difference was discussed openly and how this initial openness set the stage for future work on religious aspects of the client's life.

While the discussion of the client's specific religion and its influence in therapy provides illustrative clarity, the author's specification of the universal issues that the case studies illustrate insures that the article's scope of application will be ecumenical.

At the same time, the role of concepts and techniques specific to denominations must be recognized. Evangelical Christian, Latter-day Saint, and Orthodox Jewish clients present different needs embedded in languages and lifestyles that demand technical content adapted to their needs (Lovinger 1984, 1990; Spero 1985). A psychologist whose background and perspective derive strongly from a denominational context needs to learn how to function both in the broader ecumenical world and in the fine texture of his or her own tradition. A viable spiritual strategy must be responsive to both ends of this continuum and persist in the conceptual struggle to embrace them both. An example of this was recently noted in a newsletter article on pain management ("Using Faith," 1990). Coping skills are taught for handling suffering using two types of spiritual content ("Christian" and "God and Faith") and a nonspiritual format. Watson, Hood, Morris, and Hall (1985) nicely illustrate ways of carefully integrating denominational Christian concepts of sin and salvation with the psychology of personal growth and self-esteem. Lovinger's (1985, 1990) work reflects an attempt to touch upon common themes across religions within an egoanalytic perspective, while Jensen and Bergin (1988) attempt to identify mental health values that can be endorsed by persons of diverse denominational origins.

Conclusion

We have noted but a few of the many illustrations that could be given of substantial work in each of the seven tasks we have outlined for the development of a "spiritual strategy." It is encouraging that a literature is evolving that could form the basis for a new approach that is comparable in substance with the existing major strategies. At the same time, we must realistically acknowledge that this work is relatively primitive compared with the main secular traditions. In all areas of theory, practice and research, major work remains to be done. We hope that our outline will provide a meaningful structure and a stimulus for this challenging cause.

References

Antonovsky, A. 1979. *Health, stress, and coping.* San Francisco: Jossey-Bass.

Aust, C. F. 1990. Using the client's religious values to aid progress in therapy. *Counseling and Values* 34: 125–29.

Beit-Hallahmi, B. 1975. Encountering orthodox religion in psychotherapy. *Psychotherapy: Theory, Research and Practice* 12: 357–59.

Bergin, A. E. 1980. Psychotherapy and religious values. *Journal of Consulting and Clinical Psychology* 48: 95–105.

_____. 1985. Proposed values for guiding and evaluating counseling and psychotherapy. *Counseling and Values* 29: 101–15.

_____. 1988a. Three contributions of a spiritual perspective to counseling, psychotherapy, and behavior change. *Counseling and Values* 33: 21–31.

_____. 1988b. The spiritual perspective is ecumenical and eclectic (rejoinder). *Counseling and Values* 33: 57–59.

_____. 1991. Values and religious issues in psychotherapy and mental health. *American Psychologist* 46: 394–403.

Beutler, L., M. Crago, and T. Arizmendi. 1986. Research on therapist variables in psychotherapy. In *Handbook of psychotherapy and behavior change,* ed. S. L. Garfield and A. E. Bergin, 3d ed., 257–310. New York: Wiley.

Brandsma, J. M. 1985. Forgiveness. In *Baker encyclopedia of psychology,* ed. D. G. Benner. Grand Rapids: Baker.

Collins, G. R. 1977. *The rebuilding of psychology: An integration of psychology and Christianity.* Wheaton: Tyndale House.

_____. 1980. *Christian counseling. A comprehensive guide.* Waco: Word.

Dombeck, M., and J. Karl. 1987. Spiritual issues in mental health care. *Journal of Religion and Health* 26: 183–97.

Donahue, M. J. 1985. Intrinsic and extrinsic religiousness: Review and meta-analysis. *Journal of Personality and Social Psychology* 48: 400–419.

Donnelley, D. 1982. *Putting forgiveness into practice.* Allen, Tex.: Argus.

Fillipaldi, S. E. 1982. Zen-mind, Christian-mind, empty-mind. *Journal of Ecumenical Studies* 10: 69–84.

Frank, J. D. 1973. *Persuasion and healing.* Rev. ed. New York: Johns Hopkins Univ. Press.

Harrison, S. M. 1988. Sanctification and therapy: The model of Dante Alighieri. *Journal of Psychology and Theology* 16: 313–17.

Hope, D. 1987. The healing paradox of forgiveness. *Psychotherapy* 24: 240–44.

Hutch, R. A. 1983. An essay on psychotherapy and religion. *Journal of Religion and Health* 22: 7–18.

Jensen, J. P., and A. E. Bergin. 1988. Mental health values of professional therapists: A national interdisciplinary survey. *Professional Psychology: Research and Practice* 19: 290–97.

Jones, S. L. 1989. Rational-emotive therapy in Christian perspective. *Journal of Psychology and Theology* 17: 110–20.

Kirkpatrick, L. A. 1989. A psychometric analysis of the Allport-Ross and Feagin measure of intrinsic-extrinsic religious orientation. In *Research in the social and scientific study of religion,* ed. M. L. Lynn and D. O. Moberg, vol. 1, 1–31. Greenwich, Conn.: JAI.

Liebert, R. M., and M. D. Spiegler. 1990. *Personality: Strategies and issues.* Pacific Grove, Calif.: Brooks/Cole.

Little, G. L., and K. D. Robinson. 1988. Moral reconation therapy: A systematic step-by-step treatment system for treatment resistant clients. *Psychological Reports* 62: 135–51.

Lovinger, R. J. 1984. *Working with religious issues in therapy.* New York: Jason Aronson.

_____. 1990. *Religion and counseling: The psychological impact of religious belief.* New York: Continuum.

Martin, J. E., and C. R. Carlson. 1988. Spiritual dimensions of health psychology. In *Behavior therapy and religion: Integrating spiritual and behavioral approaches to change,* ed. W. R. Miller and J. E. Martin, 57–110. Newbury Park, Calif.: Sage.

McIntosh, D., and B. Spilka. 1990. Religion and physical health: The role of personal faith and control beliefs. In *Research on the social scientific study of religion,* vol. 2, ed. M. L. Lynn and D. O. Moberg, 167–94. Greenwich, Conn.: JAI.

Meyer, M. S. 1988. Ethical principles of psychologists and religious diversity. *Professional Psychology: Research and Practice* 19: 486–88.

Miller, W. R., and J. E. Martin. 1988. *Behavior therapy and religion: Integrating spiritual and behavioral approaches to change.* Newbury Park, Calif.: Sage.

Payne, I. R., A. E. Bergin, K. A. Bielema, and P. H. Jenkins. In press. Review of religion and mental health: Prevention and the enhancement of psychosocial functioning. *Prevention in Human Services* 9.

Propst, L. R. 1980. The comparative efficacy of religious and nonreligious imagery for the treatment of mild depression in religious individuals. *Cognitive Therapy and Research* 4: 167–78.

Propst, L. R., R. Ostrom, P. Watkins, T. Dean, and D. Mashburn. 1992. Comparative efficacy of religious and non-religious cognitive-behavioral therapy for the treatment of clinical depression in religious individuals. *Journal of Consulting and Clinical Psychology* 60: 94–103.

Rogers, C. R. 1980. Healing and growth in the therapeutic relationship. In C. W. Waymon (Chair), *The efficacy of psychotherapy: New perspectives for tomorrow.* Symposium sponsored by The Institute for Social Systems Engineering and The University for Humanistic Studies, San Diego, California, January.

Smith, J. H., and S. A. Handelman. 1990. *Psychoanalysis and religion.* London: Johns Hopkins.

Spero, M. H., ed. 1985. *Psychotherapy of the religious patient.* Springfield, Ill.: Charles C. Thomas.

Spilka, B., and R. A. Bridges. 1989. Theological and psychological theory: Psychological implications of some modern theologies. *Journal of Psychology and Theology* 17: 343–51.

Spilka, B., R. W. Hood, Jr., and R. L. Gorsuch. 1985. *The psychology of religion: An empirical approach.* Englewood Cliffs, N.J.: Prentice-Hall.

Sprinthall, N. A., and J. G. McVay. 1987. Value development during the college years: A cause for concern and an opportunity for growth. *Counseling and Values* 31: 126–38.

Using "faith" as a coping skill. 1990. *Coping Skills Development (DSC) Newsletters,* p. 1. 124–B Exchange Pl. Lafayette, LA 70503.

Watson, P. J., R. W. Hood, R. J. Morris, and J. R. Hall. 1985. Religiosity, sin, and self-esteem. *Journal of Psychology and Theology* 13(2): 116–28.

Wilson, W. P. 1974. Utilization of Christian beliefs in psychotherapy. *Journal of Psychology and Theology* 2(2): 125–31.

Worthington, E. L., Jr. 1978. The effects of imagery content, choice of imagery content, and self-verbalization on the self-control of pain. *Cognitive Therapy and Research* 2: 225–40.

_____. 1986. Religious counseling: A review of published empirical research. *Journal of Counseling and Development* 64: 421–31.

13

Psychology and the Christian Faith: 20th and 21st Century

EVERETT L. WORTHINGTON, JR.

Where there is no vision, the people perish . . .
[Prov. 29:18]

As we ready to march into the 21st century, Christian psychology needs a vision. We need more than tunnel vision fixed unblinkingly on a distant point in the future. We need more than a myopic vision that blurs beyond the outer extension of our own noses. We need a full-fledged peripheral vision to allow us to see the forces that assail us broadside. We even need a glance over our shoulder to see the paths we have already navigated. Further, we need light that illumines our path lest we stumble in the darkness and fall headlong onto our faces. With that vision and with the light, we can focus clearly on distant points and march unwaveringly without stumbling.

In the present chapter, I do four things. First, I identify three trends that have influenced where we are as a society today and where the average "everyperson" is psychologically. These are necessarily speculative and no doubt presumptuous to some degree. Second, I speculate on the implications of these trends for Christian mental health professionals. These speculations, while based on the first analysis and thus open to question, are more specific and pertinent to Christians in the psychological fields. Third, I recommend actions to bring about a vision of Christian psychotherapy. Fourth, I call Christians to be more a part of the healing community of Jesus' church.

The 20th Century

Three fundamental societal changes have shoved us where we are today: improved health with an increased life expectancy, movement to a postindustrial, communication-based society, and cultural acceptance of philosophies of relativism and postmodernism.

Improved Health

At the turn of the century, the life expectancy of the average United States citizen was about 45 years; today it is nearer 85 (United States Bureau of the Census, CPR, Series P-25, No. 1045; United States Senate Special Committee on Aging 1986). This shift has pressured us toward a new way of understanding the world—even apart from new moral issues that have been opened up in biological and health fields, such as our abilities to prolong the life of the body when the brain is dead, to splice genes and to create new forms of life, to observe and even change the process of life as early as the fertilized cell, and to keep a child alive if born even halfway through the pregnancy. Many of these moral changes have yet to create the impact that they likely will in the following century.

In the 20th century, though, the longer life expectancy has shifted the family life cycle dramatically (Carter and McGoldrick 1989). In 1900, most people in the United States were agrarian-based. The mass migration to the cities had only begun. Typically, a child was born into a family and was reared within the family until he or she was a teen. The teen then married someone from the community and quickly bore children. People often had ten or more children in those days. Thus, most child bearing occurred from between ages 15 and 30 or 35. For the 15 or so years after the last child was born, parents reared the children. At age 45 to 50, the last child left home and coincidentally parents soon expected to die (from exhaustion, no doubt). At the turn of the century, most social life of the country was organized around the nuclear family.

Today, the story is vastly different. A child is born into a family, but dual-income families, day care, institutional schools, divorce, and single-parent households mean that some children may grow up hardly seeing their family members.

Even assuming a child grows up in a family, at about 18, the child enters young adulthood in which the child is essentially on his or her own while maintaining minimal ties with the parents. College is followed by a job. Marriage is usually deferred until about 25 (on the average) and even after marriage many couples postpone having children until their mid-thirties. An increasing number of couples are remaining childless voluntarily (Spanier 1983; United States Bureau of the Census, CPR, Series P-23, No. 162, 1989; Series P-20, No. 445, 1990).

An average couple has 2 children 2 years apart and thus spends 20 years at child bearing and rearing (United States Senate Special Committee on Aging 1986). Once the last child leaves home, a couple can expect to live together for the last 30 to 40 years until (usually) the husband dies, leaving a widow alone for 5 to 10 additional years (United States Senate Special Committee on Aging 1986). This pattern is complicated, of course, by a divorce rate of well over 50%, meaning that many people spend considerably more time alone than the (atypical) couple that I have just described (Cherlin 1981).

The social ramifications of longer life are remarkable. Society is no longer organized around the family.

Marriage is a more reasonable organizing unit in modern life. Susan and David Larson (1990) and others have shown that marriage is actually good for health. Married people have better health and longer life expectancy than do unmarried people on the average. Yet, marriage is generally seen as undependable. Society has abandoned its vision of a permanent marriage covenant and substituted for it the breakable and increasingly legal marriage contract.

Consequently, life is organized not around the family or marriage but around the individual. Throughout the 20th century, better health and longer life have pushed us toward individualism. Simply put, in 1900 people depended on others and spent most of their lives largely living intimately with others. Today, people spend proportionately (and absolutely) much more time living independently and focusing on meeting their own needs (Carter and McGoldrick 1989). This focus on meeting one's own needs continues to take its toll on relationships.

Recently, a troubled couple sat across from me pouring out their woes. The woman complained, "He doesn't listen to me. I need support. I need someone who cares for me, someone who can help me up when I'm feeling down. I need a husband. It's not unreasonable to expect that a husband would meet his wife's needs, is it?"

The man's song was in a different key, but the melody was familiar. "She tries to help but every time she offers help, it comes out as a request for validation of her. She rubs my back and asks, 'How am I doing?' Even when she gives me advice, she is more interested in her helping skills than in my well-being."

Most modern people grasp at intimate relationships as ways of meeting their own needs. The idea of self-sacrifice for the relationship is unpopular except as a romantic means of self-fulfillment. If people put aside their comfort for a family member, they feel that they deserve a medal.

An individualistic focus means that people marry less frequently and cohabit more than they did previously (Spanier 1983). They establish a norm for relationships that says, "As long as I love you, I am thoroughly committed to you, but if you no longer meet my needs, I'll end the relationship and find another committed relationship." One woman I recently saw had been in three "committed" relationships within a year, which makes one wonder what an uncommitted relationship would be like.

Postindustrial, Communication-Based Society

The second great change of the 20th century was stimulated by technological developments. Society has moved from an emerging industrial nation in the late 1800s through industrialism until about 1970 to a postindustrial, communication-based society (Naisbitt 1984). Throughout most of the 20th century, our mentality as a nation was product oriented. We took pride in our ability to produce large quantities of goods quickly while meeting high standards. The result has been technical advances that have restructured society (Kipnis 1991).

The electric light. First, electric lights were invented. The development of the electric light and widespread use of electric power created a society that could be fully urban. Activity did not halt at sundown. Rather, lighting prolonged productive days in the factory and allowed cities to reorganize social life on a 24-hour cycle.

Individual transportation. Second, personal transportation developed markedly. The interstate road system has interconnected almost every concentration of population in the United States, making different regions of the country accessible to anyone. Consequently, society has developed a mobility that is not tied to mass transportation, which enhanced personal freedom, autonomy, and independence. In addition, air travel developed until intracontinental travel is easily possible within half a day and travel across the world can be accomplished within 36 hours by the average business traveler. This has exposed more people to more regions of the country and to people from other countries and cultures within the world.

Television and VCR. Third, television has been developed within the United States and Japan such that almost every home in the country has at least one television. Most children and many adults spend at least two or three hours per week night and many more hours per day on weekends in front of the television (Liebert, Sprafkin, and Davidson 1982). The content of television programs has enormously affected our culture, many would say negatively. When confronted with negative changes in culture that are blamed partly on television, television spokespeople and sponsors deny the negative influences of television. "Watching hours of crime, murder, and sex portrayed on television has no effect on children," they argue. However, the same television executives sell 30 seconds of advertising time to the same sponsors during the Super Bowl for over a million dollars, presumably because someone believes that exposure to 30 seconds of fiction (often less realistic than television programs) will have a million-dollar impact on people.

The influences of television that have affected modern culture have to do with violence, perception of family interactions, and desire for continual change.

It is estimated that the average child will observe over 40,000 television murders by the time he or she is 18 years old (Liebert, Sprafkin, and Davidson 1982). Also viewable on television—more so on cable channels—are other violent acts including rape, abuse, and all manners of property crimes. Is it any wonder that most scholars conclude that watching television violence increases aggressiveness (Friedrich-Cofer and Huston 1986; Singer and Singer 1981; cf. Freedman 1984, 1986) and that the judicial system in the United States is overcrowded and frequency of violent crimes reported each year has continually risen since 1950 (Liebert, Sprafkin, and Davidson 1982)?

Television also has influenced the average television viewer's perception of family life. Based on the ubiquitous situation comedy, people expect the average family to be populated with smart-mouthed children disrespectful to adults and to other children, and with wise-cracking, often vulgar adults, who use put-down humor to deal with others. In the situation comedy, characters say outrageous, hurtful things to each other weekly but end each episode with warm and tender feelings for each other. The following week, they show no evidence of previous hurtfulness. This teaches viewers, especially children for whom television may form their major contact with "reality," that one can say anything to another person without serious consequences.

Another way that television has undermined the fabric of society is by exposing viewing children to a world in which adults act abominably toward each other, show weaknesses and character flaws, and make egregious mistakes (Gergen 1991). Such things obviously happen in real life; however, historically, most children were never privy to its widespread portrayal on television. This has intensified estrangement between adults and children and eroded parental authority.

In addition, television is based on continually stimulating people through change. Commercials change camera angles sometimes 20 times during a 30-second spot. Programs change every 30 minutes. Trends change each year. Old shows lose popularity, new shows appear. One unintended consequence has been a normalizing, through television, of rapid societal change. People expect to be entertained constantly with new stories, new images, new thoughts—to which they respond with increased passivity (Kubey and Csikszentmihalyi 1990). That view generalizes to other aspects of their lives.

In the last ten years, VCRs have become commonplace. People watch more movies than they ever have, and the nature of those movies has been transformed by the VCR. Traditionally, movies have been viewed by groups of strangers sitting in the dark watching a bigger-than-life image.

Emotional reactions of movie-goers to movies in the past have also been bigger-than-life.

With the widespread use of the VCR, though, movies have changed. People now watch movies in well-lit family rooms, amid the distractions of home life, with one finger on the remote control pause button. To achieve a bigger-than-life emotional reaction from such a modern viewer, modern movies made with an eye to the VCR market often are more violent, more grotesque, more repulsive, more terrifying, more sexually explicit, more shocking (and consequently less restrained) than ever before. Further, the natural tendency for people to adapt to their experience coupled with the tendency for people to watch two to five video movies per week, result in demands for movie producers to make ever more emotionally evocative movies.

Cultural metaphors help give life meaning by providing individuals with mental images of how people should and actually do behave. Traditionally, cultural metaphors have been provided by heroic ballads, storytellers around the fire, later novelists, and now movie writers and producers. With the transformation of the nature of movies will inevitably come new cultural mental images of life.

Computers and communications technology. Ten years ago, I had never heard of a personal computer. I had never sent a FAX. Today, scientists and business people communicate with people from other cultures almost instantaneously. Whatever information is needed is in some computer, somewhere, accessible by telephone, modem, diskette, network, or nefarious means.

With the linking of cultures by phone, satellite, and computer has come the necessity to work with and understand other cultures. Multiculturalism has already become a buzzword for the 1990s. To understand people from different cultural traditions has thus become, by degrees, interesting, then helpful, then useful in business and politics, and now morally desirable. Further, by degrees, people have been admonished to understand cultural differences, accept the differences without criticism or challenge, and even embrace the differences.

With the change of focus away from products and the production of knowledge to the processing and communication of information and away from a (relatively) uniform culture to a multicultural hodge-podge, modern United States culture has become more complex.

With advances in technology, especially communications and computer technology, the collective cultural mentality has changed. With information not just accessible but too easily accessible, one of society's major tasks has become, not discovering knowledge, but dealing with sensory and mental overload (Naisbitt 1984). People have reacted with a societal sense of hopelessness and helplessness.

People have tried to cope with a societal sense of hopelessness in two ways. Some specialize in minute areas of expertise, decreasingly small until the information is manageable. The medical field is an example. Previously, people went to general practitioners when they broke a bone. My daughter recently broke her foot and was referred to not just an orthopedist, but an orthopedist who specialized in feet.

While some people handle communication-overload hopelessness by specializing, others simply throw up their hands in a rejection of discernment and an unwillingness to decide which things are important. If all the information cannot be accounted for, then, they think, it is better not to make *any* distinctions. This solution more often reflects the mentality of the politician and liberal artist, while specialization reflects the mentality of the scientist and technocrat. In the structure of society, a loss of clear standards for performance and decision making has led to a pervasive sense of nondiscernment.

Coupled with rising multicultural awareness, loss of standards of judgment has resulted in perception that culture is fragmented. There is no longer a majority culture. Rather, the culture is seen as complex and pluralistic. Distinctions are discerned among groups or ideas but are not evaluated on their merits. In trying to value all directions equally, the culturally pluralistic mind-set has removed the rudder of society, consigning direction to the tides rather than to purposeful decision.

Philosophy

Relativism. The technological changes of longer life and postindustrial technological social reorganization have led to increasing pressures toward individualism, abandonment of family ties, and hopelessness. They have paved the way for the widespread acceptance of a philosophy of relativism. Relativism is the belief that absolute truth does not exist; thus, all truth is thought to be relative. Criteria for which truths are *useful* are varied (with the understanding that no choice of criteria is correct in an absolute sense). Francis Schaeffer (1968) traces the origins of this philosophy to the writings of Hegel, but relativists have been around since people began to discuss the meaning of life, probably beginning about the time of Adam and Eve. However, the influence of the Italian Renaissance and the European Enlightenment, the increasing exposure in the western hemisphere to Far Eastern religions, and the technological innovations producing 20th-century western culture have made widespread acceptance of a relativisitic worldview inexorable.

Postmodernism. Postmodernism is a philosophical approach to life that has grown out of the idea that truth is relativistic. Postmodernism has permeated philosophy, art, and music for years, and is currently trickling into general culture. Postmodernism is contrasted with premodernism and modernism. (For good summaries, see Doherty 1991; Efran

1991; Gergen 1991; O'Hara and Anderson 1991; Penn 1991; cf. Minuchin 1991).

Premodernism is a philosophical worldview in which cultural presuppositions are roughly uniform. Premodern times were roughly those prior to the industrial revolution. Although there were different ideologies and opinions about the most efficient and most morally correct means to ends and even differences in desirable endpoints, the parties generally agreed on fundamental assumptions about culture, identity, and existence. In general, the number and type of choices to which people were exposed were limited in the premodern culture.

Modernism arose in the United States during the latter part of the 19th century. It developed as civilizations formed complex social and political structures. Generally this occurred as the industrial revolution brought large numbers of different types of people in proximity. Religions and worldviews ceased being matters of presupposition and began to be debated and questioned. Belief systems were at war across the culture. Yet despite the seeming chaos, an underlying thread unified culture. The Enlightenment had lauded reason as the primary arbiter of truth. Even though people could not agree on exactly what was true, most people believed that truth was discoverable through reason, properly applied. In the modern world, some idolized Aristotelian logic and others idolized Hegelian and Marxist dialectical synthesis. Regardless, a pervasive belief existed in *some* sort of reasoning. Reality was thought to be undergirded by some structure.

Modernist ideas were manifested in psychology by Freud, Piaget, Kohlberg, Fowler, and others. Freud proposed a structure for the unconscious mind—id, ego, and superego, and an underlying dynamic method. Although such a structure could not be directly observed, it was considered to be objectively there. Piaget and Kohlberg believed in universal "stages" of intellectual development, and Fowler believed in stages of religious development. Chomsky suggested that there was an inherent brain organization that gave structure to human language. In the modernist world, while the structures were unseen, they were at least inferable.

The psychotherapist in the modernist world was supposed to help a client solve problems or grow into someone who was more adjusted to the modernist world. Often this meant a person was more governed by reason and less by unconscious irrational forces. Growth was demonstrated by being integrated, connected, "together," or whole, as opposed to the troubled person, who was seen as fragmented, disintegrated, and poorly connected, either within the psyche or to interpersonal networks.

Postmodernism arrived with the loss of a sense that there were absolute truths, but even more, a loss of the will to search for absolute truths. Religious and philosophical systems are thus seen as simply social constructions of reality, of which many compete in the marketplace of ideas.

Truth is generally understood to be whatever is individually relevant. For example, a postmodern person might say, "Christianity may be true for you but not for me." Truth is seen as constructing a useful mental or psychological explanation for what happens to an individual. Truth is not expected to be consistent across situations; life is thought to be too complex for cross-situational consistency. Identity is thus fragmented, and people are encouraged to live dissociated lives, mentally separating the events of one context from those in another.[1]

The postmodern person generally feels overwhelmed with the vast number of choices available and the uncertainty over the standards that should be used to make those choices. There seem to be no clear boundaries, with life seemingly a never-ending ocean of arbitrary decisions.

In art (see Risatti 1990), postmodernism is evident in a mixing of media. For example, a painting might use oils, acrylics, chalk, and ink. A sculpture of a deformed head might be attached to the canvas. The entire sculpture-painting might sit on a chair in a room within a museum in a city in a state, and so forth. The viewer wonders what the medium of the art work is and indeed where the art work stops and the environment begins. Categories are seen by the artist as arbitrary and socially constructed, so the viewer is left to make decisions about what the art work says, exactly what is part of the art work and what isn't, and whether it is even art. In another strain of postmodern art, the artist may disavow interest in the product of an art work. Art is seen as the process of creating, and art involves having viewers observe the artist during the process of creation.

In music, chords traditionally provided a structure to music. Currently, a work of music might be composed of random sounds, suggesting that chorded sounds are socially constructed conventions, not manifestations of an underlying harmonious structure of sound. A musical composition might be scored but the instrument left unspecified so that the performer could employ a suitcase or a trash can—left to the discretion of the musician (or even the audience)—to pound out the prescribed rhythm. Even the rhythm might remain unspecified at some point in the composition to maximize the musician's freedom.

Postmodernism, as can be seen by a few brief examples, is characterized by loss of absolute truth, emphasis on individualism and choice, and advocacy of the social (consensual) construction of reality.

---

1. Each decade seems to have a "favorite" psychological disturbance. In the sixties, phobias were popular (mirroring the nuclear anxieties). In the seventies, assertiveness blossomed as struggles for individual rights became more prominent. In the eighties, the borderline personality disorder and narcissism became popular disorders, with affected people flip-flopping from rage to dependence on one hand and being self-absorbed and unconnected in relationships on the other. I would not be surprised if multiple personality disorder did not become the disorder of the nineties.

Postmodernism cannot be discounted as being merely weird, airy-fairy philosophy that is divorced from reality. The arts reflect current philosophy in a way that dramatically heightens people's awareness of their life experience. The average person in the United States today—though he or she might not be able to articulate the philosophy undergirding the feelings—generally feels overwhelmed by choices, cut off from sure standards of decision making, unsure of what is true and what isn't, and sometimes even unable to judge what is real and what isn't. In short, the average person feels postmodern.

Of course, not every person is sold out to postmodernism. People vacillate between modern and postmodern ways of thinking. They may advocate their adherence to the absolute truth of Scripture when they are at church on Sunday, but they shed that belief like a coat in a heat wave when they enter the workplace on Monday morning. They are bothered by their inconsistencies, but quickly put the inconsistencies out of their mind because there are so many other choices to make. Mental life is more a collage than an integrated painting.

Today's United States Everyperson

The confluence of these three forces—improved health care, technological progress toward a communication-based multicultural society, and philosophical relativism and postmodernism—have shaped the person of today. He or she is largely dissatisfied with a life of production and is more concerned with process—how to—than with product. The person continually feels overwhelmed, nonintegrated, stressed out, hopeless. He or she strives desperately for intimacy and community but can find only fleeting committed relationships that rub the itch but never stop it. Further, today's Everyperson has lost his or her standards for judgment and thus retreats into specialization or nondiscernment. There is a deep spiritual hunger in Everyperson.

Some will, of course, reject that hunger and adhere to the mid-20th century materialistic, modernist worldview. They will laud science, material prosperity, and no-nonsense pragmatism, but perhaps eventually find themselves, like the caterpillar in *Hope for the Flowers* (Paulus 1972), at the top of the heap having achieved only emptiness.

Increasingly, people are reaching out to feed that spiritual hunger. Yet, instead of filling it with the Bread of Life, they gorge on the junk food of a standardless spirituality—love without Truth, New Age instead of the Rock of Ages. Their religion is feeling good without moral demands. Their God is a psychological aid to coping with stress without being a leader who is Lord over life.

The New Age notes the loss of absolute standards and labels it freedom, freedom for a person to impose his or her own standards on reality rather than be shackled with someone else's cultural meaning. In the

New Age, people are admonished to shape their own meaning from their own experience. This is portrayed as a heroic enterprise, despite the angst felt by people who have no absolute standards. To the Christian, constructing one's own reality sounds less like freedom and more like making an idol. People construct the fruit of their own hands (or minds), then worship it.

Of course, there will always be a remnant of faithful Christians. They will try to live biblical Christianity in the 21st century, but the world exerts pressures toward modernity that many Christians will too little understand (Pembroke 1990). Modernity is the philosophy that change is better than stability, the new is better than the old, the modern is better than the traditional. Trained in a philosophy of relativism and nondiscerning equality of all values, even the committed Christian may find it difficult to maintain a stable, traditional, biblical worldview in which there are absolute truths mixed among the relative truths.

In such a world, the 21st-century Christian counselor and psychotherapist must function.

The Future: Implications for the Mental Health Field

Life-Cycle Changes

The life span will likely continue to be lengthened. Obviously, this will affect the age distribution of clientele, making it necessary to be aware of physical, psychological, and social effects on older adults.

Less obviously, the increasing life span will likely affect the counseling modalities that are employed in the next century. Despite the wonderful efforts of James Dobson and others, the family will almost certainly play a decreasing part in our social organization. Family counseling and therapy will likely decrease in popularity. Yet because of the shifting life cycle, marriage counseling, remarriage counseling, and even counseling unmarried couples will probably increase. Group counseling will also probably increase as lonely individuals desperately seek intimacy in ad hoc groups rather than natural family groups.

Children will be moved progressively out of the home, so school counseling will increase, and even day care counseling could become a reality. In my youngest daughter's elementary school, the counselor already runs as many group counseling sessions as are run in many counseling agencies. Obviously, counseling done in schools and government supported day care settings are likely to prohibit explicitly Christian counseling.

Businesses will more frequently employ their own mental health workers, who will be pressured to offer more stress management techniques, nutritional counseling, exercise therapy, and spiritual renewal counseling (which is specifically not tied to one religion).

The health care industry, notably insurance companies, have already exerted an enormous impact on psychotherapy by deciding who will and will not be reimbursed for how much or how little psychological treatment and who the favored and the unfavored providers are. Unless we have a health care revolution, insurance companies will likely continue to be influential. What if insurance companies do not believe that Christian counseling or psychotherapy is effective? They won't pay, and they won't put Christian psychotherapists on their lists of preferred (or acceptable) providers. They will hire additional "independent" review boards of psychiatrists and psychologists who review mental health records of patients they have not seen. These boards accept a practical mandate to reduce allowable mental health services (lest the "independent" review boards will not be reemployed by the insurance company). Unallowable mental health services could easily become those thought by the "independent" review boards not to be efficacious—such as perhaps Christian psychotherapy.

A gloomier scenario is also possible, as I mentioned in the introduction to this book. Pressure mounts for a national health system. If the government becomes involved in funding most psychotherapy, it is easily conceivable that Christian psychotherapy will go the way of Christian anything in government-sponsored programs. It could be prohibited by law.

Technological Progress

Technological progress will likely continue unabated. The personal computer has already gone through more generations than *Rocky*. Undoubtedly, within 25 years, many new technological changes will transform life into something so different from today that we cannot even imagine it. Yet, I believe the trends occurring in the last part of the 20th century will continue into the 21st—more interconnectedness throughout the world and more pressure to accept and incorporate ideas, philosophies, and even religions different from the prevailing culture.

Christian counseling will probably be in good favor because it deals with spiritual issues. There will be pressure to make a few *minor* changes, of course, such as not mentioning Jesus' name because that might offend a client, or not challenging people's behavior by ever talking about sin, or incorporating other religious techniques like meditation or other eastern religious practices. These might not seem *minor* to some, but they are, after all, the price of progress.

As communication technology becomes more suitable for work at the home, fewer people will come to work in central work settings, and more work will be conducted at home computing centers. This could change the entire demography of the country, reversing the trend toward megalopolises by placing more middle- and upper-socioeconomic status people in the rural areas. The poor, not having the resources and training to capitalize on such technological advances, will likely continue to congregate in population centers. As the wealth moves to rural areas, the poor will likely become even needier. Since they can hardly afford psychological services, their psychological treatment will be picked up by government-paid mental health workers, which again does not bode well for Christians who are drawn to helping the downtrodden being able to practice explicitly Christian treatments.

Philosophical Pressures

In the 21st century, there is likely to be a shrinkage in the numbers of materialists and (unfortunately) true Christians and a growth in numbers of those with a spiritual hunger drawn to wholistic New Age psycho-religions.

Postmodernism, which is fundamentally a rebellion against absolute meaning and against reason, will continue to take its toll on Christianity. Its belief structure erodes the foundation of biblical Christianity, which is based on absolute truth, an unseen spiritual reality and objective external reality (rather than a social construction of reality), and a reasonable God who created a reasonable world that reflects God's character.

Postmodernism will push people toward individually understood, psychologically-based religions. Many will come to the psychotherapist to try to discover meaning in life rather than come to the pastor and the church. The therapist will increasingly function as a secular priest. This is not a new idea (London 1986). On the bright side, though, as people experience a spiritual vacuum, the explicit Christian therapist might even become a sought-after therapist.

At present, the profession of psychotherapy is not qualified to fulfill such spiritual needs. Our system of values is still client-centered, and there is little movement toward value proselytization. Within family systems theory, though, in recent years postmodern philosophy has gained momentum. Life is seen as a story, a narrative constructed by the client. If the narrative is causing difficulty for the client, the therapist acts as an instigator to help the client construct a different story of reality that will be less problematic (White and Epston 1990).

With such a postmodern philosophy, it is a short step for the secular therapist to counsel the committed Christian client away from his or her Christian values toward a more "helpful" story with more "helpful" values. On the other hand, a committed Christian therapist who counseled a non-Christian to adopt Christianity would be unhesitatingly charged with unethical value proselytization.

At the present, religious therapists—Christians in particular—are ill equipped to argue these philosophical questions. There is little understanding about the ethics of sharing Christian values in therapy apart from the injunction to avoid it unless specifically asked.

Fortress Near the Forest

This is rather a dismal vision of the future. It goes against my nature to present such a vision of the role of Christian therapy within the future. I generally err by being too optimistic. The glass is almost always half full (or even fuller) with me.

Such a gloomy vision encourages the image of religious psychotherapy hiding in a fortress near a hostile forest. In some ways, I do not like the image of the fortress near the forest. It suggests that we are under deliberate attack when that is not always the case, that we are entrenched and will thus experience continual siege, damage, and destruction until the siege ends, that at best we can beat off the attacks as they are mounted (or we can pull our heads in until Jesus returns to earth to rescue us), and that while we are within the fortress, our island is being constantly eroded, which could ultimately undermine the walls of the fortress.

Until now, my vision has focused on the decaying fortress and the powerful attacking forces. With such an outward-looking vision, defeat seems inevitable.

Yet Christians have a biblical view of the future. We know that Jesus Christ is Lord of creation. We know that one day every knee will bow, every tongue confess that he is Lord (Phil. 2:10–11). We can affirm that the future is firmly held in his hand, and that we are destined with him for glory and for dominion on earth as well as in heaven.

Christians will help their brothers and sisters in Christ whatever insurance companies do and whatever the government decrees. Christians will continue to evangelize those who do not know our wonderful Lord.

Knowing the final outcome, can we expand our vision of the fortress in the forest? What is going on inside the fortress? Are we cowering against the walls with necks bowed, or are we preparing to launch a systematic counterattack?

Any effective counterattack involves two elements: combatants and support. The combatants are well-trained and well-prepared soldiers who are willing to fight the battles they are called to fight regardless of whether they *want* to fight. Further, successful combat requires ground and air support. That is, we need people who support the warriors on the front line and we need prayer warriors.

Specifically, wherever we are, we can play a part in the counteroffensive against worldliness.

What Are We to Do?

There are several courses of action to pursue as we enter the 21st century. Educator, scholar, agency counselor, private therapist, and lay person can each take different actions. Finally, in the field, as a whole, Christian mental health professionals can engage in common enterprises: safeguarding our attitude against pride, attending to contemporary ethics of Christian counseling, and striving for more excellent performance in both practice and research on Christian mental health treatments.

Educator

In general, the educator must conceptualize his or her task as not merely training excellent therapists but as training excellent therapists who value, use, and promote research and scholarship. For too many years, there has been a tension between educators and scholars, between scientists and practitioners. The educator must draw from both traditions so that research and scholarship complement rather than compete with professional training.

Scholar

The scholar too often is concerned with how many publications he or she has accumulated and not with their usefulness to practicing therapists. As a consequence, the scholar too often investigates topics that are irrelevant to the practicing therapist (Cohen, Sargent, and Sechrest 1986). Scholarship must inform practice, and conversely, practice must inform scholarship. Scholars who are not themselves therapists must maintain dialogue with practicing therapists to keep abreast of the issues that therapists deal with daily. This suggests that scholars and practitioners should actively maintain contacts with one another.

Agency Counselor

The agency counselor is often the workhorse of the mental health system, seeing a seemingly never-ending stream of clients. The agency counselor must be willing to disrupt his or her routine to promote better dialogue between the scholar, educator, and practitioner. Agency counselors can maintain conversations with educators, can offer to train practicum and intern-level counselors, and can mentor postdoctoral applicants for licensure. Further, agency counselors, because of the numbers of clients they see, can offer their support to scholars who are conducting research on issues in religious counseling. Instead of decrying the lack of relevance of most academic research on psychotherapy, the agency counselor can work to interest research scholars in conducting research on the agency's clients. Such collaboration could be the epitome of clinically relevant research—research conducted on a local sample with national implications.

The agency counselor must also become a better consumer of research. More time must be allotted for reading research and thinking about religious values in psychotherapy and for improvement at therapeutic skills.

The agency counselor can also become an active participant in scholarship. The large numbers of clients that pass through a typical agency in a short period of time make agency counselors prime candidates for conducting applied research. If the agency counselor is unsure of his or her research skills, forming a collaborative alliance with a scholar is a viable option.

Private Therapist

The private therapist perhaps of all the people in the mental health system feels the most pressure to see clients. His or her livelihood depends on how many clients are seen. Dealing with insurance companies, disgruntled clients, secretaries, office personnel, partners, and accountants takes time. Speaking to PTAs, library clubs, churches, and other sources of clients or (at least) referrals drains away the odd hours. Being unable to take a vacation without losing money and disrupting the treatment of fragile clients eventually takes its toll.

Nonetheless, the private practitioner is probably the person who can benefit the most from research and scholarship that shows the effectiveness of religious psychotherapy under the right circumstances for the right clients. Therefore the private therapist has a moral responsibility to give back to the profession. This may be done in a variety of ways. As one example, Florence Kaslow, a Jewish private practitioner in Florida, sets aside a day each week for her own writing, even though she loses a substantial amount of income through her scholarship. This keeps her fresh, recharges her intellectual batteries, and contributes her knowledge and skill to the field of family psychology. As another example, Jonathan Robinson, a private therapist in Richmond, offered his services to us (Morrow, Worthington, and McCullough 1992) as a videotaped counselor in an experimental investigation of a religious issue. Like the agency counselor, the private therapist can also contribute clients to a scholar's research efforts or can collaborate in scientific studies of ongoing counseling.

Lay Person

As a lay person, the Christian should demand accountability from the mental health field. The lay person who receives mental health care should require of the provider assurance that the treatment is generally effective and that the treatment does not influence the client's important religious values in negative ways.

Medical costs must be cut without denying mental health services to people who truly need them. The lay person is the vehicle to pressure insurance companies and mental health professionals to minimize mental health costs.

The religious lay person must encourage the pursuit of truth through research on the effectiveness of therapy and on possible unintended effects of therapy on clients' religious values. Lay people should not fear the findings that science will uncover. These will generally not conflict with the truth of Scripture. God is a reasonable God, whose natural truth and scriptural truth are part of the same fabric, though sometimes appearing different in design. The Bible asks and answers questions that cannot be addressed by science, and science provides limits for theological explanations and opens areas that the Bible does not address.

Although at times there is tension among the participants in providing and consuming mental health services, there is a common interest in providing mental health service to those in need at reasonable cost while not destroying—and while hopefully enhancing—people's values. For the Christian, there are three cautions that should be heeded.

Guard against pride. Most of you who are reading this final chapter have been called by God in some way to bring his message to others. Christians have been given "the way, the truth, and the life" (John 14:6), who is "Christ in [us], the hope of glory" (Col. 1:27). It is easy to believe that we have all the answers, too.

If our answers are arrogant and prideful, the world will not hear.

When we become Christ's, he gives us the Holy Spirit. Yet, from a lifetime of living in the world, we have a hard outer nature that often prevents the Holy Spirit from getting out of us. It is usually necessary for the Lord to break that hard outer nature before the Holy Spirit can flow freely from us making us effective helpers. As counselors, we experience breaking periodically. Further, our clients' pain is often because God is breaking their hard outer nature. We want to help people learn how their present pain can allow the sweet fragrance of the Holy Spirit, the Helper, flow out to others. We can do that more effectively when we learn to allow God to break us, too.

Attend to contemporary Christian ethics. Altogether I have painted a mixed picture of the future for Christian psychology. On one hand, there should be more openness from the professional community and from needy clients to talk of the spiritual, but institutional and especially governmental controls may prohibit or limit our free expression of the Christian faith with our clients. The ethics and morals of sharing our faith during counseling have never been adequately addressed, though there are some fine Christian ethicists—such as Don Browning and Alan

Tjeltveit—emerging. New societal conditions and new technological conditions will necessitate training an entire generation of therapists whose serious thought is aimed at Christian ethics.

Cultivate excellence in practice and research. The oft-repeated admonition that we document the effectiveness of Christian psychotherapy with solid, well-respected research could easily turn out to be not a luxury but a necessity of survival for Christian psychotherapy. Consequently, we must train more Christians in first developing and delivering excellent mental health treatments and second in psychological research. Developing excellent treatments that are distinctively Christian and are so well articulated that they compete with the best secular treatments should be a self-evident goal of the Christian concerned with mental health issues.

With research, though, Christians have traditionally had more difficulty than they have with practice. Christians must characterize the research endeavor as a high calling having a place equal in status to counseling. If we do not draw bright young researchers into conducting Christian research, we may find ourselves having well developed counseling techniques, programs, and hospitals but having no clients, insurance companies, or government agencies able or willing to pay for explicitly Christian mental health services.

In His Time

In one family that used to attend our little church was a young girl. She was born without a functioning thyroid, which caused all sorts of physical problems. After she weathered the adjustment of birth, she had to learn to deal with abnormal growth rates, handsful of medications each day, and blindness. Besides the blindness, she had no control over her eyes. Her eyeballs rolled around, and she sometimes grimaced. She thus had to learn to handle people's reactions to her.

God may not have given her excellent health, nor sight, nor—because of her eyes—a completely pleasing physical appearance, but he gave her talent. She could sing. When she was six, she would stand before the congregation and in a clear voice sing,

> In his time, in his time
> He makes all things beautiful in his time. . . .
> Lord, my life to you I bring
> May each song I have to sing
> Be to you a lovely thing
> In your time.

I still can't think of that song without getting teary and choked up. I thought of that precious girl, with her physical unloveliness, waiting with great faith for the glorified body that Christ promises us. Waiting, like in

C. S. Lewis's Narnia tale, *The Last Battle,* for the time when we can run and not be weary, walk and not faint, when we can swim up waterfalls to dash into the arms of the living God.

It has been a while since this young girl was six years old. Now, she's sixteen, tall and still blond. She has not only continued to sing, but she has taken up piano, and won a statewide competition in song writing, performing her own composition on the piano. She has swum competitively, and while not being in the top finishers, she usually places. (And I might add, I certainly wouldn't want to race her.) Her personality is mature. She's been through a lot.

I realized that God *has* made her beautiful in his time. It has not just been a wait-for-heaven beauty, but a maturing beauty, a hard-won, struggling-by-faith beauty.

The church is like this young woman. Sometimes the church is not entirely pleasing to look at. We have gestures that some find repulsive and can never get past to see the inner working of the personality of Christ within. Sometimes we Christians are amazingly blind. We grope our way through life, treading on toes, causing inadvertent pain in those we love. Sometimes, we even lose patience with our frailty and lash out at others, intentionally trying to hurt.

But like this young woman, God has put within the church a talent, fueled by Jesus' own life within. The song we sing is one of love. The opening stanza is about bringing the good news of God's redemptive love through Jesus to those who don't know about it. The middle stanza is about ministering love to those within the healing community, which is Jesus' body. The third stanza is about social justice and compassion—the "kindness and severity of God" (Rom. 11:22)—in which we work to eliminate inequities and promote love throughout the world.

Each person in Christian counseling is a priest, ministering this song within the community to which we are called. Some will be called mostly to evangelize, others mostly to counsel, still others mostly to work for social justice and compassion. Whatever we do, we sing our song directly to God.

In his time, God will call out the church to him, and we will have such a banquet that we can't imagine—I like to think about having roast turkey, fragrant dressing, creamy mashed potatoes, gravy, tangy cranberry sauce, peas, sweet potatoes. All those appetizers will be followed by the main meal where we will eat bread and wine with Jesus in celebration. All this—calorie free and with no cholesterol worries.

In his time, he is also, like with this young woman, maturing us as a healing community. He is not hampered by human difficulties and failures. He provides in them opportunities to glorify him. We are the body of Christ, called to minister healing from, within, and through the therapeutic community of the church. Christ will accomplish that healing in his way and in his time. Let us strive to stay in his will.

References

Carter, E., and M. McGoldrick. 1989. Overview: The changing family life cycle—A framework for family therapy. In *The changing family life cycle: A framework for family therapy*, ed. B. Carter and M. McGoldrick, 2d ed., 3–28. Boston: Allyn and Bacon.

Cherlin, A. J. 1981. *Marriage, divorce, remarriage.* Cambridge: Harvard Univ. Press.

Cohen, L. H., M. M. Sargent, and L. B. Sechrest. 1986. Use of psychotherapy research by professional psychologists. *American Psychologist* 41: 198–206.

Doherty, W. J. 1991. Family therapy goes postmodern. *Family Therapy Networker* 15(5): 37–42.

Efran, J. S. 1991. Constructivism in the inner city. *Family Therapy Networker* 15(5): 51–52.

Freedman, J. L. 1984. Effects of television violence on aggressiveness. *Psychological Bulletin* 96: 227–46.

———. 1986. Television violence and aggression: A rejoinder. *Psychological Bulletin* 100: 372–78.

Friedrich-Coffer, L., and A. C. Huston. 1986. Television violence and aggression: The debate continues. *Psychological Bulletin* 100: 364–71.

Gergen, K. J. 1991. The saturated family. *Family Therapy Networker* 15(5): 27–35.

Kipnis, D. 1991. The technological perspective. *Psychological Science* 2(2): 62–69.

Kubey, R., and M. Csikszentmahalyi. 1990. *Television and the quality of life: How viewing shapes everyday experience.* Hillsdale, N.J.: Lawrence Erlbaum.

Larson, S. S., and D. B. Larson. 1990. Divorce: A hazard to your health. *The Physician* 2(3): 13–17.

Liebert, R. M., J. N. Sprafkin, and E. S. Davidson. 1982. *The early window: Effects of television on children and youth.* New York: Pergamon.

London, P. 1986. *The modes and morals of psychotherapy,* 2d ed. New York: Hemisphere.

Minuchin, S. 1991. The seductions of constructivism. *Family Therapy Networker* 15(5): 47–50.

Morrow, D., E. L. Worthington, Jr., and M. E. McCullough. 1992. Observers' perceptions of a counselor's treatment of a religious issue. *Journal of Counseling and Development*.

Naisbitt, J. 1984. *Mega-trends: Ten new directions transforming our lives.* New York: Warner.

O'Hara, M., and W. T. Anderson. 1991. Welcome to the postmodern world. *Family Therapy Networker* 15(5): 19–25.

Pembroke, N. F. 1990. John Stott and Erik Erikson on the problem of modernity: Applications for the ministry of the church. *Journal of Psychology and Theology* 18: 237–43.

Paulus, T. 1972. *Hope for the flowers.* New York: Paulist.

Penn, P. 1991. Letters to ourselves. *Family Therapy Networker* 15(5): 43–45.

Risatti, H., ed. 1990. *Postmodern perspectives: Issues in contemporary art.* Englewood Cliffs, N.J.: Prentice-Hall.

Schaeffer, F. 1968. *Escape from reason.* Downers Grove, Ill.: InterVarsity.

Singer, J. L., and D. G. Singer. 1981. *Television, imagination and aggression: A study of preschoolers.* Hillsdale, N.J.: Lawrence Erlbaum.

Spanier, G. B. 1983. Married and unmarried cohabitation in the United States: 1980. *Journal of Marriage and the Family* 45: 277–88.

United States Bureau of the Census 1989. *Current population reports.* Washington, D.C.: Government Printing Office, Series P-23, No. 162, June.

United States Bureau of the Census 1990. *Current population reports.* Washington, D.C.: Government Printing Office, Series P-20, No. 445, June.

United States Bureau of the Census 1990. *Current population reports.* Washington, D.C.: Government Printing Office, Series P-25, No. 1045, January.

United States Senate Senate Special Committee on Aging. 1986. *Aging America: Trends and projections (1984–85 Ed.).* Washington, D.C.: U. S. Government Printing Office.

Index

Abortion, 184
Academic problems, 90, 96, 98
Acceptance, 169
Accountability, 276
Action, 45, 48, 49
Activity, 134
Adams, Jay, 33, 231, 232, 233
Adjustment, 114–15
Adolescence, 9, 231
Agency, 214–15, 216, 219, 220, 245, 247, 252
Agency counselor, 30, 275–76
Aggression, 50, 51, 130, 265
Agnosticism, 171–72
Alcohol abuse, 76, 80, 90, 96, 98, 184, 230, 231
Allport, G. W., 151
American Association of Marital and Family Therapists, 185, 187
American Psychiatric Association, 113, 191
American Psychological Association, 163, 194, 198, 200, 226
ethical standards, 99
Analogue research, 65
Anger, 183, 185, 187, 230
Anointing with oil, 175, 177–78, 180–81
Antisocial personality, 81
Anxiety, 51, 54, 55, 72, 90, 96, 97, 98, 157, 230
Aquinas, 211
Aristotelian logic, 22, 268
Assertiveness, 90, 96, 97, 98, 230, 269n
Assessment, 67–68
Association of Marital and Family Therapists, 25
Assumptions. See Presuppositions
Atheism, 153, 171–72
Atomism, 45
Attitudes, 220

Attributional pattern, 140
Augustine, 211
Aust, C. F., 250
Authentic living, 54, 55
Authority, authorities, 21, 22, 131, 149, 155
competing values of, 156
conflict of, 155–56
Autonomy, 44, 50, 51, 54–56, 57, 252, 264

Backus, William, 33, 233
Batson, C. D., 151
Baucom, D., 48
Bear, G., 228
Becoming, 55
Behavior, 123
and value change, 150
and value conflicts, 146–47, 154, 156
Behavioral therapy, 40, 42, 46, 50, 54, 67, 68, 137, 168
Behaviorism, 39, 40, 42, 45, 46–48, 49
Beit-Hallahmi, B., 257
Belief in God, 38, 41
Beliefs, 41, 123, 124, 146, 147, 148, 151
Benner, David, 33
Bergan, J., 32, 134
Bergin, A. E., 129, 148, 163–64, 213, 215, 225–26, 247, 257
Berry, J. T., 20
Beutler, L. E., 32, 128–30, 132, 134, 135, 145, 148, 152, 158, 219
Bevan, William, 37
Bible, 170, 195, 211
authority, 131, 149
in counseling, 88, 92, 93, 94, 169, 174, 176, 179, 180, 197, 198, 226, 227, 229, 230, 231, 232, 234, 235
memorization, 177, 178, 179
Bipolar disorder, 81
Birch, B. C., 213, 216, 217

Blacks, 136
Borderline personality, 184, 269n
Boundary conditions, 139
Bridges, R. A., 245
Broger, John C., 232
Browning, Don S., 42, 43, 44, 46, 47, 50,
    51, 53, 56, 214, 277
Butman, Richard, 32

Calvin, John, 211
Career choice, 90, 96, 97, 98
Carlson, C. R., 255
Castle metaphor, 152–53, 156–57
Central values, 149, 150–51, 156–57
Change, 88, 230, 265, 271
Character, 211
Charismatic tradition, 198, 199, 200
Child abuse, 183, 230
Choice, 56, 269, 270
Christian Association for Psychological
    Studies (CAPS), 25, 173, 175, 179,
    181
Christian counseling, 18, 19, 20–21, 99,
    168, 169–70, 172, 173, 174, 179, 181,
    272, 279
  diversity in, 100
  future of, 207
  and nonreligious clients, 136
  techniques, 100, 168–70, 192, 194, 201
Christian counselor, 87–88, 90–97, 100,
    101
Christian disciplines, 194–96, 198–200
Christian ethics, 209–15, 217, 219, 220,
    277–78
Christian faith, 217–19
Church, 279–80
Clergy, 71–77, 80, 81–82
  accessibility, 81
  lack of understanding of mental
    disorders, 82
  view of professional therapy, 156
Client
  dysfunctional religious life, 68
  expectations prior to counseling, 65–66,
    100
  highly religious, 129–32, 135–37, 148,
    151–55
  interpersonal style, 140
  medium, low religious, 132
  politically extreme, 129
  religiously extreme, 129
  religion, 65, 110–13, 129–36, 140, 186,
    187, 226, 227, 252–53
  values, 40, 67, 130, 157, 159
Clinebell, H. J., Jr., 191
Clinical values, 247

Cognitive complexity, 153
Cognitive therapy, 33, 67, 68, 167, 235,
    245, 255
Cognitive-behavioral therapy, 33, 45–46,
    48, 53, 67, 68, 233, 249–50
  Christian evaluation, 48–49
Collins, Gary, 230, 231, 232, 233
Comfort, 88
Commitment, 123, 124, 250
Communications technology, 262, 264,
    266, 270, 272
Community, 146, 211, 250, 270
Community counseling, 29, 31
Compassion, 279
Competence, 46
Computers, 266
Confession, 172, 192, 197, 198, 250, 251
Confidentiality, 230
Consensus values, 100, 101
Consistency, 269
Constantine, L. L., 131
Contemplative tradition, 198, 199, 200
Context, 216, 218, 219
Contrition, 251
Conversion, 192
Coping function of religion, 115–16, 118
Counselee. See Client
Counseling
  anticipations for, 132, 138
  content, 172
  definition, 29, 30
  flexibility in, 93, 100
  philosophy of, 230, 231
  process, 172
  theories of, 31–33
Counselor
  annihilation of client's religion, 111–12
  orientation, 89–92, 94, 96–99, 101
  preference, 90
  professional identification, 66
  relationship with client, 65, 66, 140, 247
  religious values, 66–67
  training, 72
Counselor Preference Questionnaire
    (CPQ), 90
Courage, 151
Crabb, Larry, 33, 230, 231, 232, 233
Creation, 117
Crisis counseling, 230
Cross-cultural counseling, 248
Cults, 127
Cultural conformity, 109, 111
Cultural diversity, 128
Cultural mandate, 53
"Cultural nones," 157

Davis, C. S., 136
Davison, M. L., 158
Day, J. M., 109
Day care counseling, 271
Death, 231
Deep metaphors, 43, 44
Defensiveness, 251
Delay in gratification, 250
Deliberative motif, 211
Deliverance, 195, 197, 198
Demon possession, 180
Denominations, 256–58
Depression, 45, 51, 72, 81, 90, 96, 97, 98, 157, 178, 180, 184, 185, 187, 230, 250, 255
Determinism, 45, 49, 53, 54, 211
Diagnosis, 110, 112–13, 118, 230
Diagnostic Interview Schedule (DIS), 73, 76
Differentiated faith, 151
Discernment, 195, 197, 198
Discipleship counseling, 232, 233
Discipleship groups, 31
Disraeli, Benjamin, 22–23
Dittes, James, 116
Divorce, 75, 262, 263
Dobson, James, 271
Dogmatism, 152n
Dombeck, M., 247, 255
Donahue, M. J., 213
Donnelley, D., 251
Drakeford, J. W., 33
Draper, Edgar, 110
Dream interpretation, 200
Drucker, Peter, 107, 109
Drug abuse, 76, 80, 96, 230, 231
DSM III-R, 73, 80, 113–15, 118
Duncan, L. A., 20
Dupont, P. A., 20
Dysfunction, 171

Eastern religions, 136, 256, 272
Eating disorder, 90, 96, 97, 98
Eclecticism, 21, 33, 254–56
Ecumenical therapy, 256–57
Education and therapy, 10, 275
Edwards, Jonathan, 211
Edwards, T. H., 192
Efficacy, 44, 49
Egan, Gerard, 230, 231
Ego, 50
Ehrenwald, Jan, 10
Elderly clients, 75, 77
Ellis, A., 115, 171, 231
Emotional distress, 158
Emotions, 22, 45, 48, 49, 54, 55, 57

Empiricism, 39, 40, 41, 45, 49, 216, 217, 220, 254
Enigmas, 115
Enlightenment, 108, 267, 268
Enns, C. Z., 86
Environment, 49
Environmentalism, 45
Epidemiological Catchment Area (ECA) Study, 73–75, 77, 80–81
Epistemology, 39
Epperson, D. L., 137
Ethical egoism, 51
Ethics, 42, 44
  in counseling, 99, 101, 135, 211, 274
Ethnic prejudice, 151
Evangelical tradition, 198, 199, 200
Evangelism, 232, 235, 252, 274, 277, 279
Evans, C. S., 45, 213, 214, 217, 218
Evolution, 212
Excellence, 278
Exercise therapy, 271
Existential questions, 151, 152
Existential therapy, 53–55, 245
  Christian evaluation, 55–57
Expediency, 249
Experiencing, 45, 48, 56
Extramarital affairs, 230
Extrinsic religion, 151, 254

Faith, 112–13, 210
  and adjustment, 115
  and physical maladies, 114
  and stress, 114
Falsification, 40, 41
Family, 245, 247, 262–63, 265, 267, 271
Family problems, 178, 180
Family systems theory, 273
Family therapists, religion, 163
Family therapy, 29, 30, 40, 139, 231
Fasting, 195, 197, 198
Feelings, 48, 123
Fellowship, 250
Feminist theology, 245
Feminist therapy, 86, 99–101, 136–37
Fillipaldi, S. E., 251
Fischer, E. H., 155
Fisher, S. F., 184
Fiske, D. W., 217
Fitzgibbons, R. P., 183
Flanigan, B. J., 184
Flooding, 48
Forgiveness, 88, 92, 93, 94, 101, 135, 151, 169, 170, 175, 176, 179, 183–88, 189, 192, 195, 196, 197, 226, 246, 250–51
  and anger, 185, 186–87
  and depression, 185, 186–87

Formal lay counseling, 227–29
Fowler, J., 268
Frankena, William, 51
Frankl, Viktor, 55
Free expression, 248
Free will, 139n
Freedom, 54, 56, 57, 211, 213, 214–15,
    217, 219, 220, 250, 252, 264, 270–71
Freud, Sigmund, 10, 42, 44, 50, 52, 53, 66,
    67, 68, 171, 214, 252, 268
Friendship counseling, 31
Fundamentalism, 86, 152n
Future, biblical view, 274

Gartner, J. M., 129
Gascoyne, S. R., 100
Gergen, K. J., 217
Gestalt therapists, 42, 137, 168
Glasser, William, 231
Glossolalia, 192
God
    power, 246
    presence, 246
    sovereignty, 56, 139n
    wisdom, 246
Goldsmith, W. M., 151, 155
Goodness, 214, 217, 219, 220
Gorsuch, R. L., 156
Grace, 57
Graduate training programs, 193–201
    accreditation, 193, 194, 198, 200
Grammar networks, 43, 48
Gratification, 50, 51–52, 53
Grief, 230
Griffith, E. E., 191
Group counseling, 29, 30, 31, 271
Growth, 163, 212, 268
Guilt, 72, 157, 230, 248

Hackett, G., 86
Handelman, S. A., 255
Happiness, 108
Hauerwas, S., 217
Haugk, Kenneth, 228, 231, 233
Healing, 191, 195, 197, 198
Health. See Physical health
Health care industry, 17, 18, 270, 272
Hedonism, 51
Hegel, G. W. F., 22, 267, 268
Heggen, C. H., 156
Helpee. See Client
Helplessness, 266
Henry, Carl, 211
Holiness tradition, 198, 199, 200
Holy Spirit, 21, 170, 233, 235, 277

Homework, 176, 180, 226
Homosexuality, 90, 96, 97, 98
Honesty, 163, 250
Hood, R. W., Jr., 253
Hope, 88
Hope, D., 183, 250–51
Hopelessness, 266–67, 270
Hulgus, Joyce, 234
Human nature, 134, 230, 244–46
Humanism, 163, 169, 245
Humanistic psychology, 39, 40
Humility, 49
Hunt, Skip, 233–34
Hutch, R. A., 256
Hypnosis, 200

Id, 50
Identification, 131, 149
Identity, 117, 163, 245, 247, 269
Identity crisis, 9, 10
Idolatry, 57, 271
Image of God, 56
Immigration, 127–28
Implosion therapy, 48
Importance, 153
Impressions of the Counselor
    Questionnare (ICQ), 89–92
Inauthentic living, 55
Inconsistencies, 270
Independence, 252, 264
Individual counseling, 29, 30
Individualism, 42, 53, 55, 248, 263, 267,
    269, 273
Industrialism, 264, 268
Informal lay counseling, 227–29
Information, 266–67
Informed consent, 85, 99, 101
Inner conflict, 52
Inner harmony, 151
Inner healing, 177, 178
Inspiration, 117
Instinctualism, 44
Institutions, 38, 106
Insurance companies, 17–18, 19, 272, 277
Integration techniques, 179
Integrative review of research, 23–24
Integrative therapy, 33
Integrity, 117, 245
Intention, 216, 217, 219, 220
Internal drives, 49–52
Interpretation, 216, 217, 218
Interventions, 174–75, 179, 180, 181
    See also Religious interventions
Intimacy, 245, 270
Intrinsic religion, 151, 254

Intuition, 22
Isolation, 54, 55

Jacobson, N., 47
James, William, 115, 220
Jensen, J. P., 163–64, 225–26, 247, 257
Jesus Christ, 246
Johnson, Rex E., 234
Johnson, W. B., 19
Jones, S., 32, 43, 45, 53, 245, 255
Journal keeping, 195, 196, 197
Journal of Psychology and Christianity, 11, 88
Justice, 169

Kant, Immanuel, 40, 211
Karl, J., 247, 255
Kaslow, Florence, 276
Kierkegaard, S., 218, 220
King, R. R., 172
Kohlberg, L., 268
Koltko, M. E., 149, 153–54, 155, 157
Kopp, S., 171
Kosmin, Barry, 106
Kuhn, Thomas, 22, 40

Larson, David, 263
Larson, D. B., 192
Larson, Susan, 263
Latter-Day Saint tradition, 246n
Lay Christian counseling, 31, 227–35
Lay person, 276–77
Laying on of hands, 180
Leaders, 131, 149
Lesmeister, R., 136
Lewin, Kurt, 24
Lewis, C. S., 279
Lewis, D. A., 86
Lewis, Hunter, 21–22
Lewis, K. N., 86, 136–37
Liberation theology, 245
Libertarianism, 53
Libido, 50–51
Liebert, R. M., 243–44
Life expectancy, 262–63
Lindbeck, G. A., 218
Logic, 22
Logical positivism, 39
London, P., 145, 171
Long, E. L., Jr., 211
Long, V. O., 156
Love, 49, 169, 252
Lovinger, R. J., 32, 248, 251, 257
Lukens, H. C., Jr., 233
Luther, Martin, 211

Maladaptive thoughts, 167
Malony, H. Newton, 33, 115, 117, 163
Mapping of values, 145, 147, 157–59
"Marginal nones," 157
Margolin, G., 47
Marital problems, 90, 96, 98, 178, 180, 231
Marital therapy, 29, 30, 45, 46, 47, 50, 131, 139, 150, 159, 230, 271
Marriage, 247, 262–63
Martin, J. E., 255, 256
Marx, Karl, 268
Materialism, 45, 49, 270, 273
McGee, R. S., 33
McMinn, M. R., 210
McVay, J. G., 247, 256
Meaning, 213, 215–17, 219, 220
Meaninglessness, 246
Medical costs, 277
Meditation, 176, 195, 197
Medium central values, 130, 131, 148, 152, 156, 158, 159
Mega-churches, 31
Meier, P. D., 33, 231
Mental disorders, 10, 72
Mental health professionals, 71–77, 80, 130, 273
    accessibility, 81–82
    ambivalence about religion, 171, 181
    training in religious intervention, 193
Mental health values, 163
Mental status, 113, 115
Mercy, 169
Metabeliefs, 149, 153–54
Metaphors, 44, 266
Metaphysics, 41–42, 44, 57
Meyer, M. S., 248
Meylink, W. D., 156
Middle Ages, 108
Miller, W. R., 255, 256
Minirth, F. B., 33, 231
Minirth-Meier clinics, 30
Misbelief therapy, 233
Mischel, W., 130
Misdiagnosis, 129, 148
Modernism, 268, 270
Modernity, 42, 271
Mohline, Richard J., 234
Moral development, 250
Moral dilemma, 250
Moral good, 44, 46, 47, 50
Moral law, 215
Moral reconation therapy, 250
Moral values, 210
Morality, 215
Morris, M., 19
Motivation, 220

Movies, 265–66
Mowrer, O. H., 33
Multiculturalism, 266–67, 270
Multiple personality disorder, 269n
Music, 269
Mysteries, 115
Mystical experience, 192

Narcissism, 269n
Narramore, Clyde, 33
Narrative, 216–20, 273
National Association of Social Workers, 18
National health system, 18, 272
Natural selection, 44
Naturalism, 39, 42, 45, 46, 49
Needs, 50–51, 53, 249, 263
Nelson, A. A., 193, 234
Neumann, J. K., 99
Neurotic anxiety, 54
New Age movements, 109, 128, 270–71, 273
Newbigin, Lesslie, 108
Newton, Isaac, 108
Niebuhr, H. R., 217
Nondiscernment, 267, 270, 271
"Nones," 157
Nonmoral good, 44, 46, 47, 50
Nouthetic counseling, 33, 232
Nuclear family, 262
Nugent, M. D., 131
Nurturance, 247
Nutritional counseling, 271

O'Donohue, W., 41–42
Obedience, 195, 197
Objectivity, 53, 212
Obsessive compulsive disorder, 81
Older adults, 271
    See also Elderly clients
Oppression, 245
Organizational values, 37
Ostrum, R., 19
Outpatient psychotherapy, 29

Packer, M. J., 216
Pain, 50
Panic disorder, 76, 80
Parenting problems, 90, 96, 97, 98, 230
Pastor. See Clergy
Pastoral counseling, 30, 72, 132
Pathological religion, 111, 113
Peace, 184
Perceptions, 146, 220
Personality, 130, 151, 243–44
Personality theory, 244, 246

Persuasion. See Value persuasion in counseling
Peucher, D. R., 19
Phenomenology, 53
Phobias, 269n
Physical health, 114, 115, 163, 247, 253, 262–63
Piaget, Jean, 268
Pleasure principle, 50, 51
Pluralism, 267
Poor, 273
Post-positivism, 40–42, 214
Postmodernism, 262, 267–70, 273
Potency, 149, 153–54
Power, 245
Powerlessness, 246
Pragmatism, 42, 270
Prayer, 170, 195
    in counseling, 88, 92, 93, 94, 164, 172, 174, 176, 180, 195, 197, 198, 226, 227, 229, 232, 234, 235
Precision, 157
Premarital counseling, 31, 72, 230
Premarital sex, 86
Premodern times, 268
Prescriptive motif, 211
Presuppositions, 42, 43, 45, 57, 58, 139, 268
Pretherapy information, 67, 85–87, 99–101, 138
Pride, 277
Private therapists, 276
Process theology, 245–46
Progress, 272
Propst, L. R., 19, 33, 135, 200, 249–50, 255
Prosperity, 270
Pruyser, Paul, 111
Psychiatric inpatient treatment, 29–30
Psychiatrists, 77
    accessibility, 81
Psychoanalysis, 9, 39, 49–53, 54, 137, 167
    Christian evaluation, 52–53
Psychodynamic psychology, 40, 66–67
Psychological healing, 183
Psychologically-based religions, 273
Psychologists, 41, 42, 77
    accessibility, 81
    religion, 163, 171–72, 226–27
Psychology, 57
    and spiritual nature, 218
    and theology, 193, 210, 212
Psychopathology, 29, 54, 72, 130, 230
Psychotherapy, 9–11, 20, 29, 42, 43, 167–68
    and spiritual direction, 192
    Christian evaluation, 58

as value-laden, 246–47
See also Counseling; Therapy
Public service, 250
Purpose, 163

Quackenbos, S., 200
Questing Intrinsics, 151–52

Rambo, L. R., 220
Rapha Hospital programs, 30
Rasmussen, L. L., 213, 216, 217
Rational Emotive Therapy, 33, 245
Rationalism, 216
Rationality, 44, 45, 48–49, 108, 245
Reality therapy, 231
Reason, 108, 268
Reciprocity, 45, 46–49, 50, 53
Redemption, 117
Reductionism, 45, 49
Referral, 72, 81, 95, 130, 132, 156, 230,
    247–48, 253
Relationships, 53, 56, 97, 134, 183, 184,
    211, 230, 231, 247, 263–64, 270
Relativeness, 249
Relativism, 53, 212, 217, 262, 267, 270–71
Relaxation techniques, 176, 178, 179
Relevance, 269
Religion
    correction, 112
    demise, 10
    dysfunction, 171
    functions, 114, 115–17, 118
    importance for clients, 226
    and life, 106–9
    and mental health, 106–7
    privatization, 107, 109
    and psychotherapy, 109, 128, 138, 164,
        256
Religious cognitive therapy, 255
Religious counseling, certification in, 201
Religious diagnosis, 105, 107, 110, 112–18
Religious diversity, 248, 249
Religious imagery, 192
Religious interventions, 37, 176, 177–79,
    227, 229, 231, 234–35
Religious interventions questionnaire, 173
Religious maturity, 68, 110, 112, 114, 115,
    117, 151, 170, 220
Religious orthodoxy, 72
Religious status interview, 111–13, 114,
    117, 118
Religious traditions, 198–201
Religious upbringing, 157
Religious values, 19, 32, 38, 123, 124, 210,
    218, 234, 247
    abuses of, 136

in family therapy, 139
Judeo-Christian, 163
in marriage counseling, 139
and psychotherapy, 10–11, 18, 20, 21,
    32, 38, 133, 139–40, 218–20
See also Values
Renaissance, 267
Repentance, 57
Research, 23–24, 110, 113, 118, 278
Response efficacy, 45–46, 48
Responsibility, 55, 56, 247, 250
Richards, P. S., 158
Richardson, F. C., 42, 48
Ridley, C. R., 19
Rieff, Philip, 51
Rightness, 214, 219, 220
Roberts, Robert C., 43
Robinson, Jonathan, 276
Rogers, Carl, 39, 67, 156, 214, 231
Rokeach values survey, 124, 151, 157,
    158–59
Rosenthal, D., 212
Rotter's incomplete sentences blank, 157
Rychlak, J. F., 214–15

Salience, 149
Salvation, 57, 72, 151, 246, 257
Sanctification, 57, 117, 251
Sarbin, Theodore, 107
Satir, Virginia, 231
Schaeffer, Francis, 267
Schizophrenia, 80–81
Schizophreniform disorder, 77, 80
Scholarship, 275–76
School counseling, 271
Schwartz, B., 212–13
Science, 22–24, 108, 210, 212–13, 216, 219
    and faith, 209–10, 212
    and metaphysics, 41
    philosophy of, 40, 212
Science of chaos, 139
Script analysis, 200
Scripture. *See* Bible
Secular counseling, 32, 130, 132, 134–38,
    149, 169, 172, 173, 174, 175, 179,
    192, 226, 249, 273
    fear or distrust of, 81–82
    techniques, 169, 177, 178, 179, 180
    See also Traditional counselor
Secularization, 107, 109, 118
Security, 116
Self-actualization, 10
Self-consciousness, 54–55
Self-control, 163, 247
Self-esteem, 246, 257
Self-exaltation, 49

Self-exploration, 97
Self-fulfillment, 263
Self-image, 230
Self-understanding, 44
Sell, K. L., 155
Seminary education, 72–73, 82
Sensitivity, 247
Sermons, 31
Sexual issues, 90, 96, 97, 98
Sexuality, 50
Shafranske, E. P., 163
Sharing religious faith. *See* Evangelism
Shepherd Scale, 89
Shut-ins, 231
Shweder, R. A., 217
Sierra Project, 109
Simplicity, 195, 196, 197, 198
Sin, 92, 93, 94, 147, 230, 246, 257
Situation comedies, 265
Situational values, 151
Skinner, B. F., 44, 46, 214
Smith, D., 33, 54
Smith, J. H., 255
Social constructionist thought, 217, 245,
    268, 269, 273
Social identity, 107
Social justice, 279
Social justice tradition, 198, 199, 200
Social psychology, 136
Social security, 77
Social skills, 10
Social stigma, 155
Social workers, 77
    accessibility, 81
Society for the Scientific Study of
    Religion, 253
Sociology, 106
Solitude/silence, 195, 197, 198
Solomon, C. R., 33
Specialization, 267, 270
Spiegler, M. D., 243–44
Spilka, B., 245
Spiritual guidance, 30, 193
Spiritual discernment, 170
Spiritual growth, 135
Spiritual health, 88
Spiritual history, 195, 196, 197
Spiritual humanism, 154
Spiritual hunger, 270
Spiritual interventions. *See* Religious
    interventions
Spiritual maturity. *See* Religious maturity
Spiritual needs, 273
Spiritual reality, 244, 253
Spiritual renewal counseling, 271

Spiritual strategy, 243, 244, 246, 249, 253,
    256, 257, 258
    empirical dimension, 253–54
Spirituotherapy, 33
Sprinthall, N. A., 247, 256
Stages of development, 136, 268
Statistics, 23
Steinbron, Melvin J., 228
Stephen Series, 228, 230, 231, 233
Stress, 114, 140, 247
Stress management, 271
Strong, S. R., 172
"Structural nones," 157
Strupp, H. J., 139
Stuart, R. B., 46
Sturkie, J., 228
Sublimation, 52, 53
Suicide, 230, 231
Superego, 50
Survival, 212
Swamp metaphor, 152–53, 155, 156–57,
    159
Sweeten, G. R., 233
Symptoms, 113, 115
Systemic values, 37–38

Tan, S. Y., 31, 232
Taylor, C., 217
Teaching, 176
Technological progress, 272
Teen pregnancy, 230
Telecommunications, 128
Television, 264–65
Theology, 211
    and psychology, 44, 213
    traditional, 220
Theoretical reflection, 24
Therapeutic success, 159
Therapist
    disagreement with pastor, 156
    neutrality, 39
    politically extreme, 129
    religion, 127, 132, 133–35, 154, 156,
        163–64
    religiously extreme, 129
    as secular priest, 273
    style, 139
    values, 130, 139
    See also Counselor
Therapy
    goals, 135, 139, 211
    events, 140
    religious content, 133
    setting, 140
    as value-free, 10
    values, 58, 139

Time, 134
Tjeltveit, Alan, 38, 277–78
Toleration, 100, 131, 132, 149, 152, 153, 155, 248
Tournier, Paul, 33
Traditional counselor, 86, 87, 90, 92–97, 99, 100, 101, 248, 249
Traditional values, 153, 247
Tragedies, 115
Transactional Analysis, 33
Transcendence, 107, 109
Transportation, 264
Trust, 250
Truth, 267, 269, 273, 277
Turner, J. L., 155
Tweedie, D., 56

Unconscious, 49, 167
Universalistic values, 247
Urbanization, 264
Utilitarianism, 44

VCR, 264–66
Value acceptance, 100
Value ambiguities, 152
Value ambivalence, 157
Value change, 129, 146, 148, 150, 154, 212
Value clarification, 10
Value conflicts, 146–47, 154, 157–59
  in marital therapy, 159
  with nonreligious clients, 147
  with religious clients, 147
Value convergence, 128, 150
  and therapy success, 148
Value dilemmas, 249
Value dimensions, 131, 149
Value dissimilarity, 32, 128–29, 149n, 153, 154, 158, 159, 247, 248
Value-free counseling, 67, 88, 214
Value-informed counseling, 67
Value intrusion by therapists, 137, 138, 252
Value neutrality, 39, 100, 145, 212
Value persuasion in counseling, 85, 95, 100, 128, 273–74
Value resistance, 155
Value similarity, 32, 65, 86, 92, 94, 95, 101, 128–29, 148, 149n, 154, 158

Values, 10, 11, 18, 19, 37–39, 42, 43, 44, 57–59, 124, 146–47, 155, 210, 211, 213–14, 245, 246
  in behavioral paradigm, 46
  in psychoanalysis, 52
  in psychotherapy, 43, 57, 130, 214
  in cognitive-behavioral therapy, 45
  of significant others, 155
Van Wicklin, J. F., 151
Verification, 40
Veterans Administration, 77
Victimization, 178
Violence, 265–66
Virkler, H. A., 154
Virtue, 211, 213, 214, 219, 220
Vision, 261
Vitz, P. C., 216
Vocational counseling, 230

Walters, R. P., 231
Watkins, P., 19
Watson, P. J., 151–52, 257
Watzlawick, Paul, 23
Web of belief, 41–42, 43
Welfare, 77, 80
Welter, P., 231
Wholistic person, 49
Wichern, F., 33
Widows, 75, 77
Wilson, W. P., 19, 193, 234, 250
Wisdom, 151
Wittgenstein, Ludwig, 40
Wolberg, A. R., 184
Women clients, 75, 77
Woolfolk, R. L., 42, 48
Work, 50, 52, 53, 247, 252
Worldviews, 32, 57
Worship, 195, 197
Worth, 163
Worthington, E. L., Jr., 19, 20, 21, 32, 33, 100, 129–30, 131, 132, 146, 148–49, 152, 153, 155, 156, 158, 159, 172, 174, 175, 179–80, 193, 194, 231
Wright, H. Norman, 33, 231, 234

Yalom, I., 54
Yinger, Milton, 115

Zone of toleration, 131–32, 149, 152, 153, 155, 158, 159